Water Markets
in Theory and Practice

Studies in Water Policy and Management
Charles W. Howe, General Editor

Water Markets
in Theory and Practice

Market Transfers, Water Values, and Public Policy

Bonnie Colby Saliba
and David B. Bush

Studies in Water Policy and Management, No. 12

Westview Press / Boulder and London

Studies in Water Policy and Management

Copyright © 1987 by Westview Press, Inc.

Published in 1987 in the United States of America by Westview Press, Inc.; Frederick A. Praeger, Publisher; 5500 Central Avenue, Boulder, Colorado 80301

Library of Congress Cataloging-in-Publication Data
Saliba, Bonnie.
  Water markets in theory and practice.
  (Studies in water policy and management; #12)
    1. Water transfer—Southwestern States. 2. Water
transfer—Government policy—Southwestern States.
3. Water-supply—Southwestern States. 4. Water-supply—
Government policy—Southwestern States. I. Bush,
David B. II. Title. III. Series: Studies in water
policy and management; no. 12.
HD1695.A165S25 1987   333.91'00979   87-21687
ISBN 0-8133-7465-0

Composition for this book was provided by the authors.
This book was produced without formal editing by the publisher.

Printed and bound in the United States of America

⊗ The paper used in this publication meets the requirements of the American National Standard for
   Permanence of Paper for Printed Library Materials Z39.48-1984.

3-28-90

Contents

PART ONE
WATER MARKETS IN THEORY

PART TWO
WATER MARKETS IN PRACTICE

Tables

Figures

Foreword

   This timely book, number twelve in the Westview
Studies in Water Policy and Management Series, comes out
in the midst of rapid changes in water institutions and
management practices in the Western United States. New
water resources are becoming more difficult and expensive
to develop, while competition for existing supplies
continues to intensify. While market transfers of water
rights are increasing in number, a greater emphasis is
being placed by private individuals, water management
agencies, and the courts on matters of public interest in
water: instream flows, water for wildlife and wilderness,
water quality and area-of-origin protection.
   The Saliba-Bush book explains in careful detail the
workings of existing Southwestern water markets. What is
a water market, who is buying, selling and leasing, how
are trades arranged, how do laws and policies affect
market transactions, what prices are being paid and how do
the characteristics of water rights affect their market
value? Use of observed prices along with alternative
approaches to valuing water rights are addressed, as is
the issue of evaluating whether or not market transfers
allocate water resources efficiently and fairly.
   This book will be valuable to those who approach
water markets from a practical point of view, and will be
equally stimulating and informative for those interested
in broad policy and theoretical issues.

Charles W. Howe
General Editor

_____

   Charles W. Howe is professor of economics at the
University of Colorado, Boulder, Colorado. He has been a
teacher and a consultant in several developing countries,
specializing in natural resource economics. His books
include <u>Benefit-Cost Analysis for Water System Planning</u>,
<u>Natural Resource Economics</u>, and <u>Management of Renewable
Resources in Developing Countries</u>.

Acknowledgments

The research for this volume was supported by grants from the U.S. Forest Service and the U.S. Geological Survey. Support was also provided by the Arizona Agricultural Experiment Station, the University of Arizona, and U.S. Dept. of Agriculture Western Regional Research Project W-178 "Water Management and Conservation in Western Irrigated Agriculture."

The authors gratefully acknowledge suggestions provided by the following individuals who reviewed material presented in this volume: F. Lee Brown, Robert E. Dietrich, Charles W. Howe, Helen M. Ingram, Larry J. MacDonnell, William E. Martin, Susan C. Nunn, Steven J. Shupe, Gary D. Weatherford, and Robert A. Young. We also appreciate suggestions on the text and maps provided by Thomas Brown of the U.S. Forest Service Rocky Mountain Experiment Station.

Invaluable production and administrative assistance was provided by Cathy Campanella and Jo Robb. Technical editing was provided by Genevieve Gray, graphics and artwork by Linda Phipps and Wally Varner, and computer and equipment support by Annie Hudecek.

Bonnie Colby Saliba
David B. Bush

Part One

Water Markets in Theory

1
Water Markets—What Are They and Why Do They Develop?

WHAT CHARACTERIZES MARKET PROCESSES?

This chapter identifies alternative processes for transferring water, distinguishes markets from other transfer processes, outlines the role of economic incentives and institutional arrangements in water market development and argues that economic rather than legal considerations have prevented markets from becoming more active and widespread.

A few definitions of terms will be helpful in the discussion which follows. A "water resource" is a source of water supply (such as a lake, reservoir, stream or aquifer) and a "water right" is a collectively recognized access to water resources under specific conditions defined in the right, such as point of diversion, season, location and purpose of use, and quantity of withdrawals. While water resources are regarded typically as the inalienable property of a community as a whole ("the people of New Mexico," for instance), water rights often are held by individuals, businesses and government agencies and, in many areas, may be bought, sold or leased. A "market" consists of the interactions of actual and potential buyers and sellers of one or more interrelated water commodities. Negotiated transactions generate prices and conditions of sale and use for each commodity. The term "market" generally refers to a set of transactions taking place continuously over a period of time. When relatively few transactions take place the market is considered "thin", and a key market function-- the establishment of a "going" price--may be lacking.

Market transfers are only one of many processes by which water is reallocated in the western United States. Other reallocative processes include the following:

At-cost Administrative Transfers. Water may be leased for a rate that covers costs associated with the transfer but does not confer economic gain on the lessor. A number of such transfers took place in California during the drought years of the late 1970s. Authorized by the Emergency Drought Act of 1977, the Bureau of Reclamation purchased water from users who were willing to reduce their use temporarily and resold it to water users who needed water to protect long-term investments in orchards and other perennial crops. The price was set to cover Bureau acquisition costs and conveyance charges.(1) The 1977 Act stipulated that the purchase price "could not confer any undue benefit or profit to any persons compared to what would have been realized if the water had been used in normal irrigation of crops adapted to the area."(2)

Forfeiture and Abandonment. Water rights can be lost due to intent to abandon the right or to long periods of continuous nonuse (five years in many states). Under either of the above circumstances the right could become available for appropriation by others. Weatherford and Shupe(3) note that while forfeiture and abandonment proceedings have been infrequent, they may occur more often as water scarcity and competitive pressure for water rights become more acute.

Eminent Domain. Public agencies and utilities are often authorized to condemn and obtain title to water rights. Reallocation of water rights through eminent domain is constrained by lack of public funds to compensate rights holders and by political opposition. Condemnation of riparian rights and compensation of rights holders to permit construction of the Friant Dam in California's Central Valley Project is one example of the exercise of eminent domain.(4)

Litigation. Law suits challenging existing water allocations have the potential to force water transfers. Thus far, litigation by native American tribes to establish and protect tribal water rights generally has been resolved by developing new water sources rather than by transferring water from non-Indian users. However, some reallocation seems inevitable if the many tribal claims still unsettled are to be resolved.(5) Litigation based on the Public Trust Doctrine has resulted in some modification of water use by existing right holders. For instance, the 1983 Mono Lake case held that diversions from tributary streams serving Mono Lake by the Los Angeles Department of Water and Power, based on a permit issued in 1940, had to be modified to protect the unique scenic, recreational and scientific resources associated with the lake and its environs.(6)

Legislative Settlements of Conflicting Claims. Congress and state legislatures sometimes take a hand in settling conflicting water claims with resultant clarification, if not reallocation, of water rights. Two recent examples include the Fort Peck-Montana Compact which allocates disputed claims to the Missouri River and the 1982 Southern Arizona Water Rights Settlement Act which addressed conflicts over groundwater pumping between the Tohono O'odham tribe and other water users in the Tucson area.(7) The settlement includes a transfer of treated effluent from the City of Tucson to the Secretary of the Interior for use in water exchanges to provide water to the Tohono O'odham.(8)

Water Project Redesign. During the long time lapses between public water project authorization, appropriation and construction, regional economies change with resultant pressures to alter initial project allocations among alternative water uses. Both the Central Arizona Project, authorized in 1968 and currently under construction, and North Dakota's Garrison Diversion Project initially were envisioned as primarily irrigation projects but have undergone significant shifts in the proportion of project water allocated to agricultural industrial and municipal users. Weatherford and Shupe (9) are of the opinion that it is not yet clear whether these shifts in the proportions of project water going to various water using sectors require Congressional action, such as amendment of project authorization or reauthorization.

Given that a variety of reallocative processes exist, what differentiates market reallocation of water rights from other processes? The following characteristics may be said to distinguish market transfers from other transfer processes and from transfers of other property rights:

1. Water's value is recognized as distinct from the value of land and improvements. Water is bought and sold for its own sake, not merely as an incidental part of a land transfer. In Arizona, for instance, where irrigation rights may only be transferred if the buyer purchases the irrigated land to which the rights are appurtenant, land

acquisition is often incidental to the real
purpose of the transaction, which is acquisition
of water rights.
2. Buyers and sellers agree to reallocation volun-
tarily, believing it is in their own best interest
given the alternative opportunities available to
them.
3. Price and other terms of transfer are negotiable
by the buyer and the seller and are not
constrained to be "not for profit" or "at cost."

The term "water markets", as used in this study,
refers to transactions which satisfy these three conditions. Such transactions may include sale or lease of fee
titles, water use permits, conservancy district shares and
project contract rights; or conditional water leases for
drought year use; or even exchanges of water rights with
varying priority dates and arrangements to use conserved
water. Water resources which may be involved in market
transactions include groundwater, native and imported
surface water, artificially recharged and recovered water,
effluent and conserved water.

WHY DO MARKETS DEVELOP?

The motivating force behind market development is
mutual perception by potential buyers and sellers that
economic gains may be captured by transferring water to a
location, season or purpose of use in which it generates
higher net returns than under the existing use patterns.
The economic returns to buyers must be large enough (or be
perceived as large enough) to outweigh the costs of
obtaining water through the market process. Even if the
net benefits to prospective buyers of transferring water
are positive, a second criterion must be satisfied for a
market transfer to occur. A market transaction must be
attractive relative to all other processes by which buyers
could achieve their water supply objectives. The costs of
the market process, including political costs and legal
uncertainties associated with market transfers, must be
less than the costs of alternative means of obtaining
water--such as hooking up to an existing water service or
contracting for water deliveries from a public water
project.

This study of market transactions in six western
states suggests that more market transfers are occurring,
and in more areas, in the 1980s than occurred in the 1970s

or 1960s.   Data on applications filed for water rights
transfers in seventeen western states over the years 1963
to 1982 indicate a substantial increase in transfer
applications over that twenty year period.(10) While many
of these applications either were not approved or were not
for market transfers, the data do support the notion that
interest in market transfers is growing.   Given the
conditions necessary for a market transaction, there are
several reasons why the level of market activity may be
increasing.

The southwestern states have experienced rapid rates
of population and economic growth since the Second World
War.   Concurrent with this growth, there has also been a
significant structural change in regional economies.
While irrigated agriculture remains the predominant water
user in the Southwest, the nonagricultural sectors of the
economy now employ all but a fraction of the work force
and generate a large proportion of income.   The construction, manufacturing, service, and government sectors of
the economy are competing successfully for land and water
resources once devoted to agriculture.   These economic
trends, which are discussed further in Chapter 3, make it
more probable that the first condition for a market
transaction will be satisfied--that there are net benefits
to be gained in transferring water to a new use.

Historically, water for new users in the West has
been provided through appropriating water rights to which
no previous claims had been established and through
constructing water development projects to capture, store
and transport water for areas where local supplies are
perceived as inadequate. The costs of such projects were
subsidized heavily by the federal government. During this
era there was little incentive to bid water rights away
from existing users because appropriation of unclaimed
water and subsidized or relatively inexpensive supply
development were attractive alternatives to market
transfers.   But surface water supplies are now fully
appropriated in many areas and some states have set limits
on new groundwater pumping so that it is no longer an
inexpensive and easy matter to appropriate new water
rights.   The costs to project beneficiaries of water
development have risen for several reasons: the best
reservoir sites have been used, environmental considerations and conflicting water claims have prompted
litigation resulting in project delays and costly impact
studies, and in recent years the federal government has
been less willing to subsidize project costs.   These

changes, which are discussed in detail in Chapter 3, make
it more likely that the second condition for a market
transaction will be satisfied--that market transfers will
be an attractive means of obtaining water supplies
relative to other alternatives.

While market transactions are primarily a response to
economic incentives, institutional arrangements play a
central role in market development. The term
"institutions" as used here shall mean the set of
political and legal norms and organizations which
coordinate and govern individual activities.(11) Commons
describes institutions as defining what "...individuals
must or must not do...what they may do without
interference from other individuals...what they can do
with aid of collective power...and what they cannot expect
the collective power to do in their behalf."(12)
Prospects for increasing net returns to water use may be
the driving force behind markets but laws and policies
affect the cost of market transactions and the
attractiveness of market transfers relative to other means
of transferring water. The institutional environment
determines the transaction and development costs associated with market transfers.

Transaction costs are incurred in searching for
trading partners; in identifying legal and hydrologic
characteristics of water rights (priority date, return
flow obligations, etc.); in negotiating price and arrang-
ing financing and other terms of transfer; and in
satisfying state laws and transfer approval procedures.(13) Development costs are often incurred in putting
water to new uses or moving it to new locations. Development costs may include storing, transporting and treating
water for the new use. Buyers will not undertake a
transfer unless returns to water in their intended use
outweigh both the price paid to the seller and all transaction and development costs borne by the purchaser.
Sellers will not agree to a transfer unless the price they
receive compensates them for the stream of future profits
sacrificed by giving up water rights plus any out-of-
pocket transaction costs borne by the seller.

Transaction and development costs influence the
profitability of a given transfer and can, therefore,
affect the level of market activity. State laws impose
transaction cost on market participants in the form of
transfer approval requirements such as court hearings,
title searches and hydrologic studies to determine
transfer impacts. Institutional arrangements affect

development   costs of transporting and treating water.
For instance, conveyance charges, priority of canal use
and other conditions for using existing public project
canals to transfer non-project water can affect the
economic viability of a transfer that requires conveyance
systems to move water from the seller to the buyer.
Institutions that restrict market activities and make
transactions more costly are not necessarily wasteful.
They are an expression of the concerns that members of
society and policy makers have about reallocating water
through market processes.   The role of institutional
conditions for transfers and their impact on transaction
costs and the level of market activity are discussed in
detail in Chapter 4.

WHY ISN'T THERE MORE MARKET ACTIVITY?

    As Brown, et al. note, only a small proportion of
water resources in the West have been, or are soon likely
to be, reallocated through market processes.(14)   If all
that is needed for market transfers to occur is for net
benefits to the purchaser to be positive and for markets
to be an attractive mechanism for obtaining water relative
to other possibilities, then why do we not see more market
transactions?   It is argued here that economic, rather
than institutional, considerations are responsible for
limited market activity.   Young (15) notes that water has
relatively low economic value at the margin.   The value of
the first units of water available to a city, household or
farm may be very high, but the value of an additional unit
of water above and beyond existing supplies is often quite
low.   Given that market transactions often are costly to
implement and that water can be costly to convey and store
relative to its marginal value, it is not surprising that
more market transfers do not occur.   The excess of
benefits over costs for market transactions simply is not
high enough in some areas to induce more market activity,
especially if lower cost nonmarket alternatives for
obtaining water supplies are still available.

    In areas characterized by low net returns to water
transfers, potential buyers and sellers have limited
incentives to lobby for laws and policies that promote
market development.   In those areas where net returns to
market transfers are high, legal impediments to transfers
often are not enforced or are modified to facilitate
transfers.   Economic incentives for market development

Marginal value of water (margin note)

generate pressure for institutional innovation. Implementation of laws that restrict water transfers may indicate
that policymakers do not expect the gains from market
transactions to outweigh the political and economic costs
of allowing active markets to develop. As Martin argues,
"It will only take time for more formal water markets to
develop...I am not worried that major opportunities for
economic development are being foregone. Outmoded institutions seem to evolve into new institutions when economic
opportunities really exist."(16)

NOTES

1. R.W. Wahl and F.H. Osterhoudt, "Voluntary Transfers of Water in the West." In National Water Summary
1985, U.S. Geological Survey, 1986.
2. C.T. Lee, "The Transfer of Water Rights in
California." Governor's Commission to Review California
Water Rights Law (Staff Paper #5). Sacramento, December,
1977.
3. G.D. Weatherford and S.J. Shupe, "Reallocating
Water in the West." American Water Works Association
Journal 78:63-71, October, 1986.
4. Ibid.
5. J. Folk-Williams, What Indian Water Means to the
West. Santa Fe: Western Network, 1984.
6. C.F. Wilkinson, "Western Water Law in Transition." American Water Works Association Journal 78:34-49,
October, 1986; J.E. Thorson, "Public Rights at the Headwaters." American Water Works Association Journal 78:72-
78, October, 1986.
7. S.J. Shupe, "Water Management in Indian Country."
American Water Works Association Journal 78:55-62,
October, 1986; R.B. Collins, "Indian Reservation Water
Rights." American Water Works Association Journal 78:48-
54, October, 1986.
8. H.T. Ingram, T. McGuire, and M. Wallace,"Poverty,
Power and Water Resources on the Papago Reservation."
University of Arizona and the Ford Foundation, Department
of Political Science, Tucson, 1984.
9. Weatherford and Shupe, op. cit.

10. Higginson-Barnett, Consultants, "Water Rights and Their Transfer in the Western United States." Report to the Conservation Foundation by R.K. Higginson and J.A. Barnett. Salt Lake City, 1984.

11. I. Fox, "Institutions for Water Management in a Changing World." Natural Resources Journal 16:743-758, 1976.

12. J.R. Commons, Legal Foundations of Capitalism. Madison: University of Wisconsin Press, 1968, p.6.

13. A detailed discussion of transaction costs associated with New Mexico water transfers is provided in R. Khoshakhlagh, F.L. Brown and C. DuMars, "Forecasting Future Market Values of Water Rights in New Mexico," final report on Project No. 3109-209, New Mexico Water Resources Research Institute, July, 1977.

14. L. Brown, B. McDonald, J. Tyseling and C. DuMars, "Water Reallocation Market Proficiency and Conflicting Social Values," in Water and Agriculture in the Western U.S., ed. Gary Weatherford. Boulder, Colorado: Westview Press, 1982.

15. R.A. Young, "Why are There So Few Transactions Between Water Users?" American Journal of Agricultural Economics Vol. 68:1143-1151, December, 1986.

16. W.E. Martin, "The Economics of Water Transfers: When Do Markets Develop?" Proceedings of Symposium on Arizona Water Markets and Transfers, Tucson, Arizona, November, 1986.

2
The Market Model
of Water Allocation

DESIRABLE CHARACTERISTICS OF ALLOCATION PROCESSES

When water becomes economically scarce, conflicts
over access begin to develop and a water allocation
process of some kind must evolve. Water is said to be
economically scarce when there is no longer enough
available to allow all users to have as much as they want
without giving up something else of value in order to
obtain it. Where water is abundant, there is no reason
for anyone to pay to obtain it since more can be used
without giving up something else and there is little
reason to develop rules for water use and allocation.
However, water is economically scarce in areas of the West
where undeveloped water supplies and unappropriated water
rights are no longer readily available. Decisions must
therefore be made about who will have access to water and
under what conditions.
Howe et al. (1) outline six characteristics desirable in
water allocation processes:
1. There should be flexibility so as to allow water
   to be shifted in location, season and purpose of
   use in response to changing social and economic
   conditions.
2. There should be secure expectations of water
   availability for established right holders,
   giving water users a basis for making long-term
   investment and planning decisions.
3. Opportunity costs associated with water use and
   transfer must be accounted for by water right
   holders so that their decisions are based on a
   complete assessment of costs and benefits.

Opportunity costs are the stream of net benefits that are foregone when one resource use alternative is chosen over other alternatives.

4. Collective values related to water must be incorporated into the allocation process so that water use and transfer decisions reflect not only private interests but also broader social values.

5. Predictability of the allocation process helps water users know what to expect and to adjust gradually to changes. Prevailing requirements (the "rules of the game") should be clear and not subject to unanticipated changes.

6. Fairness requires that uncompensated costs must not be imposed on third parties and the public, and that water transfers are noncompulsory.

HOW DOES MARKET ALLOCATION COMPARE?

Howe et al.(2) have argued that market processes meet the above six criteria better than alternative allocation processes--administrative or judicial reassignment of water rights, for instance. They note that markets guarantee flexibility and security of water rights since all rights holders are permitted to participate in the market but none are required to do so. The opportunity to buy and sell forces rights holders to consider water's opportunity cost. Transactions are fair in the sense that buyers and sellers will only participate if they believe they have something to gain. Markets allocate economically scarce water resources by compelling buyers to evaluate the benefits of acquiring additional quantities of water at the expense of foregoing something else of value.

Reliance on market processes is consistent with the belief that individuals are the best judge of their own well-being and have the right to make economic decisions in pursuit of their own self-interest. Markets disperse the capacity to make resource allocation decisions among individuals who control resources. In a "free" market, resource ownership is primarily vested in private individuals and firms and the role of government is limited to facilitating individual decision-making through clarification and enforcement of property rights and contractual agreements.

Individual writers have displayed a wide range of opinions about the appropriateness of the market as a water allocation mechanism. Howe et al.(3) recognize the inherent weaknesses of market processes but suggest ways in which these weaknesses can be strengthened. Tregarthen(4) asserts that there is general agreement among economists that the market is capable of allocating water rights, and that the market is constrained by rules that limit its efficiency because jurists and policymakers don't perceive the virtues of an unfettered market which are so apparent to economists. Quinn(5) notes that very few water transfers resemble a "pure" market transaction in which water is treated like other routinely exchanged commodities and that in those situations which do approach the market paradigm, serious implementation issues have had to be addressed and overcome. Nunn et al.(6) argue that even though rural-to-urban market transfers may appear economically efficient and involve willing sellers, there are significant hidden costs and social impacts not adequately reflected in market transactions. Brown and Ingram (7) emphasize the social consequences of market transfers, quoting a member of the Tohono O'odham tribe on the leasing of tribal water rights. "...[M]oney," he said, "is just spent and the people are left with nothing. With water, there is something in the future."(8) To appreciate this wide spectrum of opinion on market transfers, it is important to understand the competitive market model for resource allocation and then to explore how actual water market processes differ from this model.

The virtue of the competitive market system as a mechanism for coordinating economic activities and allocating society's resources is a time-honored theme among economists. Adam Smith (9) described the market process as an "invisible hand" which uses price signals to guide self-interested individuals and profit-maximizing firms to buy, sell and pursue those activities in which they have a comparative advantage. Thus, Smith argued, the value of output is maximized, all participants are better off and resources are allocated and used efficiently.

The concept of efficiency was refined by the Italian economist Vilfredo Pareto around the turn of the century. A change in resource allocation is said to be "Pareto efficient" if the reallocation can improve at least one individual's well-being without decreasing the well-being of anyone else. Many resource transfers involve trade-offs; they make some individuals better off and leave others worse off, and so cannot be evaluated using the Pareto efficiency concept. Pareto efficiency has, therefore, been modified to extend its relevance. The

Kaldor-Hicks compensation criterion is a widely used modification which states that a reallocation is efficient if it represents a <u>potential</u> Pareto improvement--that is, if the gainers from the reallocation would be able to compensate fully the losers for their sacrifice in well-being and still be better off themselves.(10) This definition of efficiency, the conceptual foundation of benefit cost analysis, requires that benefits from any resource transfer must exceed all costs. This is how the term "efficiency" will be used in this discussion.

The Kaldor-Hicks compensation criterion has been criticized widely as a basis for public policy. Resource policy recommendations based upon it are contingent on current resource allocations and tend to reinforce the status quo.(11) The ethical, conceptual and practical difficulties of valuing changes in individuals' well-being and the problems of identifying those who would be beneficially or adversely affected by a water transfer also make implementation of efficiency criteria a complex and subjective process. Nevertheless, cost benefit analysis based on Kaldor-Hicks remains the standard economic approach to evaluating water project proposals and water policy alternatives. The efficiency of market allocation processes will be discussed and evaluated in Chapter 7, using information on market transfers in the Southwest.

A HYPOTHETICAL COMPETITIVE MARKET FOR WATER

To illustrate the workings of a competitive water market, assume that water rights are tradeable in standard units, that they are homogeneous and that they are demanded for only two purposes--irrigation and urban water service. Suppose further that water supplies are fixed and that there are no transaction costs incurred in transferring water. How, then, will market processes allocate water between the two sectors?(12)

The value that a particular water user or water-using sector places on any given quantity of water can be expressed as a marginal value (or demand) function which shows the value of the last unit of water added or deleted as a function of the quantity of water used. Figure 2.1 shows hypothetical urban, agricultural and aggregate marginal value functions for water at a fixed point in time. The negative slope of the demand function reflects the economic concept of diminishing marginal utility.

15

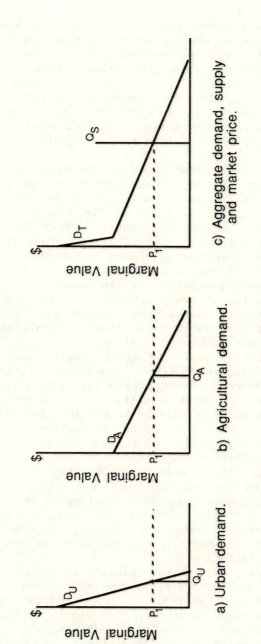

FIGURE 2.1   Urban, Agricultural and Aggregate Demand Functions

a) Urban demand.

b) Agricultural demand.

c) Aggregate demand, supply and market price.

Water uses are ranked by users according to their value. Domestic water users, for instance, might rank water for drinking and cooking highest and water for lawn-sprinkling or for washing cars at a lower value. As a household has more water available, it will put it to lower and lower valued uses. This phenomenon is called diminishing marginal utility. As more units of water become available to particular water user, that individual or firm is willing to pay less and less for each additional increment of water.

If we draw a graph relating the quantity of water a user will buy (on the horizontal) to the price of water (on the vertical), the graph will trace out the "marginal" value of water, or the value of the last unit used, for every quantity on the horizontal. This is called the marginal value product (MVP) of water. Next, if we add up all the quantities that all users in a region will buy at each price, then the aggregated graph will represent the regional demand for water, or the amount of water people will want to buy at every alternative price. Diminishing marginal utility makes the demand for water slope downward--as more water is available, people are willing to pay less for each additional unit.

Different types of water users have somewhat different marginal value functions. Urban users (illustrated by D_U in figure 2.1a) generally attach a higher value to the first units of water they use than most farmers would be willing to pay for that same initial quantity of water. Irrigated agriculture also has a downward-sloping demand curve for water (D_A in figure 2.1b). The negative slope shows that the first quantities of water available to a farm are the most valuable because they will be applied to crops for which the highest returns can be obtained. Additional water will be applied to the next most profitable set of crops, and so on. The aggregate marginal value function, D_T, is the horizontal summation of the agricultural and urban demand schedules as is shown in figure 2.1c.

Now, how does a market allocate water among the users represented by D_T? Suppose the total amount of water available is Q_S. In order to have a market, Q_S must be owned by persons or firms, the rights to Q_S must be transferrable, and claims to ownership of Q_S must be secure. Suppose these conditions are satisfied. An individual holding a right to use a portion of Q_S would be willing to give up (sell) some or all of their right if the market price for a right to a unit of Q_S exceeds the value of a unit of Q_s to the right holder. Anyone who does not own a right, but has a use for water, will be willing to buy a right to unit of Q_s if the market price is less than the value of a right to a unit of Q_s to the potential buyer.

The market price occurs at P_1 in figure 2.1, where the aggregate demand curve (D_T) intersects the supply function (Q_s). this example, Q_s is vertical to indicate fixed water supplies. If the going price in the market for water rights were below where demand intersects supply, there would be more persons in the buying mode than there would be in the selling mode. Buyers would be competing with one another for the available water, and would bid the price up towards P_1. Only when price equals P_1 does the market for water clear--that is to say, everyone who has a water right has a use valued higher than the market price, and everyone who does not have a water right is not willing to pay the going price to obtain one.

At the market clearing price the agricultural sector uses Q_A units of water and the urban sector uses Q_U units. Note that the value of an additional unit of water is equal for each use and is equal to the market price. If this were not so, more transactions would occur. However, there is nothing to be gained by reallocating water from one sector to the other since water has the same marginal value in both sectors.

Figure 2.1 portrays water demand, supply, and price formation in a static framework. As population and income levels grow or agricultural commodity prices and production technologies change, demand and supply curves shift and new prices evolve, as shown in figure 2.2. Suppose that urban growth caused the urban marginal function $D_U{}^1$ to shift upward to $D_U{}^2$, implying that the larger group of urban users represented by $D_U{}^2$ collectively are willing to pay more for the same units of water than the smaller population represented by $D_U{}^1$ was willing to pay. At the original allocations of water between urban users and agriculture, $Q_A{}^1$ and $Q_U{}^1$, the marginal value of water is no longer equal between the two sectors. It is now higher in urban use and urban users would be willing to buy a specific quantity of water from irrigators--that specific quantity which will reestablish equal marginal values between irrigation and urban uses. This adjustment is shown in figure 2.2 in the increase of the market clearing price from P_1 to P_2 and the transfer of $\bar{Q}$ units of water (where $\bar{Q}=Q_A{}^1-Q_A{}^2=Q_U{}^2-Q_U{}^1$) from

18

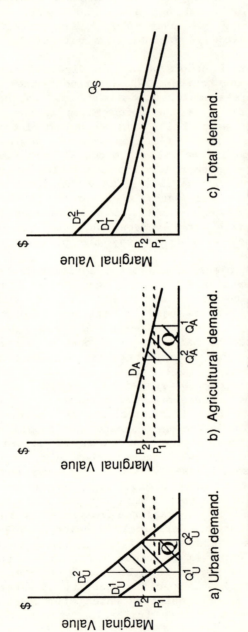

FIGURE 2.2 Reallocation Of Water From Agricultural To Urban Users.

irrigation to urban use. Figure 2.2a shows the original and new urban marginal value functions ($D_U{}^1$ and $D_U{}^2$) and the original and new market allocation of water to urban use ($Q_U{}^1$ and $Q_U{}^2$) and figure 2.2b shows the unchanged irrigation demand curve (D_A) and the competitive market allocation of water to agriculture before and after the transfer ($Q_A{}^1$ and $Q_A{}^2$).

The economic implications of this transfer are also illustrated in figure 2.2. It is assumed, for illustrative purposes, that the transfer has no impact on markets for other goods and services. The market reallocation of water to satisfy increased urban demand has increased the total benefits realized by water users. Total benefits are the sum of all the marginal benefits and so benefits are represented by the area under the marginal value curves.(13) The shaded area in figure 2.2a shows the increase in urban benefits from the additional water, while the shaded area in figure 2.2b shows the decrease in agricultural benefits due to decreased water for agriculture. The shaded areas do not indicate overall changes in well-being attributable to the transfer. Agricultural water users are exchanging one form of wealth for another--water for dollars. They will only agree to sell the water if they are paid a sum greater than or equal to the value of the water to them in agricultural use. Urban users will not experience an increase in well-being equal to the entire shaded area in figure 2.2a because they have to make a payment to irrigators in order to obtain the additional water. The net benefits of the transfer--when the increased benefits of water use in urban areas, the losses due to decreased water use in irrigation and the payment from the urban area to irrigators are all accounted for--are represented by the shaded area in figure 2.2a minus the shaded area in figure 2.2b. If this amount were not positive, there would have been no economic incentive to transfer water. The distribution of these net benefits between agricultural sellers and urban buyers depends on their bargaining skills and the prices they negotiate.

A perfectly functioning market would ensure that transfers occur automatically whenever the net benefits from a transfer are positive. Beneficial reallocations take place when a change in demand stimulates a change in marginal values. Under the competitive market model, when marginal values are not equal among water users, gains from an exchange are possible and a transfer between

willing buyers and sellers will bring marginal values back
into equilibrium.
Three conditions must be satisfied for a buyer and seller
to consummate a water transfer:

1. The buyer must expect the returns from the water
   rights purchase (which may be contributions to
   some production process, investment returns or
   returns to real estate development) to exceed all
   costs associated with the purchase including the
   price paid to the seller, water storage, treatment
   and conveyance costs, and legal costs to implement
   the transfer.
2. The seller must receive a price offer that equals
   or exceeds the return he gives up and that covers
   any costs he has incurred in transferring the
   water. A farmer, for instance, must consider the
   net returns to water in irrigation, any decreases
   in the value of his land, improvements and
   equipment due to reduced water, available for
   irrigation and expected appreciation in the value
   of the water right over time.
3. The buyer must view a market purchase of water
   rights as an economically attractive method of
   obtaining water relative to other possibilities--
   such as contracting for public project water or
   hooking up to a water service organization.

These conditions can be summarized in the following two
inequalities:(14)

Buyer's Returns - Buyer's Costs Associated with Transfer	>	Returns Foregone by Seller	+ Seller's Costs Associated with Transfer

Buyer's Costs Associated with Transfer	<	Costs of Alternative Means of Obtaining Water Supplies

Use of these conditions to evaluate a particular
proposed transfer requires that all returns and costs be
expressed in comparable units, such as discounted present
value.(15)

The description of the market process thus far has
assumed fixed water supplies. A competitive market could
also, hypothetically, ensure that an efficient quantity of

water is provided. Economic efficiency requires that another unit of water be supplied whenever the cost of supplying it is less than the benefits generated by supplying it, and only then. This implies that the optimal quantity is that for which the marginal cost of supplying an additional increment of water equals exactly the marginal value of that additional increment. For quantities less than the optimum, benefits of supply expansion exceed the costs, while for quantities greater than the optimum, water supplies are too expensive at the margin and this results in net losses. Profit-maximizing suppliers of water would respond to increases in the marginal value of water by providing more water, up to the quantity where marginal costs rise as high as marginal value. The costs of supplying an additional unit of water can be expressed as a marginal cost function which indicates the change in the total cost of providing water resulting from an incremental change in the quantity of water supplied.

The process of inducing suppliers to provide more water is illustrated in figure 2.3a which shows a regional water market in equilibrium with a demand (marginal value) function, a marginal cost function and a market clearing price of P_1 at quantity Q_1. At Q_1 the marginal cost of supplying an additional increment of water just equals the marginal value of an additional increment so there is no incentive to supply more water. Suppose regional economic growth causes an upward shift in the demand curve from D_1 to D_2 without altering the marginal cost function, as shown in 2.3b. At Q_1, the marginal value of additional water exceeds the marginal cost of providing it and profit-maximizing competitive water suppliers would respond by providing more water until marginal cost again equals marginal value. In figure 2.3b this occurs at Q_2 and a price of P_2.

For a water market to provide efficient allocation, use and supply of water resources, the following criteria must be satisfied:

1. All economic agents must behave as price takers; no single individual or firm can strategically affect market prices because simultaneous exchanges among many buyers and sellers jointly are what determine market price.

2. All economic agents must have access to complete information on legal and hydrologic characteristics of water rights and the costs of alternative means of obtaining water.

22

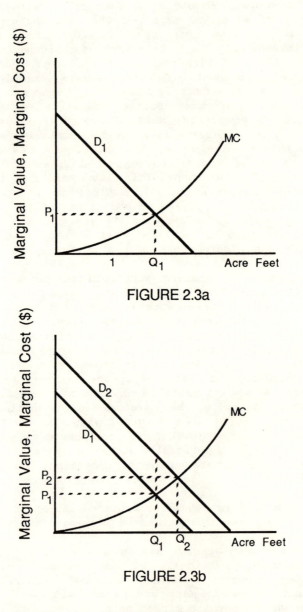

FIGURE 2.3a

FIGURE 2.3b

FIGURE 2.3   Efficient Water Supply Expansion

3. Property rights for water resources must be
   a. completely specified and enforced so that all individuals know the privileges and restrictions associated with holding a water right and the penalties for their violation;
   b. exclusive so that the benefits and costs associated with water use and transfer decisions accrue to the decision makers (buyers, sellers, right holders), not to third parties;
   c. comprehensive so that all attributes and uses of water that generate value can be represented by water rights, including water quality, instream flow levels and so on; and
   d. transferable so that water right holders may transfer rights in response to an attractive offer and water resources can gravitate to their highest value uses.

A market economy operating under these conditions has many desirable consequences. Prices for all goods and services, including water, will be equal to both marginal cost and marginal value in various uses. Prices will guide producers to supply the combination of goods and services that has the maximum value to buyers given available resources, current technology, consumer preferences and the distribution of income and resource ownership. Firms, in maximizing profits, will buy and use water and other inputs to minimize the costs of production and will produce items which have the highest market value. Consumers, in maximizing satisfaction subject to their budget, will purchase goods and services based on their own tastes and preferences, bidding up prices for those items most desired and thus signaling firms to produce those items. Market prices will adjust to changes in technology, resource availability and consumer preferences, signaling production patterns to shift to whatever combination of goods and services currently has the highest market value.

Finally, problems of unsatisfied water demand or excess water supply are resolved through voluntary responses of water right holders and prospective water users. Prices adjust to allocate water and other goods to those willing to pay the most for them so that anyone willing to pay the going price can obtain water. Price changes also stimulate changes in production patterns. When a particular good is in excess supply, its price falls and it becomes less profitable to produce. Prices for those goods in excess demand rise and those goods become more profitable to produce.

To summarize, a competitive market creates and maintains production, consumption and exchange patterns that cannot be improved upon by any alternative arrangement given current technology, preferences and wealth distribution.

DEVIATIONS FROM THE COMPETITIVE MARKET MODEL

Water markets, along with markets for many goods and services, are not perfectly competitive and deviate significantly from the model just described. These deviations, often referred to as market failure, will be discussed in four broad categories which are briefly defined in this chapter and which will be treated in more detail in Chapters 6 and 7, where their implications for water valuation and for water policy will be discussed. A fifth category, equity and collective values, will also be introduced although it is related to the distributional impacts rather than the economic efficiency of market water transfers, and so is not typically considered a market failure in the economics literature.

External Effects of Market Activities

When water use and transfer decisions have impacts on individuals who were not party to the decision process or transfer negotiations, some values are affected that are not considered in buyers' and sellers' decisions. These third-party effects are termed "externalities." They occur because property rights in water are difficult to completely specify and make exclusive--the mobile nature of water makes third-party impacts almost inevitable. When water use and transfer decisions involve externalities, prices no longer convey accurate information about opportunity costs. In particular, market transactions fail to account for costs imposed on third-parties and thus market prices fail to reflect these costs.

Public Goods Characteristics of Water Resources

Some water uses can provide benefits to more than one individual simultaneously, a characteristic called nonrivalry or joint consumption. It may also be difficult to limit benefits received to those who pay for them, a

characteristic called nonexcludability. The benefits
generated by water use for urban greenbelts and parks and
the aesthetic and recreation value of water on public
lands are both nonrival and nonexcludable. Since the
market allocates goods by excluding those who will not pay
the going price, the nonexcludability characteristic means
that market prices cannot effectively allocate water for
these uses. To further complicate matters, even if
exclusion were possible, to exclude individuals from the
benefits of nonrival goods would reduce the total value
that these water uses can generate. Uses of water which
have public good characteristics cannot be efficiently
allocated through market processes, either because it is
impractical to charge a price (due to nonexcludability) or
because it is not desirable to exclude individuals who
benefit from the water use at zero cost to others (due to
nonrivalry).

Imperfect Competition

When individual buyers or sellers can influence
market prices, a market is characterized as imperfectly
competitive. Under these circumstances, prices may no
longer reflect the marginal value of water in alternative
uses and may not provide market signals that result in
efficient water use and transfer. Imperfect competition
can arise for a number of reasons, two of which are
relevant to this discussion. First, because supply or
distribution costs typically decrease on a per acre-foot
basis as the quantity of water provided by a particular
organization increases, larger providers may undercut
smaller providers resulting in a small number of water
suppliers or distributors who have power over price. The
second reason, often related to the first, is public
policies which affect the number of prospective water
providers. Public policies often result in only one water
service company or one irrigation project serving an area.
If these organizations participate in market transfers,
their control over local water resources may influence
market outcomes.

Risk, Uncertainty and Imperfect Information

The efficiency of competitive markets assumes
accurate information is available on water quality,
availability, and costs of supply over time so that
individuals may decide how much supply uncertainty is

acceptable to them and at what price. Opportunities for
redistributing risk exist when some water users are
willing to pay more than others to protect themselves
against supply shortfalls. The consequences of water
shortages for a city may be more serious than the
consequences of water shortages for an irrigator. A market
potentially could distribute the risks of supply
shortfalls between those willing to bear some risks if
they are compensated for doing so--irrigators, for
example--and those willing to pay to protect themselves
from supply uncertainty--cities or industrial users.
Examples of risk sharing in water markets include city
purchases of options to use irrigation water rights in
drought years. Markets to redistribute risk typically are
incompletely developed due to uncertainty about the nature
of the risk and asymmetric information which could allow
parties which have special information on the nature of
the risk to take advantage of any risk allocation process.

Equity and Conflict Resolution

Policymakers may intervene in market allocation
processes in pursuit of objectives such as redistribution
of economic gains from water use, settlement of water
right conflicts, revenue generation to repay water project
costs, public control over strategic water resources and
enhancement of specific interest groups' objectives.
Public policies can affect the efficiency of market
processes. Public policies which affect the cost of water
to specific users may impair the ability of the market
price system to reflect accurately opportunity costs and
to induce efficient water use. An example is the
longstanding federal policy of subsidizing irrigators.
Providing water to irrigators at less than the marginal
cost of supplying that water prevents farmers from
accounting for the full opportunity costs of irrigation
water use. As a result, marginal values of water in
irrigation may be less than the marginal costs of
providing irrigation water and may also be less than
water's marginal value in alternative uses.

THE POTENTIAL FOR INEFFICIENCY IN MARKET TRANSFERS

While the competitive market model has a number of
attractive features, both the nature of real world
markets, with the imperfections described, and the nature

of water resources suggest that water markets will not necessarily ensure efficient use and transfer of water. Young(16) summarizes characteristics of water itself which make it difficult and costly for market processes to efficiently allocate water. Since water is highly mobile (it flows, evapotranspires and seeps), it is difficult to define and measure property rights in water. Supply can be highly variable across seasons, years and locations, and water quality varies as well. The diversity of uses to which water can be put, along with the mobility of water, create interdependencies among water users. Many off-stream uses of surface water, such as irrigation, return a proportion of water diverted back to the stream system and these return flows are used by downstream users. Transfer of a water right can change these return flow patterns and affect water availability for downstream users. Water has instream values related to recreation, fish and wildlife, and aesthetics. Instream and offstream water values come into conflict when water is diverted at locations and in seasons for which instream values are high.

The potential for inefficiency in water market transactions when the competitive market criteria are not satisfied can be illustrated by an example of a hypothetical conflict between instream and offstream water uses. Suppose that a power company holding water rights is negotiating with a growing city over a water transfer to the city that would reduce instream flows on a particular stretch of river. The transfer will reduce hydroelectric power generation and the city is willing to fully compensate the power company for this loss.(17) The situation thus far is illustrated in figure 2.4. $Q_U{}^1$ and $Q_H{}^1$ represent the initial allocation of stream flow, represented by Q_S, between the city and the hydropower plant. Note that the marginal value of water for city and hydropower uses are equal at this allocation, as efficiency requires. D_H represents the marginal value of water instream on this stretch of the river in hydropower production and D_U represents the city's willingness to pay for various quantities of river water. The urban marginal value function has shifted upwards from $D_U{}^1$ to $D_U{}^2$, making water's marginal value higher in urban use higher than in hydropower and prompting the transfer negotiations. The market price rises from P_1 to P_2. Assuming no impacts on the market for any other goods or services, the gains associating with transferring water to urban use appear to outweigh the losses associated with

28

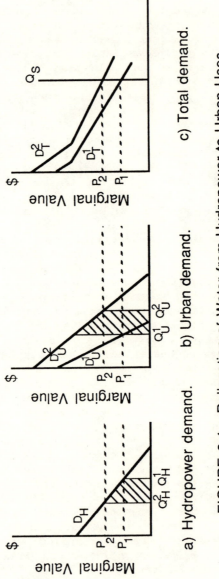

a) Hydropower demand.　　b) Urban demand.　　c) Total demand.

FIGURE 2.4　Reallocation of Water from Hydropower to Urban Uses

removing water from hydropower production since the shaded area in figure 2.4b (urban gains) is larger than the shaded area in figure 2.4a (hydropower losses). The shaded areas in figure 2.4a and 2.4b do not represent net changes in well-being for the hydropower firm and the city because they do not indicate the transfer of money from the buyer to the seller. The power company must receive a sum greater than or equal to the hydropower value of the water they give up (the shaded area in figure 2.4a) and the city must negotiate a payment to the seller that is less than or equal to the benefits generated by the additional water for urban use (shaded area in figure 2.4b). Otherwise the two parties would not agree to the transfer. The overall net benefits of the transfer are equal to the shaded area in figure 2.4b minus the shaded area in figure 2.4a. The distribution of these benefits between the buyer and the seller depends on their negotiating skills and the price they eventually agree upon.

To illustrate the potential for an inefficient transfer (one for which losses outweigh gains), let us suppose that stream flow has recreation value and that this value is unaccounted for in hydropower-urban transfer negotiations. Suppose that this recreation value, when added to the demand (marginal value) function for hydropower, implies a higher marginal value for instream flows. In figure 2.5a, D_I represents overall demand for instream flow--hydropower value plus recreation value. Recreation value unrecognized in market negotiations has several implications for market efficiency. First, the original allocation between urban use and instream flow was itself inefficient. Unrecognized recreation values made the marginal value of water instream higher at the original allocation (Q_U^1, Q_H^1) than the marginal value of water in urban use. The marginal value of water instream at Q_H^1 is actually MV_I^1 (shown in figure 2.5a) and more water should have been left instream, in order to equate marginal instream values with marginal values for urban use,which were MV_U^1 at the original allocation (shown in figure 2.5b). Second, the proposed transfer of water from hydropower generation to the city may generate net losses, rather than net gains when recreation values are considered as shown in figure 2.5. The shaded area in 2-5a represents the losses to both sets of instream users, the hydropower plant and recreationists. City users, represented by D_U^2, may not be willing to make the transfer if they must compensate not only hydropower but

30

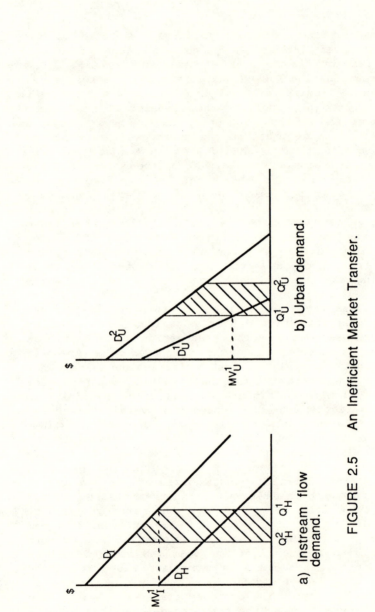

a) Instream flow demand.

b) Urban demand.

FIGURE 2.5   An Inefficient Market Transfer.

also recreationists for the loss in instream values. City
users are willing to pay no more than the shaded area in
figure 2.5b, which represents the value to urban users of
additional water. If the shaded area in figure 2.5b is
less than the shaded area in figure 2.5a the transfer
generates net losses. However, if institutional
arrangements do not cause buyers and sellers to account
for other values that may be affected by the transfer
(recreation values in this example), then the proposed
transfer may be beneficial to the buyer and seller even
though it is actually inefficient from an overall social
perspective. The possibility that private and social
interests regarding water transfers may diverge has been
recognized by western state policymakers. Legal
arrangements to address this divergence are described in
Chapter 4.

SUMMARY

Competitive markets have many desirable attributes
but the interdependencies and public goods characteristics
associated with water resources imply that a perfectly
competitive market is not a feasible water allocation
process. Chapter 5 describes the ways in which water is
allocated through a combination of market and nonmarket
processes in the western states and Chapter 7 evaluates
the efficiency of existing markets operating with the
imperfections discussed in this chapter.

NOTES

1. C.W. Howe, D.R. Schurmeier and W.D. Shaw, "Innovative Approaches to Water Allocation: The Potential for
Water Markets, " Water Resources Research 22:439-445,
1986.
2. Ibid.
3. Ibid
4. T.D. Tregarthen, "Water in Colorado: Fear and
Loathing of the Market Place." In Water Rights, ed. T. L.
Anderson, San Francisco: Pacific Institute for Public
Policy, 1983, p. 119-136.
5. T.H. Quinn, "Water Exchanges and Transfers to
Meet Future Water Demands in Southern California." In

Water Marketing, ed. S.J. Shupe, Denver: University of Colorado College of Law, September 1986, p.5-34 to 5-48.

6. S.C. Nunn, H. Ingram, R. Grimes and S. Eden, "Learning the Limits: Water Management in the Colorado River Basin." Paper presented at Western Social Science Meetings, Reno, Nevada, April, 1986.

7. F.L. Brown and H.M. Ingram, Water and Poverty in the Southwest: Conflict, Opportunity and Responsibility. Tucson: University of Arizona Press, 1987.

8. The tribal reservation is adjacent to the City of Tucson and has been the subject of large scale land and water development proposals.

9. A. Smith, An Inquiry into the Nature and Courses of the Wealth of Nations. 2 vols., ed. E. Cannon, London: Methuen and Co., Ltd., 1904.

10. N. Kaldor, "Welfare Propositions of Economics and Interpersonal Comparisons of Utility." The Economic Journal Vol. 49, No. 195, September, 1939, pp 549-52. J.R. Hicks, "The Foundations of Welfare Economics." The Economic Journal Vol. 49, No. 196, December, 1939, p. 696-712.

11. For an in-depth discussion, see D.W. Bromley, "Land and Water Problems: An Institutional Perspective." American Journal of Agricultural Economics 62:834-844, December, 1982.

12. The authors gratefully acknowledge the detailed comments of S.C. Nunn, Department of Economics, University of New Mexico, in clarifying this discussion of market processes.

13. The use of areas under market demand curves as measures of benefits and costs is discussed further in Chapter 6 where consumer and producer surplus measures are described.

14. These inequalities are adapted from R.A. Young, "Why Are There So Few Transactions Between Water Users?" American Journal of Agricultural Economics Vol.68:1153-1151, December, 1986.

15. The costs and returns of a water transfer typically are spread over a number of years. In order to determine whether returns outweigh costs, the stream of costs and returns over time must be reduced to a single number. The present value concept explicitly recognizes the time value of money by converting a stream of payments over time into the current worth of that stream of payments at a particular interest (or discount) rate.

16. Young, op. cit. See Note 13.

17. This heuristic example does not discuss the complex economic trade-offs and institutional arrangements affecting hydropower and off-stream use water conflicts. For a thorough discussion of such conflicts in the Pacific Northwest see W.R. Butcher and P.R. Wandschneider, with N.K. Whittlesey, "Competition Between Irrigation and Hydropower in the Pacific Northwest," in Scarce Water and Institutional Change, ed. K. Frederick. Resources for the Future, Washington D.C., 1986.

Part Two

Water Markets in Practice

3
Historical Development and Overview of Southwestern Water Markets

While much of the water market activity in the Southwest is a relatively recent phenomenon, the hydrologic, legal, and economic conditions that have contributed to the formation of water markets have been evolving for many years. Economic development of the arid and semiarid regions of the United States was facilitated by development of physical and social infrastructures to capture and manage scarce water resources. Native Americans and then Spanish colonists were the first to practice irrigation. Beginning in the mid-19th century, Anglo farmers followed suit, occupying the fertile bottomlands, damming rivers, and digging canals to create a green patchwork of irrigated fields throughout the West. While ranching and mining have contributed significantly to the economic development of the western United States, irrigated agriculture was the primary influence responsible for early and sustained economic growth. Demand for irrigation water provided the impetus for extensive investment in water infrastructure and also for development of water laws and institutions.

This chapter summarizes water resources development and changing patterns of water use and economic growth as they pertain to market formation in the Southwest. Characteristics of water rights which affect market values are outlined, and different types of market transactions are described. The chapter concludes with a discussion of current forces affecting market development.

WATER RESOURCE DEVELOPMENT: PHYSICAL AND INSTITUTIONAL
INFRASTRUCTURE

While water resource development in the West has
depended heavily on federal assistance, the contributions
of private reclamation projects should not be under-
estimated. From the Mormon villages of the Great Basin
states, to the cooperative agricultural colonies of
eastern Colorado and central California, to the ditch
companies and acequias of the Salt River and Rio Grande
River valleys, it was private capital that financed water
resources development. By 1910, over 13 million acres of
western lands were irrigated by private ventures. Between
1900 and 1910 the number of irrigated acres roughly
doubled, with private enterprise accounting for nearly all
of the increase.(1) Federal assistance in water resource
development began in the 20th century in response to the
demand for larger and more capital-intensive reclamation
projects than private investors were able and willing to
undertake on their own. Over 45 million acres of land
currently are under irrigation in the United States.
Eighty-five percent of the U.S. irrigated acreage is
located in the seventeen western states.(2) Approximately
20 percent of the water used in the West now comes from
federal water projects, and the rest is supplied by
private, local, and state water resource developments.(3)

Legal Development

Frontier settlers developed innovative institutional
arrangements in order to manage scarce water resources in
the West. Water resource administration in the humid
regions of the United States, adopted from the English
system of common law, operated under the presumption that
water resources were abundant and that users were never
located far from their source of supply. The riparian
doctrine vests water rights in the land adjacent to a
watercourse. This system generally gives license to the
holders of riparian rights to use whatever quantities of
water they desire, provided that other riparian users are
not affected adversely.

The legal doctrine of prior appropriation was
developed first by miners in California during the gold
rush of 1849 to settle conflicting claims to streamflows
used in mining operations. The appropriation doctrine
reflects a fundamental reality of water use in arid areas
--potentially productive lands frequently are located

distant from riparian areas. Riparian water law was not suited for development of water resources in the Southwest because it provided for the use of water at locations adjacent to watercourses only. While ownership and use of riparian water rights is limited strictly to riparian locations, appropriative water rights are not. Appropriative water rights are assigned to, but are not necessarily restricted to, specific locations and purposes of use. Under most appropriation systems, the location and purpose of use of a water right may be changed, subject to the permission of the state's agency for regulating water use. By the turn of the century, the appropriation system was accepted almost universally throughout the West as the legal basis for defining and allocating property rights in water.(4)

The nature of the appropriation system requires controls on water use in order to prevent serious conflicts among users. Offstream uses of water tend to be consumptive in nature. That is, not all the water withdrawn from the water resource is returned to the system. Appropriators of water are interdependent in that water used and released by one user is recaptured, used, and subsequently released by another user, and so on. As the number of appropriators on a common surface water or groundwater system grows and the rate of water consumption becomes significant, use of the water resource eventually may be stretched beyond its capacity to satisfy all demands. The consumptive uses of some appropriators will reduce the availability of water for others. It is the responsibility of state agencies to control the use of appropriated water rights by determining and enforcing the maximum quantity of water that may be used under each water right. Quantity limits may be expressed in terms of a maximum rate of flow (such as cubic feet per second) or a maximum volume diverted (such as acre feet per year).

Absolute limits on quantity are not sufficient to control water use under the appropriation system, however. The level of flow in western surface waters can vary tremendously from one season to the next. In some periods there might be more than enough water to serve all water rights, while in other periods there may be only enough to serve a fraction of the total demand. Administrators of western water have two alternative means of adjusting water use to variations in water availability. One possibility is to prorate water supplies among all users according to their existing claims to water--i.e., if flows are 20 percent below normal, all users might be

required to cut back on water use by 20 percent. The other
alternative is to institute a priority system, whereby in
times of inadequate flow some users are denied access to
water until the rights of other, higher priority water
rights are satisfied. Priorities typically are determined
on the basis of when each water right was established, the
older (senior) rights being considered superior to the
newer (junior) rights. Following the example of the gold
rush miners in California, most state agencies chose the
prior appropriation system of water rights over the
prorationing appropriation system, although in many areas
of the West a hybrid system of priorities and prorations
is practiced. Since priority systems of water rights
predominate throughout the West, in general the terms
"appropriation" and "prior appropriation" are used
interchangeably.

Conditions on the use of appropriative water rights
form a legal framework for defining water rights. The
framework provides each individual water right an absolute
measure in terms of quantity, and a relative measure in
terms of priority vis-à-vis other water rights. It
provides a basis for water users to understand the extent
and limit of their water rights, and on this basis, users
develop expectations of the economic returns they can earn
in exercising their rights. Users then are able to make
informed (economically rational) decisions about
undertaking investments in water resources and about
buying and selling water rights. Under the appropriation
doctrine, water rights are relatively well-defined and
exclusive, providing users with the means to determine the
value of the rights in use. Appropriative water rights
are also generally transferable, so that right holders
have an incentive to consider the value of water in
alternative applications and to exploit opportunities to
move water from lower to higher valued uses and to new
locations.

Rising Water Costs and Tightening Pursestrings

The water economy of the Southwest in the second half
of the twentieth century is characterized by rapidly
rising costs of developing new water resources and
increasing competition for existing supplies. The total
cost for the Central Utah Project, currently under
construction, is estimated to be $1.8 billion.(5) Funding
for the proposed Animas-La Plata Project was pushed
through Congress only after the original design was scaled

down considerably, reducing estimated construction costs from over $800 million to $572 million.(6) The Central Arizona Project, considered one of the last large federal water projects, will cost over $3.4 billion to complete.(7) Faced with growing budgetary constraints, the federal government is less willing to commit funds to large water projects. Although federal assistance is not expected to be withdrawn completely, conditions for providing money are becoming more stringent. Recently the federal government adopted new policies requiring state and local governments to provide more financial support for water projects directly, in some cases shouldering as much as half the project costs.(8) In addition, federal funding is increasingly difficult to obtain without broad support from a wide range of political and economic interests. For example, both the Central Arizona Project and the Animas-La Plata projects are linked closely to efforts to settle native American water rights claims. Many observers expect that conflict resolution objectives rather than economic development goals will provide the primary momentum for future federal funding of water projects.(9)

The Changing Mission of Water Service Organizations

Water service organizations historically have had a two-fold mission: first, to develop the physical and institutional infrastructure to make water available for use, and second, to define, maintain and protect the rights of users to have access to the water provided by the organization. Efficiency of water use historically has not been a concern of water user organizations. So long as water supplies were inexpensive to develop and additional undeveloped resources were available, there was little pressure to put water resources to their highest valued uses.

Emphasis in public water resource policy has begun to shift from supply enhancement towards supply and demand management. The role of the U.S. Bureau of Reclamation is evolving from supplying capital for large new water projects to facilitating more efficient use of existing supplies.(10) State and local governments are beginning to stress the importance of improving efficiency in water use by adopting policies designed to promote water conservation and the reallocation of water resources from lower to higher valued uses. Interest in flexible institutional processes to reallocate existing water

resources has led to an exploration of the potential for
voluntary market exchanges.

In summary, the history of the western United States
has been marked by ambitious development of water supplies
and rapid economic growth. Settlers in the West created
both the physical and institutional infrastructure
necessary to facilitate extensive development and use of
water. By the middle of the twentieth century
sophisticated systems of capturing, storing, treating, and
distributing appropriated waters were in place throughout
the West.

The doctrine of prior appropriation has been a
significant force in the development of western water
markets. It provided users with secure, quantifiable and
transferable property rights in water, creating
circumstances favorable for marketing water. Rapid
economic and population growth continues in the western
United States, but the era of inexpensive water supplies
has ended. Rising water costs have driven users to
consider ways of improving the efficiency of use of
existing water supplies, including market reallocation of
water resources.

THE CHANGING SOUTHWESTERN WATER ECONOMY

Several important points about water supply and use
in the Southwest over the period 1960 to 1980 may be
observed from the data summarized in Tables 3.1, 3.2 and
3.3. First, the aridity of the Southwest has not prevented
rapid growth and economic expansion. The rate of
population growth in every southwestern state has been in
excess of the average rate of population growth
nationwide. Economic expansion in this region has kept up
with increasing population, as indicated by significant
increases in real per capita income. Real per capita
income in Arizona, Colorado, and New Mexico increased at
rates in excess of the national average over the period
1960-1980.

A second observation is that municipal and industrial
uses of water in the Southwest are small relative to
agricultural uses. Proportions of water diverted for
public supply nationwide (7.6 percent) and in the
Southwest (7.2 percent) are about the same. However, while
over two-thirds of the water diverted outside the
Southwest is for industrial purposes, the great majority
of all diversions in the Southwest--nearly three-quarters

Table 3.1: Trends in Population, Personal Income, and Irrigation in the Southwest and U.S.

Region	Population		Real Per Capita Personal Income*		Irrigated Acreage	
	1980 (1000's)	%Change 1960-1980	1980 ($)	%Change 1960-1980	1980 (1000's)	%Change 1960-1980
Arizona	2,731	106.7	11,775	58.0	1,146	-0.5
California	23,771	49.8	14,560	44.1	8,482	14.7
Colorado	2,903	64.1	13,390	59.1	3,315	23.5
Nevada	807	177.3	14,236	39.2	855	57.5
New Mexico	1,305	36.8	10,522	56.0	848	15.9
Utah	1,472	63.6	10,208	39.8	1,125	5.9
Southwestern States	32,989	56.3	13,867	45.5	15,771	16.2
All Other States	194,167	22.2	12,468	55.2	33,904	73.0
US Total	227,156	26.2	12,671	54.4	49,675	49.8

* Per capita income is expressed in 1986 constant dollars, adjusted by the GNP price deflator index.

Adapted from:
U.S. Department of Commerce, Bureau of the Census, Census of Agriculture, Washington, DC, 1960, 1978, and 1982.
U.S. Department of Commerce, Bureau of Economic Analysis, State Personal Income: 1929-1982, Washington, DC, 1984.

Table 3.2: Withdrawals of Water for Offstream Use
(Acre feet per year)

Region	Public Supply* 1980 (1000's)	Public Supply* % Change 1960-1980	Irrigation, Livestock, and Rural Domestic* 1980 (1000's)	Irrigation, Livestock, and Rural Domestic* % Change 1960-1980	Self-Supplied Industrial* 1980 (1000's)	Self-Supplied Industrial* % Change 1960-1980	Total 1980 (1000's)	Total % Change 1960-1980
Arizona	627	294.3	7,953	51.5	281	92.5	8,861	59.5
California	4,592	57.7	42,416	108.7	13,956	23.5	60,964	76.5
Colorado	659	102.2	15,229	49.6	1,015	174.3	16,903	55.4
Nevada	261	193.3	3,520	75.0	281	430.2	4,062	88.6
New Mexico	236	95.0	4,059	99.0	82	60.8	4,377	97.9
Utah	840	241.5	3,677	-1.8	659	97.3	5,176	19.7
Southwestern States	7,215	87.6	76,854	76.5	16,274	32.8	100,343	68.2
All the Other States	30,870	61.3	97,729	77.2	279,578	88.9	408,177	83.6
US Total	38,085	150.9	174,583	76.9	295,852	84.6	508,520	80.3

Adapted from:
  K.A. Mackichan and J.C. Kammerer, Estimated Use of Water in the United States, 1960, Geological Survey Circular 456, Washington, DC, 1961.
  Wayne B. Folley, Edith B. Chase, and William B. Mann, Estimated Use of Water in The United States, 1980, Geological Survey Circular 1001, Washington, DC, 1983.

*Public supply refers to water withdrawn by public and private water suppliers and delivered to a variety of users for domestic, household, public, industrial, or commercial use. Water for rural use includes self-supplied household use, drinking water for livestock, and other uses such as dairy sanitation, evaporation from stock watering ponds, and cleaning and waste disposal. Irrigation use is the direct application of water to crops for promoting growth or improving yields. Self-supplied industrial use includes cooling water for thermoelectric power generation and other self-supplied uses in the production of products including (but not limited to) steel, chemicals, paper, minerals, and petroleum refining.

Table 3.3: Water Withdrawn by Region by Type of Use in 1980
(percent of total)

	Public Supply	Irrigation, Livestock, and Rural Domestic	Self-Supplied Industrial	Total
Southwestern States	7.19	76.59	16.22	100.00
All Other States	7.56	23.94	68.50	100.00
US Total	7.49	34.33	58.18	100.00

Source:

Wayne B. Solley, Edith B. Chase, and William B. Mann, Estimated Use of Water in the United States in 1980, Geological Survey Circular 1001, Washington, DC, 1983.

of the total--are used for irrigation. Approximately one-third of all irrigated acreage and close to half of all irrigation water use in the United States is concentrated within the six southwestern states.

A third observation is that the historical rates of change among the three major types of water use between 1960 and 1980 differs in the Southwest from elsewhere in the country. In the Southwest, use of water for public supply grew the fastest over this period, followed by irrigation and industrial uses. Outside the Southwest, industrial water use increased the most, followed by irrigation use and public supply.

There are strong indications that expansion of irrigation activity is slowing nationwide, prompted by the reversal of historical growth trends in western and southwestern irrigated agriculture. Since the late 1970s, declines in irrigated acreage and irrigation water use in the principal irrigated western states have overshadowed modest increases in irrigation elsewhere in the nation.(11) Meanwhile, western population and non-agricultural economic activity continue to grow at rapid rates.

Young's 1982 study of regional and state economic development in the West indicates that the water economy is passing from the "expansionary" phase to the "mature" phase.(12) During the expansionary phase, the incremental cost of new water supplies remains relatively constant, in real terms. Ample undeveloped water resources are available to meet expanding demands. Extensive development of water-intensive industries, particularly irrigated agriculture, takes place. Economic growth is reflected by expanding water supplies. The mature phase, characterized by full development of inexpensive water sources and by growth and shifts in the economy away from primary industries such as agriculture, results in rapidly rising water costs and greatly increased interdependencies among water users.(13)

Kelso, Martin, and Mack(14) described the transition of Arizona's water economy from the expansionary to the mature stages. During the period from 1929 to 1940, the state economy was relatively stable and total water use held steady at about three million acre feet per year. Rapid economic change and growth began in the early 1940s, with tremendous expansion in the agricultural and government sectors. Irrigated land increased from 0.5 to 1.3 million acres, population grew by 80 percent, real personal income more than tripled, and water use more than doubled, from 3 million to 6.5 million acre feet per year. Beginning in the early 1950s, the structure of the economy began to change again. Agricultural production remained stable and mining increased slightly, while all other sectors grew at rapid rates. Between 1953 and 1968 personal income more than tripled and the state's population doubled. In spite of this phenomenal growth, total water use increased only from 6.5 to 7.8 million acre feet per year. During the 1970s, state population grew by over 1,000,000, but there was relatively little change in total water use.

The character of the "water problem" in the arid regions of the United States is changing as the structure of the Southwestern economy changes. The historical record of economic development in the Southwest shows that in a maturing water economy, gradual transfers of water from lower-valued to higher-valued uses, and from stagnant to expanding economic sectors, can provide adequate resources for development without requiring significant new increases in water supplies. Most recent economic growth and expansion in water demand originates among municipal and commercial users, while the majority of water rights are held by irrigated agriculture, an economic sector of diminishing relative economic importance in many areas of the West. If incremental reallocations of water from agricultural to nonagricultural uses can continue to occur, existing water supplies may be adequate to support future economic growth. (15)

Water markets provide an opportunity for mutually beneficial transfers of water from agriculture to nonagricultural uses. Southwestern irrigated agriculture continues to face low commodity prices and other difficulties competing in international markets. Much of the water used in western agriculture is applied using relatively water-intensive flood irrigation systems, for the production of relatively low valued forage and grain crops. (16) Driver suggests that western agricultural income could be maintained or even enhanced with less water than currently is being used. A shift to higher-valued crops or to more water conserving irrigation technologies could sustain agricultural income levels while consuming less water. However, such conversions would require substantial new investments. The market transfer of incremental quantities of water out of agriculture could fuel nonagricultural economic growth and provide the agricultural sector with financial resources to make investments in irrigation and production efficiency that might not otherwise be possible.(17)

The economic sectors in the Southwest that are undergoing the greatest expansion currently use only a minor fraction of total regional water supplies. More than 80 percent of the nation's fresh water is consumed by irrigated agriculture, and the arid western states account for ninety percent of all irrigated acreage.(18) Relatively small shifts of water out of agriculture could support significant nonagricultural economic expansion and net growth throughout the Southwest. Eighty-nine percent of Arizona's water is consumed by irrigated agriculture, mines consume less than 3 percent, while all other uses consume only 8 percent. In 1980, agriculture contributed only 2 percent to Arizona's personal income. The remaining 98 percent of personal income was generated by the sectors of the economy that consumed only 11 percent of the state's water supplies.(19) A transfer of only 5 percent of the water currently used in agriculture could support an additional 1.5 million people, an increase of 50 percent over Arizona's 1985 population. In Colorado, it has been suggested that if irrigators could reduce their consumptive use by 5 percent, the amount of water available for municipal and industrial use would nearly double.(20)

MARKET TRANSFERS--AN OVERVIEW

Types of Transfers

Market transfers of water rights can take many forms, depending on the legal characteristics of the water right, transactions and development costs, and preferences of the buyer and seller. Market transfers may be divided into four basic categories: sales, leases, options, and negotiated adjustments. Each arrangement is briefly explained here and examples will be provided in Chapter 5's descriptions of actual market transfers.

Sales of water rights involve the transfer of title including all benefits, costs, obligations, and risks associated with that right. Most transferable water rights are perpetual, so a sale implies the permanent transfer of all legal claims existing under the right.

Leases of water rights are temporary transfers, occurring for terms ranging from a single season to many decades. Since the title to a leased water right remains with the owner, the lessee usually will not incur all the benefits, costs, risks, and obligations that otherwise would be associated with the right. Water users may lease water rights for a variety of reasons. Sometimes lessees are unable or unwilling to commit the resources necessary to acquire a perpetual water right and find it beneficial to limit their ownership of water rights, leasing additional water only when they require it. Alternatively, some users may have only a short-term demand for additional water, or a long-term but highly variable demand. In still other cases, a user's demand for water may be both long-term and stable, but their existing supplies may be highly variable. Leasing arrangements provide flexibility in such circumstances.

Water rights options typically are contracts signed between potential buyers and sellers in which the terms of the contract specify the quantity, price and other conditions under which water may be transferred. Options contracts exist for both sales and lease transactions. Water rights options contracts are characterized by their flexibility and relatively low cost. Options are an attractive alternative when buyers are uncertain as to if and when they will want additional water rights but desire the certainty of knowing that they can buy a given quantity of water at a given price.

Negotiated adjustments do not involve a direct transfer of water rights from one party to another. Instead, they are an agreement under which one or both parties to the transaction agree to take certain actions which would result in the buyer benefiting from increased access to water. Negotiated adjustments are particularly useful when outright transfers of water are difficult or expensive but adjustments in the pattern of water use could release supplies for other uses. An example of a negotiated adjustment is where a municipal water user finances improvements in an irrigation district's facilities, resulting in a reduction in system losses. The "saved" water is then made available for use by the municipality. As another example, junior appropriators of water on a stream system may negotiate agreements with senior appropriators to use water "out of priority," thereby increasing the quantity or reducing the variability of their water supply.

Water Right Characteristics and Market Values

Water rights are distinguished by physical, legal, and institutional characteristics that determine the circumstances and terms under which they may be used and transferred. Two general characteristics of water rights affect their value in a market setting--security and flexibility. These characteristics are briefly introduced here. Factors affecting water rights values will be discussed in detail in Chapter 6.

The more secure a water right is relative to other water rights, all other considerations being equal, the more valuable is the right to potential buyers and sellers in a water market. Two kinds of security in water rights should be distinguished, legal and hydrological. Legal security is the guarantee that right holders will continue to enjoy the benefits of control, use, and development of their water rights, unaffected by unpredictable and capricious acts by others. Hydrological security is the assurance that the capacity of the water resource is sufficient to satisfy the users' claim to water within the legal constraints of their rights. Water rights that draw on highly variable resources, such as intermittent streams, are less secure than other water resources, such as high-volume perennial streams, lakes and reservoirs, or groundwater aquifers.

Potential buyers will not be willing to pay much for water rights that are relatively insecure and unreliable. However, security is not in itself a sufficient measure of market value. In order for a water right to be an attractive market commodity, security must be accompanied by flexibility. There must be a means by which users may alter the location, purpose, or timing of use of the water rights in response to changing economic conditions.

Security and flexibility provide a basis for market development. Both security and flexibility are highly developed for many marketed resources--land, petroleum and timber, for example. Security and flexibility are primitive or nonexistent for some other resources--such as rights to scenic views. Water rights stand somewhere between these extremes. Many water markets exist only in rudimentary form, but they are becoming increasingly active and sophisticated as property rights in water continue to develop.

CURRENT TRENDS AFFECTING WATER MARKET DEVELOPMENT

Young(21) and Hirschleifer, DeHaven, and Milliman(22) observe that water management traditionally has been viewed as an engineering problem. Many water administrators are engineers by training and experience, and prefer to view water use in terms of absolute "needs" or "requirements" that must be met through structural solutions. Non-structural means of balancing water supply and demand, such as marginal cost pricing or the reallocation of water resources from lower to higher valued uses have been neglected in favor of structural means, such as the development of additional storage and conveyance facilities. Driver, in his report to the Western Governors' Task Force, notes that traditionally the concept of efficiency in water policy management has meant engineering efficiency rather than economic efficiency.(23) He argues that

> ...An exclusive focus on improving the engineering efficiency of a particular water use can lead to unproductive expenditures if the value of that use is less than the value of some other use of that water, a possibility as long as water prices do not communicate the value of water in alternative uses...Economic efficiency addresses the value of the use of scarce water resources available to society...leads to consideration of net values of water use and whether the institutions that affect western water allocation are sufficiently flexible to permit water to be allocated to uses at any time that result in westerners gaining maximum value from the region's water.(24)

Western water institutions evolved to promote economic development through assuring a secure supply of water and protecting property rights in water once they were established. Now, they are under pressure to do many other things, such as encourage more efficient uses of water, protect the environment, and accommodate new water interests.(25) Chapter 4 summarizes recent policy developments which indicate that public interest, area of origin, and instream flow considerations are increasingly important in western water management, as is resolution of native American claims. Weatherford observes that growing interest in efficient and equitable water allocation and

the movement away from structural (engineering) approaches
to non-structural (legal, institutional, and economic)
approaches to water problems is causing an "identity
crisis" among many long-established western water
institutions.(26)

Despite the difficulties that institutions are
encountering in adapting to changing conditions, Driver
argues that water institutions generally need only a "fine
tuning" rather than a comprehensive overhaul. In his
report to the Western Governors' Association, Driver
presents a series of proposals for modifications in state
and federal water policy and management. These proposals
include the implementation of more economically rational
water pricing structures, authorization of interregional
water transfers, improved conjunctive management of
alternative water supplies, recognition of new values in
water (such as instream recreational uses), improved
collection and dissemination of data related to water
rights and water use, and improved cooperation in the
apportionment and management of interstate waters.
"Market-driven transfers", he concludes, "are the linchpin
of the strategy to improve water use efficiency in the
West."(27)

Several western states have implemented innovative
systems to encourage market transfers. In the early 1980s,
California passed legislation recognizing water marketing
as a beneficial use of water deemed "surplus" to the needs
of a water service organization.(28) Several years
previously, California established an emergency "water
bank" in response to the worst drought in the state's
history. The purpose of the bank was to permit the
redistribution of water allocations from state and federal
water projects between willing buyers and sellers. In
Idaho, a state water bank for renting surplus irrigation
water for agricultural and other uses has been in
operation since 1980.(29) In 1987, Arizona enacted an
amendment to its state water code to permit limited
leasing of some groundwater rights independently of the
land to which the rights are appurtenant.(30) These and
other market-related policies will be discussed in more
detail in Chapters 4 and 5.

The federal government is beginning to assume a more
active role in water marketing as well. An agreement
worked out among the Bureau of Reclamation, the state of
Wyoming, the city of Casper, and the Casper-Alcova
Irrigation District led to the transfer of salvaged
irrigation water to municipal use.(31) Other federal

water project facilities are serving as potential conduits
for the market transfer of privately or locally developed
water supplies. In lieu of constructing some components
of the Bureau of Reclamation's Central Utah Project (CUP),
the Central Utah Water Conservancy District is in the
process of purchasing thousands of acre feet of water
rights from five irrigation districts. These water rights
would be made available to CUP beneficiaries.(32) In
Arizona, several municipal governments and private
developers are hoping to transport water from rights
purchased in remote areas of the state via the Central
Arizona Project aqueduct.(33)

While public policies slowly are being modified to
facilitate market transfers of water, the private sector
is undergoing changes as well. A growing number of
individuals throughout the West are working as legal
counsel, financial advisors, appraisers, brokers, and
technical experts for water rights buyers and sellers. A
few groups have established funds exclusively for the
purpose of investing in water rights.(34)

Information is essential for making sound business
and public policy decisions regarding water transfers.
More formal information channels are developing as markets
become more sophisticated. Several publishers, consulting
firms, and financial services agencies are competing to
provide the best and most timely information on water
marketing. Water Market Update is a monthly newsletter
devoted to reporting water market activity and related
policy developments throughout the western United States.
The Water Strategist, a California-based newsletter,
describes itself as a national "quarterly analysis of
water marketing, finance, legislation, and litigation."
The publishers of U.S. Water News, a monthly newspaper
about national and international water resource
management, recently has begun offering its own business
publication called Water Investment Newsletter, which it
bills as "the only investment newsletter directed
specifically at the water market." A Denver-based
organization, Water Exchange, Inc., provides subscribers
with detailed information on available water rights and
water rights prices throughout the state of Colorado.
Professional and academic conferences on the subject of
water transfers and water marketing are held regularly and
are attended by representatives from government, the
private sector, universities, and environmental and other
special interests groups.

Weatherford and Shupe (1986) note that during the era of building large new federal water projects, an "iron triangle" alliance among certain committees in Congress, the state and federal agencies, and local project beneficiaries dominated public water policy.(35)   While these forces are still strong in the West, their influence appears to be waning.   In place of the old political alliances, a new triad of values may be emerging--a "new iron triangle"--representing public concern for water use efficiency, social equity, and environmental quality.(36) These concerns are receiving increased attention by policymakers and, as will be discussed in Chapter 4, policies that reflect these concerns affect the nature and extent of western water market activity.

NOTES

1. T.L. Anderson, Water Crisis: Ending the Policy Drought. Baltimore: John Hopkins University Press, 1983.
2. U.S. Department of Commerce, Bureau of the Census, "1984 Farm and Ranch Irrigation Survey." Prepared for U.S. Department of Agriculture, Economic Research Service, AG84-SR-1, June, 1986. (Hereinafter cited as "Farm and Ranch Survey").
3. Western Governors' Association Resolution 86-011. Colorado Springs, Colorado, July 8, 1986. (Hereinafter cited as "Western Governors' Resolution").
4. S. Shupe, "Western Water Rights Under State Law." Tribal Water Management Handbook, Oakland, California, AILTP/American Indian Resources Institute, 1985.
5. Personal communication with R. Cook, Bureau of Reclamation, Provo, Utah, 1987.
6. "Pact Made on Animas-La Plata." U.S. Water News September, 1986, p.9.
7. U.S. Department of Interior, Office of Inspector General, Review of the Status of the Central Arizona Project, W-WS-BOR-08-85. Washington, D.C.: April, 1986.
8. "Reagan Signs $16.3 Billion Bill for Water Projects Using Local Funds," Philadelphia Inquirer Nov. 16, 1986.
9. C.F. Wilkinson, "Western Water Law in Transition." American Water Works Association Journal, October, 1986, p.39.

10. B. Driver, "Western Water: Tuning the System." Report to the Western Governors' Association from the Water Efficiency Task Force. Denver, Colorado, June 23, 1986. (Hereinafter cited as "Tuning the System").

11. U.S. Department of Commerce, "Farm and Ranch Survey."

12. R. Young, "Direct and Regional Economic Impacts of Competition for Irrigation Water in the West." Prepared for Conference on Impacts of Limited Water for Irrigated Agriculture in the Arid West. Asilomar Conference Center, Pacific Grove, California, September 28 - October 1, 1982.

13. A. Randall, "Property Entitlements and Pricing Policies for a Maturing Water Economy." Unpublished working paper, Department of Agricultural Economics, University of Kentucky, 1982.

14. M. Kelso, W.E. Martin, and L.E. Mack. Water Supplies and Economic Growth in an Arid Environment. Tucson: University of Arizona Press, 1973.

15. Ibid.

16. U.S. Department of Commerce, "Farm and Ranch Survey."

17. B. Driver, "Tuning the System."

18. U.S. Water Resources Council, The Nation's Water Resources 1975-2000, Second National Water Assessment. Washington, D.C., December, 1978.

19. F. Welsh, How to Create a Water Crisis. Boulder, Colorado: Johnson Books, 1985.

20. T.D. Tregarthen, "Water in Colorado: Fear and Loathing of the Marketplace." In Water Rights, ed. T. Anderson, San Francisco: Pacific Institute, 1983.

21. R.A. Young, "Why Are There So Few Transactions Between Water Users?" American Journal of Agricultural Economics Vol 68:1143-1151, December, 1986.

22. J. Hirschleifer, J.C. DeHaven, and J.W. Milliman, Water Supply: Economics, Technology, and Policy. Chicago: University of Chicago Press, 1960.

23. B. Driver, "Tuning the System."

24. Ibid, p. 83.

25. Ibid.

26. Water and Agriculture in the Western U.S.: Conservation, Reallocation and Markets, ed. G. Weatherford. Boulder, Colorado: Westview Press, 1982.

27. B. Driver, "Tuning the System." Summary Report, p.11.

28. California Water Code, Sections 109, 380-387, 1010-1011.

54

29. R.W. Wahl and F.H. Osterhoudt, "Voluntary Transfers of Water in the West," <u>National Water Summary 1985</u>. United States Geological Survey Water Supply (Paper 2300), Washington, D.C., 1986 (hereinafter cited as "Voluntary Transfers.".

30. Arizona State House Bill 2334. April, 1987.

31. R.W. Wahl and F.H. Osterhoudt, "Voluntary Transfers."

32. S.J. Shupe and J.A. Folk-Williams (eds.), <u>Water Market Update</u> Feb. 1987, Vol.1,No.2, p.1.

33. Personal communication with K. Kohlhoff, Water Resources Manager, City of Mesa, 1986.

34. Personal communication with A. Parker, Western Water Rights Management, Inc., Denver, 1986.

35. G.D. Weatherford, and S.J. Shupe, "Reallocating Water in the West." <u>American Water Works Association Journal</u> 78:71, October, 1986.

36. <u>Ibid</u>.

4
The Legal Setting
for Market Transfers
in the Southwestern States

The legal setting for market transfers includes statutory law, case law and federal, state and local policies that evolve in response to statutory and case law. Laws and policies affect market activity in many different ways. Some policies affect the uses to which water rights can be applied and the value of water in alternative uses. These policies can provide incentives for water transfers. State laws define the conditions under which transfers may occur and affect the transaction costs incurred by market participants in transferring water. Laws and policies that are changing or ambiguous affect market activity by making the conditions that must be satisfied uncertain. This chapter focuses on the role of state water law and water transfer policies, although a brief summary of federal policies that affect market transfers is also included.

It should be understood that state and federal laws and policies are only one part of the complex institutional environment within which markets operate. Local organizations also play a significant role in determining the nature and extent of market transactions. The impact of local institutions will be discussed in Chapter 5, where individual market areas are described in detail. The impact of a state's policies on specific market transfers can vary considerably depending on the local situation. State laws provide an overall framework within which market participants operate, but the decisions of individual water right holders and the policies of local water user organizations determine the way in which water markets actually develop and function.

This chapter begins by reviewing the various forms of property rights in water that are encountered in the

Southwest. Seven themes in western state water law which
have an impact on market activity are outlined, along
with a description of current policies in the southwestern
states related to each theme. Finally the impacts of
various federal policies on western water markets are
discussed.

PROPERTY RIGHTS IN WATER

Overview

     One of the most basic functions of water law, as
far as markets are concerned, is to define property
rights. These property rights define and limit the rights
of members of society with respect to water resources and
allow right holders to form secure expectations regarding
benefits stemming from their rights. A water right does
not simply give a right holder access to a specific water
resource. In addition, it defines the duties of other
possible claimants and water users with respect to the
right holder.(1) A surface water diversion right, for
instance, is meaningful because it imposes duties on other
water users to behave in a way that does not impair the
right.
     Water law, by defining the rights and duties of
water users relative to one another and to the rest of
society, provides a basis for market exchanges. In order
for market participants to estimate the value of a water
right they must be able to form expectations about the
benefits associated with owning the right and the degree
to which the right is protected from impairment by others.
When property rights in water are ambiguous, buyers and
sellers cannot ascertain the nature of the privileges and
duties that are being transferred. Although well-defined
property rights in water and unambiguous policies
regarding transfers are important for market development,
market transfers do occur even when there are significant
uncertainties. When economic gains from a transfer are
large, it can be worthwhile for the transactors to clarify
legal uncertainties surrounding the transfer. Tregarthen,
for instance, describes the uncertainty and high cost of
determining the transferable quantity of appropriative
surface water rights in Colorado. In spite of the
uncertainty and expenses associated with Colorado water
court proceedings, water transfers occur routinely.(2)

There are five basic types of water rights in the West; riparian rights, appropriative rights, use permits, allotments, and mutual stock. While each of these five categories has general distinguishing characteristics, water rights are difficult to classify unambiguously because water administration varies from one state to another. This classification of water rights therefore is somewhat arbitrary but gives a flavor of the diverse forms that property rights in water have taken in the Southwest.

Riparian rights were the basis for the first systems of water law in the United States. Under the riparian system, rights to use water reside with the owners of land adjacent to a watercourse. The water is available for use only on those lands and may not be transferred to any other lands. As riparian water rights are virtually inseparable from the lands to which they are attached, generally they cannot be transferred independently from the land.

Appropriative rights evolved to serve the needs of water users in arid and semi-arid environments, where water often must be transported considerable distances from the source to the place of use. Under the appropriative system, water rights usually are assigned for use on specific lands but the assignment is not necessarily permanent. With the approval of the state water agency, appropriative water rights usually may be reassigned to another location or the purpose of use changed. However, in order to avoid adverse impacts on other holders of water rights, the transferable quantity may be limited to the consumptive use historically associated with the exercise of the right or other restrictions may be placed on the transfer of the right.

Most appropriative water rights are subject to two major conditions. The first is that the water must be put to "beneficial use." Water right holders who do not use their rights fully or who use water "wastefully" may lose their rights or face a reduction in the quantity of water associated with their rights. The second condition is that appropriative rights typically are managed under a priority system, whereby senior right holders have preferred access to water over junior holders. Priority of use generally is established by the date when the user initially appropriates water--the earlier the date, the higher the priority of the water right.

Use permits are granted in some states to recognize appropriative water rights. In addition, some states issue use permits for groundwater withdrawals. Water use permits, other than those which recognize appropriative water rights, are not necessarily granted in perpetuity, are not always subject to beneficial use limitations, nor are they generally ranked by priority among right holders. Sometimes water use permits are issued for specific purposes and are not transferable to other uses.

Allotments divide a water resource among various users according to a formula established through interstate compact, interagency negotiations, or by the governing board of a water service organization. The basis of the allotment system is a contractual agreement to deliver a certain quantity of water per unit of time. Allotments are difficult to market because transfers may violate the terms of the original agreement. Amending the agreement to permit a transfer of water may require the consent of many separate parties and frequently involves multiple jurisdictions with conflicting objectives.

Mutual stocks, like allotments, represent claims to water supplied by an organization. The organization, often a private water company, controls a certain quantity of water which it has the authority to distribute to stockholders within its service area. Each share of stock represents a fixed proportion of the total water service obligation of the company. The more stock a water user holds, the more water the user can receive. Within the service area of the water service organization, this type of water right is readily transferable so long as no specific legal restrictions on the use of the water are violated.

Water rights sometimes exhibit aspects of more than one basic category. Mutual irrigation company stock, for example, typically represents a bundle of collectively owned and managed appropriative water rights. When the water is used for its originally decreed purpose (for example, irrigation) and remains within the company's service area, the rights "behave" like mutual company stock, subject primarily to the rules and regulations of the water purveyor. If, however, the company's water is transferred outside the service area or its use is changed from that specified in the original decree, then the transfer is governed by state laws applicable to appropriative rights. Transfers of appropriative rights are a concern of the state water authority, which monitors beneficial use of water rights and protects the interests of other right holders.

Each of these five broad classifications of property
rights in water are found in one or more of the
southwestern states. While riparian rights to surface
water are recognized in California and Utah, they apply to
a small fraction of each state's water resources. All six
southwestern states have adopted the appropriation
doctrine as the prevailing system of water rights for
surface water. Arizona manages groundwater withdrawals in
its Active Management Areas under a use permit system.
Allotments are a common means of allocating water from
publicly funded water projects. Examples include contracts
to receive water from the Central Arizona Project, and the
Central Valley Project, and the State Water Project in
California. Rights to use water managed by irrigation
districts and multiple purpose water service organizations
in Utah and Colorado are often in the form of mutual
stocks. As will be apparent from the area-by-area
descriptions of market activities in Chapter 5, the
transferability and market value of each form of water
right varies depending on local economic conditions and
the legal setting for water transfers in each state.

Water Rights and Risk-Sharing

The way in which property rights in water are defined
affects how risks of water shortages are shared among
right holders. The prior appropriation system operating
on the "first in time, first in right" principle places
the risk of water supply shortfalls on junior right
holders. Junior appropriators and new water users desiring
increased protection against risk may buy senior water
rights or may negotiate options to exercise senior rights
in dry years or may develop storage and delivery systems
to reduce the variability of flows available to junior
right holders.

Howe et al. contrast the risk-sharing arrangements of
the prior appropriation system with those of a
proportional rights system in which water users share
available water supplies based on the proportion of water
rights held.(3) Holding 5 percent of the water rights in a
proportional rights system would entitle one to 5 percent
of the available water supplies each year. Mutual stocks
are a form of proportional rights. A water user in a
mutual water company who wishes increased protection
against supply uncertainty can purchase more shares of
company stocks. Tregarthen argues that mutual water
companies evolved as a response to the risk of supply

shortfalls in Colorado. Many high priority rights there
are held by mutual water companies and since sale and
rental of company stocks do not require water court
proceedings, exchanges that redistribute risk can take
place without large transaction costs.(4)   Howe et al.
observe that a proportional rights system allows low cost
sharing of risk among homogenous water users (i.e.
irrigators), but argue that the priority system is
advantageous when heterogeneous users are involved (i.e.,
irrigators, cities and industries) because senior rights
can be transferred to those sectors which place the
highest value on reliable water supplies.(5)

Market transactions allow water users to buy more
protection against supply shortfalls than their current
water rights holdings provide them. One of the dominant
motivations for water transfers in the southwestern states
is risk management. Urban water purveyors throughout the
Southwest are acquiring senior irrigation rights to
protect current and future water users in their service
areas against supply fluctuations.

STATE WATER POLICIES AND THEIR IMPACT ON WATER MARKETS

Seven themes in western state water policies are
identified as playing an important role in water market
development. Some are important because they provide
incentives for water transfers to occur. These include
beneficial use and forfeiture statutes, and policies on
transfer of conserved water. Other themes are important
because they define the conditions under which transfers
may take place, what state authorities must consider in
approving transfer proposals and the costs of implementing
transfers. These themes include appurtenancy of water
rights to land, protection of vested water rights, area of
origin considerations, public interest provisions and
instream flow maintenance. Each theme's influence on
market development and activity is discussed. Relevant
statutes and case law for each of the six states are
summarized. Laws that apply specifically to interstate
transfers are omitted because the market transactions
described in this book are all intrastate transfers.
Interstate reallocations of water rights have thus far
been implemented through legislative and judicial
processes rather than through market transfers.

Beneficial Use and Forfeiture/Abandonment Provisions

Requirements that water rights be put to some beneficial use and provisions that make rights subject to forfeiture after a period of non-use are found in the water law of most southwestern states, though they do not apply to all water rights in each state. These laws are relevant to water markets for several reasons. First, "beneficial use" defines those categories of water use for which a water right may be granted. Uses which have not been declared "beneficial" and for which a water right may not be granted--instream flow maintenance in some states, for instance--cannot be represented in market transfers of water rights. Second, the beneficial use doctrine implies an obligation on the part of right holders to apply water beneficially. Forfeiture and abandonment laws make the retention of a water right contingent upon exercising the right. These requirements can provide water right holders with an incentive to sell or lease their rights rather than not use them and risk forfeiture, although their impact on incentives to sell or lease varies with state implementation and enforcement procedures. Weatherford and Shupe argue that forfeiture and abandonment provisions may be more rigorously enforced as local competition for water grows.(6)

Arizona law states that the quantity of surface water that may be used is limited to the amount necessary for beneficial use and lists domestic, municipal, irrigation, stock watering, water power, recreation, wildlife and mining as uses for which surface water may be appropriated.(7) A surface water right ceases and the water reverts to the public and is again subject to appropriation after five successive years of non-use.(8) Groundwater is not subject to the appropriation doctrine in Arizona though statutes require that groundwater which has been withdrawn shall not be allowed to waste.(9) The groundwater rights formalized following Arizona's 1980 Groundwater Management Act need not be exercised regularly and are not subject to forfeiture for non-use.

California codes do not purport to list all recognized beneficial uses but do list domestic, irrigation, frost protection, power, municipal, mining, industrial, recreational, fish and wildlife protection and enhancement, stock watering and water quality maintenance as beneficial uses.(10) Appropriative rights are limited to the amount of water reasonably required for the use to be served and this quantity is determined on a case-by-case basis by the state's Water Resources Control Board (WRCB). An appropriative right can be forfeited in whole or in part if the water is not put to beneficial use for a period of five years.(11) The California constitution prohibits waste, misuse or unreasonable use of any water rights recognized under California law.(12)

The limit and measure of water rights in Colorado is based on beneficial use, though specific beneficial uses are not listed in Colorado statutes. Colorado case law and statutes recognize an obligation to maximize beneficial use of appropriative water rights, including tributary groundwater.(13) Abandonment in Colorado requires both non-use and intent to abandon and the State Engineer regularly brings abandonment proceedings when periodic investigations indicate some portion of a water right has not been beneficially used. There is no specific provision for water rights forfeiture in Colorado.(14)

Nevada statutes state that stock watering, recreation, energy and heating are beneficial uses.(15) Wildlife uses are inferred(16) and administrative policies consider other customary uses (domestic, municipal, mining, milling, irrigation, industrial, power, etc.) as beneficial uses. Water rights are based on the quantity required for beneficial use. Groundwater rights may be forfeited after five years of non-use. To establish abandonment for surface water rights, continuous non-use for five years must be accompanied by intent to abandon.(17)

New Mexico codes require beneficial use for both groundwater and surface water rights. Beneficial uses are those uses which do not result in waste and the State Engineer has statutory authority to prevent waste.(18) Water rights are subject to forfeiture proceedings after four consecutive years of non-use if water was available during each of those four years.(19)

Utah does not define specific beneficial uses statutorily although domestic use, stock watering, irrigation, mining, municipal and power are all mentioned.(20) State statutes and case law specify that the quantity of appropriative rights is based on the extent of beneficial use of the water.(21) A water right may be forfeited after five consecutive years of non-use.

Appurtenancy of Water Rights to Land

Attachment of water rights to a specific parcel of
land is implicit for riparian rights and has been
established in case law for appropriative rights.
However, implementation of the appurtenancy doctrine
varies among the southwestern states and thus the doctrine
has different implications for market transfers in each
state. In most states, the appurtenancy doctrine simply
requires that approval be obtained from the appropriate
state agency before water rights may be transferred from
one point of diversion or location of use to another.
This requirement generally imposes only minor transaction
costs on market participants. However, where the
appurtenancy doctrine is interpreted as permanently
attaching a water right to a particular parcel of land,
market transfers can become more costly and complex. Land
must be purchased in order to acquire water rights and so
water buyers may become the reluctant owners of undesired
land.

In Arizona, appropriative surface water rights may be
acquired only by purchasing the land to which the rights
are appurtenant.(22) The same party must own both the
water rights and the land. This requirement also applies
to irrigation groundwater rights and to a large portion of
the nonirrigation groundwater rights recognized under the
1980 Groundwater Management Act.(23) However, the party
owning both the water rights and the land may seek
approval from the Arizona Department of Water Resources to
transfer the rights from the land to which they are
currently assigned to a new parcel.(24)

In California, permits and licenses (which authorize
all appropriative rights initiated after 1914) specify a
place of use for each water right. The California Water
Resources Control Board must approve any change in the
place of use. Riparian rights are limited to use on land
contiguous to the water source and within the watershed of
the stream and may not be transferred apart from the
land.(25)

Colorado law requires that water rights be assigned
to a particular place of use but water rights may be
transferred to new locations with the approval of the
state water court.(26) Nevada law specifies that water
rights are appurtenant to the place of use specified in
the granting of the right but this place of use may be
changed by applying for a transfer.(27) Likewise, in New
Mexico, water rights are assigned to a specific location

but can be severed and transferred to a new location.(28) In Utah, also, appropriative water rights are granted for use on specific lands but the location of use may be changed by having a transfer application approved by the State Engineer.(29) Utah codes specifically note that water rights may be conveyed separately from land and that rights represented by shares of stock in a corporation are not considered appurtenant to the land on which they are being used.(30)

Use and Transfer of Salvaged or Conserved Water

Water users may be able to reduce the water diverted for beneficial uses as water use patterns and technologies change over time. Brown et al. discuss the example of an irrigator who holds a quantity of water rights that enable him to produce a particular combination of crops.(31) Adoption of a water conserving technology (lining of irrigation ditches or investing in sprinkler irrigation, for instance) would be a more attractive proposition to the farmer if the water conserved could be used to expand his irrigated acreage, applied to nonirrigation uses on his property or sold to another water user. State policies that permit application of conserved water to new land and new uses and that allow conserved water to be leased or sold would reward water conservation efforts and could also reduce disincentives for water conservation generated by the "use it or lose it" aspects of forfeiture and abandonment laws. Such policies could provide an incentive for water market transactions, even allowing water right holders to finance water conservation investments by selling and leasing conserved water. However, laws in the southwestern states on use and transfer of salvaged or conserved water vary considerably.

In Arizona, while there appear to be no specific statutes on the issue of transferring conserved water, case law establishing the appurtenancy of water rights to land appears to preclude transfers of salvaged or conserved water to lands other than those to which the water right was originally assigned. In Salt River Users' Association v. Kavocovich, the Arizona Court of Appeals ruled that irrigators who lined their ditches could not apply "saved" water to irrigate adjacent land.(32)

California codes, on the other hand, specifically provide that conserved water may be sold, leased, exchanged or otherwise transferred subject to state law applicable to transfers. In addition, appropriative water rights that are not fully exercised because reclaimed water is being used instead, or because of water conservation efforts, are not subject to forfeiture.(33)

In Colorado, legislation allowing use of salvaged water has been introduced several times but has not been passed. An individual who reduces the quantity of water needed for a beneficial use may apply to water court seeking permission to use or sell salvaged water. Court approval is required even when salvaged water will be used on the same land to which the water right is applicable. The applicant bears the burden of demonstrating that existing rights will not be impaired, and proceedings are costly and impractical for small amounts of water. If a water user delays in applying for permission, he risks having the quantity of the water right diminished to the post-conservation consumptive use quantity.(34) Colorado case law specifically holds that actions taken to reduce water consumption by phreatophytes (deep rooted plants such as cottonwoods) will not be regarded as producing salvaged water available for sale or for use on other lands.(35)

Nevada law takes the position that "since beneficial use is the limit and extent of a right, a water user has no right to his inefficiencies." Conserved water is considered unappropriated and any applicant may file to appropriate it.(36) Nevada statutes declare that water transfers are a valid course of action when it becomes impracticable or uneconomical to use the water beneficially on the land to which it is appurtenant.(37) However, this has not been interpreted as allowing transfer of conserved water and the State Engineer has consistently denied applications to transfer conserved water.(38)

In New Mexico, salvaged water may be transferred if the applicant can demonstrate clearly that there is no impairment to other water right holders, including junior appropriators.(39) In Utah, use of conserved or salvaged water cannot result in extension of water right to other land or in increased consumptive use. Conserved water may be considered unappropriated, as in Nevada.(40) As in the other southwestern states, Utah case law implies that the primary consideration in determining whether transfer of conserved water shall be allowed is injury to other perfected rights.(41)

Protection of Third-Party Water Right Holders

While all six states require that water rights shall
not be impaired by transfers, implementation of this
policy varies greatly. Procedures to protect the rights
of third-party water users against impairment resulting
from transfers are a primary source of transaction costs
associated with market transfers. Costs of demonstrating
nonimpairment to state authorities typically are borne by
the applicant for the transfer and often include
engineering and hydrologic studies and legal counsel.
When such costs are high relative to the value of the
water being transferred they can prevent transfers from
being implemented. Transfer approval procedures to
protect other right holders thus can affect the level of
market activity.

Arizona statutes require that the amount of water
diverted or used after a transfer shall not exceed the
vested rights existing at the time of the transfer.(42)
Regulations as to the spacing of wells seek to protect
groundwater users from the impact of changes in nearby
pumping activity but no statute specifically addresses the
possibility that changes in groundwater pumping resulting
from a transfer may impair surface water rights. Arizona
statutes do, however, recognize the possibility that
interbasin transfers of groundwater may impair other water
users and an exporter of groundwater potentially is liable
to pay damages to affected individuals in the basin of
origin.(43) This provision appears to be affecting market
transactions in Arizona. City governments and businesses
who purchase land in remote basins to import groundwater
pumped from beneath those lands to the Tucson and Phoenix
areas are concerned about damage claims and some buyers
plan to buy out all existing groundwater users in the
basin of origin in order to forestall litigation and
compensatory payments(44), and to control groundwater
depletion in the basin of origin.

The California water code requires that water
transfers must not operate to the injury of any lawful
user, and the petitioner for the transfer must demonstrate
nonimpairment to the satisfaction of the Water Resources
Control Board (WRCB).(45) For appropriative rights
initiated before 1914, a transfer may be made without
prior approval of the board and a party challenging the
transfer has the burden of demonstrating that vested
rights have been impaired.(46) An applicant for transfer
must obtain the approval of the WRCB. Criteria for

approval and disapproval have not been clear, but new
transfer approval procedures and criteria are in the
process of being developed.(47)   California codes allow
for a trial period before transfers will be regarded as
final so that effects of the transfer on other right
holders can be recognized and accounted for.(48)

In Colorado, water rights may be transferred so long
as vested water rights are not injured. Transfers of
appropriative rights are accomplished through water court
proceedings.   These proceedings can be expensive as third
party right holders may raise objections and parties
typically are represented by attorneys and other experts.
The transferable quantity of a right is determined by the
court based on historic beneficial use and prevention of
injury to other rights.(49) Tregarthen and Brown et
al.(50) describe   court   cases   demonstrating   the
difficulties that may be encountered and the costs that
may be incurred in quantifying transferable rights in the
Colorado water court system.   Return flows are very
important in Colorado's water economy because such a large
proportion of the state's water use relies on surface
water sources.   Protection of right holders relying on
return flows is an important issue but the adversarial
nature of Colorado water court proceedings makes
transfers of appropriative rights complicated and costly.

Nevada statutes require that existing rights (both
decreed rights and permits) must be protected when a
transfer is evaluated and the applicant has the burden of
proving noninjury.(51) Parties wishing to transfer water
rights must file an application with the State Engineer.
If the transfer is approved, a permit is issued indicating
the new location and/or use.(52)

New Mexico law requires that nonimpairment of
existing rights be demonstrated before any application for
transfer will be approved by the State Engineer.
Typically applicants submit engineering or hydrologic
studies and other documents addressing the issue of
impairment along with their transfer application. The
applicant must publish a notice of intent to transfer
water rights for three consecutive weeks and protests
may be filed up to ten days after the last publication of
intent.   Protests may be resolved privately and the
protestor can indicate resolution of a dispute by signing
a waiver of impairment. If the protest is not resolved
privately, the applicant may request a hearing with the
State Engineer's office to resolve the issue of
impairment. At such hearings both the transfer applicant

and the protestors pay court fees and typically bring in expert witnesses. The State Engineer's staff also prepare reports and examine the evidence of applicant and protestors.(53) Costs of resolving the issue of third party damages are thus distributed among the transfer applicant, parties protesting the transfer and the office of the State Engineer.

In Utah, transfer applications are evaluated by the State Engineer who must consider whether other vested rights will be impaired. Utah statutes provide for the transfer of water rights by deed in a manner similar to transfer of other real estate.(54)

Area-of-Origin Issues

Water transfers can negatively affect business activities, local government fiscal capacity and the quality of public services in areas from which water is being transferred. Transfers of irrigation water rights often involve retirement of irrigated acreage with associated reductions in agriculturally-linked economic activities in the area of origin and in property tax base. Permanent transfer of water rights may foreclose options for future economic development in area of origin. If, at some point in the future, economic conditions make expanded irrigated agriculture, new industrial activities, or residential development economically attractive, water may not be available locally to pursue these opportunities. While some studies (55) suggest that direct and indirect economic impacts of water transfers on the area of origin generally are small from the perspective of a state's economy, such impacts are a significant concern to area-of-origin residents. In addition to economic impacts, concerns have also been raised regarding the effect of water transfers on community cohesion, local traditions and cultural values, the political viability of local governments and irrigation districts, and riparian environments in the area of origin.(56)

In most western states, local government units are not involved formally in the transfer approval process. Local jurisdiction over appropriative rights is generally pre-empted by state law. In contrast to effects on vested water rights, consideration of area-of-origin impacts generally is not incorporated into transfer approval procedures. However, there are recent indications that area-of-origin concerns are receiving more attention from state policy makers. Area-of-origin issues have the

potential of affecting the conditions under which inter-
basin transfers will be approved and the costs of
implementing such transfers.

Recent Arizona legislative activity indicates a
growing concern with the impact on rural areas of
agricultural-to-urban water transfers. Legislation passed
in 1987 allows payments in lieu of property taxes by
cities who purchase and retire farmland to taxing jurisdictions in the area of origin.(57) Payments to local
governments by municipal buyers of irrigated land have
been made in lieu of property taxes and these payments add
to the municipalities' costs of acquiring water
rights.(58) The 1987 legislative session saw the introduction of numerous other bills addressing area-of-origin
concerns--including a proposal for a temporary moratorium
on transfers of irrigation rights and bills addressing
transfer impacts on local government bonding capacity. No
other effective area-of-origin measures were passed in the
1987 session.(59) Arizona statutes do provide that "no
right to the use of water on or from any watershed or
drainage area which supplies or contributes water for the
irrigation of lands within an irrigation district, agricultural improvement district or water user association
shall be severed or transferred with the consent of the
governing body of such...".(60) There are no reported
court challenges to this law.(61) Transfer applicants
routinely provide evidence to the Arizona Department of
Water Resources that water organizations in the watershed
of origin have consented to the proposed transfer, as a
condition for transfer approval.

Early California statutes attempted to give the area
of origin the legal ability to recapture specific state
held water rights but this provision has not been
successfully invoked. Long-term water exporters in areas
dependent upon imported water naturally resist recapture
by the area of origin and the conditions under which
recapture would be permitted are not spelled out clearly
in the statutes. California's Burns-Porter Act of 1959
provides for compensation to northern California for water
transferred south through the State Water Project.
Compensation is provided in the form of flood control
funding, recreation and fisheries enhancement projects and
loans for small water-related projects.(62)

Colorado law requires that conservancy district
projects which transfer water out of basin must protect
current and future consumptive water users in the basin of
origin and must not increase the cost of obtaining water

in the future. In practice this has caused importing
conservancy districts to build "compensatory storage"
facilities in the basin of origin. As a part of
negotiations concerning the Windy Gap Project and the
Azure Reservoir and Power Project, a ten million dollar
escrow fund was set up by the importing conservancy
district for use by the basin of origin to plan and
construct water projects.(63)   Colorado statutes also
provide that when an action of statewide concern is
proposed in a county, that county commissioners may hold
hearings on the proposed action and issue or deny a permit
to allow the proposal to be implemented. Eagle County
commissioners have invoked this statute in order to obtain
permitting authority over the Homestake II transmountain
diversion project which would provide water for the
cities of Aurora and Colorado Springs(64). Water court
proceedings generally are not a forum in which area-of-
origin concerns can be addressed because harm to vested
water rights is the only criterion that Colorado water
courts are required to routinely consider in evaluating
transfer proposals.(65)

Nevada requires that county commissions be notified
of transfers across county lines and the commissioners may
make nonbinding recommendations to the State Engineer
regarding transfer approval.(66)

New Mexico statutes provide for reserving a share of
a basin's water supply for use in the basin of origin,
although criteria for determining what share should be
reserved are not well defined.(67)   Area-of-origin issues
have been raised in New Mexico in response to a number of
proposed transfers. The impacts on local culture of water
transfers out of traditional acequia irrigation to
nonagricultural uses are a key issue in the Sleeper
decision in Rio Arriba County. The Sleeper case is
discussed further in the following section on public
interest considerations. The rights of irrigation
districts to block transfers of water out of their service
area were examined by New Mexico courts, in the Cox case,
but no definitive conclusion was reached on the
jurisdiction of irrigation districts. In Cox, the Middle
Rio Grande Conservancy District in the Albuquerque area
sued to prevent the Cox family from transferring water
rights outside district boundaries. However, the Coxes'
water right predates the creation of the district and the
district's jurisdiction over transfer of those rights is
unclear.(68) Irrigation district jurisdiction over rights
initiated after the creation of a district is not entirely

clear either. The State Engineer takes the position that rights perfected prior to the creation of an irrigation district may be transferred without the approval of the district, but that transfers of water rights initiated as a result of the formation of a district and held in the name of the district require approval by district authorities before a transfer may occur.(69)

Neither Utah statutory law nor case law addresses directly the impact of water transfers on the area of origin. Utah has an active and viable farm economy dating from the early years of Mormon settlement. Concern with the impact of transfers on the agricultural sector have arisen in the context of energy development.(70) Area-of-origin concerns in Utah appear to have been addressed through negotiation on a case-by-case basis rather than through legislation.

Public Interest and Public Trust Considerations

Many western states explicitly include a public interest or public welfare clause in their statutes referring to water right appropriations and sometimes in their statutes referring to water transfers. However, with few exceptions, the public interest is not statutorily defined; instead definitions have evolved gradually in case law. Wilkinson notes that public interest considerations are becoming better defined and are playing a more prominent role in western water policy. While acknowledging that application of public interest criteria to water transfers is still in the early stages of development, Wilkinson argues that future transfer proposals increasingly will be required to account for a wide range of public interest concerns, in addition to the usual concern for protecting other water right holders.(71) These views are echoed by other observers who see evidence in recent court decisions and policy initiatives that public interest considerations will play a key role in water market development and transfer approval procedures.(72)

Arizona includes public interest language in its statutes regarding appropriation of water but the terms "public interest" and "welfare" are not defined statutorily.(73) Case law and administrative policy have thus far construed them as referring to impacts on groundwater recharge in Active Management Areas (AMAs), where groundwater overdraft is a central policy concern.(74)

California was the first state to constitutionalize public interest principles by requiring, in 1928, that all water development and use be in the interest of the people and for the public welfare.(75)   Public welfare is not statutorily defined but a recent California court decision, National Audubon Society v. Superior Court of Alpine County, construed public interests as those protected by the Public Trust Doctrine including rights to fish, hunt, boat, and swim as well as preservation of trust lands and waters to serve as ecological units for scientific study, open space, fish and wildlife habitat and scenic resources.(76)   The emphasis on public interest considerations in water use and transfer has been reinforced by a 1986 California court decision that interprets the public interest as encompassing water quality.(77)

In Colorado, public interest language is not explicitly included in statutes related to appropriation or transfer of water rights. However, state appropriation of water rights, through the Colorado Water Conservation Board, for maintaining instream flows is one manifestation of public interest considerations in Colorado water policy.(78)

Nevada statutes require rejection of transfer applications if the transfer threatens to prove detrimental to the public interest.(79)   What constitutes the public interest is not statutorily defined and the public interest criterion is applied to transfer applications by the State Engineer on a case-by-case basis.(80)

New Mexico statutes for surface water appropriations have always contained a public interest clause, and the groundwater code passed in the 1930s was amended in 1983 to include public interest considerations for ground water use.(81)   In 1985 amendments to the surface water and groundwater codes explicitly extended public welfare considerations to water transfers.(82) Public welfare, while not statutorily defined, is one of the criteria the State Engineer must consider in evaluating transfer applications. The New Mexico Supreme Court ruled as early as 1910 that the State Engineer (then a territorial engineer) must consider benefits to the public in weighing the merits of alternative water allocations.(83) The State Engineer exercises discretion in interpreting the relevancy of public interest considerations on a case-by-case basis.

A recent court decision has led to some new
developments on what constitutes the public interest in
New Mexico water transfers. A 1985 state district court
decision found that a proposed transfer of agricultural
water rights to a resort project not only impaired the
rights of other agricultural water users but also was
contrary to the public interest. Judge Encinias, who
wrote the opinion overturning the State Engineer's
approval of the transfer, said:

> "...It is simply assumed by the Applicants that
> greater economic benefits are more desirable
> than the preservation of a cultural identity.
> This is clearly not so...This region of northern
> New Mexico and its living culture are recognized
> at the state and federal levels as possessing
> significant cultural value, not measurable in
> dollars and cents. The deep-felt and tradition-
> bound ties of northern New Mexico families to
> the land and water are central to the
> maintenance of that culture....I am persuaded
> that to transfer water rights, devoted for more
> than a century to agricultural purposes, in
> order to construct a playground for those who
> can pay is a poor trade, indeed."(84)

The New Mexico Supreme Court is reviewing the
district court decision and the arguments presented by the
transfer applicants to refute the district court's
conclusion. Final jurisdiction over transfer approval
lies with the courts but, regardless of the outcome of
the appeal, future water transfer proponents will have to
recognize that water transfers out of agriculture may
encounter strong local opposition in this area.(85)

Utah statutes allow the State Engineer to consider
the public interest or public welfare in evaluating
applications to appropriate water but these terms are not
statutorily defined. The public interest provision is not
applied routinely in evaluating applications for
appropriation or transfer.(86) Early Utah case law
establishes that water appropriations must be in the best
interest of the public.(87) Utah statutes also require
the State Engineer to reject applications for water rights
appropriations which will "unreasonably affect public
recreation or the natural stream environment."(88)

Like public interest provisions in state statutes,
the Public Trust Doctrine has the potential to influence

the conditions under which water transfers may be approved
and the costs of implementing market transfers. The
Public Trust Doctrine is an ancient concept originating in
English law, reflecting the historical rights of the
citizenry at large to coastal navigation and fishing and
prohibiting alienation of public rights to coastal
waters.(89)   It mandates government consideration of
public values in coastal zones and it is being applied to
an increasing range of resource issues. Several state
court decisions, including California's National Audubon
case, have implied that the doctrine applies to the public
interest in inland waters.(90)   This extension of the
doctrine is still evolving and it remains to be seen how
significantly the Public Trust Doctrine will affect water
transfers.

Some western states have affirmed the Public Trust
Doctrine while others view it as contrary to state
authority over water use.   California's Water Resources
Control Board, for instance, has interpreted the National
Audubon decision as affirming the Board's responsibility
to consider public trust values in future water allocation
decisions, as well as to re-examine past decisions. A 1986
California court decision authorizes the Board to protect
public trust values in issuing water right permits for the
(federal) Central Valley Project and the State Water
Project.(91)   The Nevada State Engineer, on the other
hand, regards the Public Trust Doctrine as contrary to the
public policy of Nevada because it is perceived as
inconsistent with the doctrine of prior appropriation.(92)
However, only courts can actually determine whether the
doctrine applies to specific cases and state agencies do
not have the legal authority to abdicate public trust
responsibilities established by common law under the
Public Trust Doctrine.(93)

Instream Flow Protection

Water transfers can affect recreational, ecological
and environmental values associated with instream flows.
While all states protect water rights, protection of
instream flows that are not relied upon by water right
holders is not a routine consideration in transfer
approval proceedings. Many states recognize instream flow
maintenance for recreation and wildlife as a beneficial
use. In some states public agencies are authorized to
purchase water rights to maintain flows.   Only a few
western states allow a private party to hold a water right

for the purpose of maintaining instream flows for
recreation, wildlife or aesthetic purposes. Generally,
water rights for instream flow maintenance are few in
number relative to rights for consumptive uses and most
instream flow rights are recent appropriations and have
low priority relative to other water rights. Free flowing
waters not protected by a water right have no legal
recognition and thus create no legal basis for protesting
transfers which will have adverse impacts.

Population growth in the Southwest has resulted in a
shift from rural to urban residents. New urban residents
not only demand water for domestic and industrial use,
they also demand recreational opportunities and aesthetic
amenities which rely on water remaining in stream. As
social values increasingly incorporate the importance of
flowing waters, instream flow considerations will have a
greater impact on market transfers. Groups interested in
protecting instream flows may choose to purchase senior
appropriative rights rather than to acquire a junior right
through a new appropriation. Where instream flow maintenance is recognized as a beneficial use so that water
rights may be held for that purpose, market transfers
could become an important means of accomplishing instream
flow protection.

While instream flow protection may provide a motivation for market transactions, instream flow issues could
also make transfers more complicated and costly to
implement. Eventually, as public interest and public
trust concerns play a greater role in water transfer
policy, instream flow impacts may be considered routinely
in approval of transfers between consumptive users.
Livingston and Miller characterize conflict of interests
between consumptive water users desiring to transfer water
rights and interest groups seeking to protect instream
flows as stark, unavoidable and pervasive.(94) Shupe (95)
notes that since instream flow rights typically are year-
round rather than seasonal, and since they often extend
along a stretch of a stream rather than being diverted at
a single point, they are particularly constraining for new
water development and for water transfers. Consequently,
establishment and enforcement of instream flow rights will
continue to generate controversy.

While Arizona statutes do not explicitly recognize
appropriations for instream flow maintenance, a 1976 court
case held that surface water may be appropriated for
instream recreation and fishing.(96) The Arizona
Department of Water Resources (ADWR) issued two permits to

the Nature Conservancy in 1983 to appropriate water for instream flow.(97) As of mid-1987 over twenty-five minimum instream flow permit applications were pending before ADWR and an Instream Flow Task Force had been appointed to assist ADWR in formulating new criteria and procedures for granting permits.(98)

In California, case law has ruled against appropriation where there is no diversion or other physical control over the water.(99) However, instream uses are declared to be reasonable and beneficial and the State Board must consider impacts on instream uses in approving new appropriations and transfers.(100)

In Colorado, the Colorado Water Conservation Board (CWCB) may appropriate water for instream flow and lake level maintenance.(101) Private entities are not authorized to appropriate water for instream flow protection but may dedicate water rights to the CWCB for instream flow maintenance. Appropriations by the board typically have been junior rights and thus do not guarantee minimum flows.(102) The CWCB has made appropriations on over 6,000 miles of streams and more than 500 lakes since the enabling legislation was passed in 1973. The CWCB is also responsible for filing objections to water transfers which may impair instream flow rights.(103)

Appropriations for instream flow and storage in lakes without a physical diversion have been granted in Nevada in specific instances. Instream flow appropriations must be acquired through the same process as any other appropriation.(104) A 1987 county district court decision determined that the federal government, representing public interests, can hold instream rights under Nevada law but rejected an application by the Bureau of Land Management for instream rights to water livestock and wildlife on public lands. Both decisions are being appealed to the Nevada Supreme Court.(105)

New Mexico has no statutes pertaining to appropriation of water for instream flow maintenance, though recognition of instream flow rights has been considered in recent legislative sessions.(106) Case law and decisions by the State Engineer imply that diversion structures are necessary for water right appropriations.(107) There is, as of yet, no case law and no administrative precedent for considering impacts on instream flow levels (other than those which affect vested water rights) in evaluating a transfer proposal.(108)

A Utah statute enacted in 1986 allows the State
Division of Wildlife Resources to acquire established
water rights to maintain flows for fish habitat. The
division must have legislative approval to acquire a right
for instream flows.(109)

IMPACT OF FEDERAL POLICIES ON MARKET DEVELOPMENT

Many different federal policies have an effect on
water market development and water transfers in the
Southwest. A thorough discussion is beyond the scope of
this book so the federal role will only be briefly
summarized here.(110)   Wilkinson(111) argues that state
domination of western water policy gradually has been
eroded in the years since World War II, though the states
continue to play the central role in allocating and
enforcing rights to use water. Significant federal in-
volvement in western water issues stems historically from
national interest in settling the West and decades of
federal participation in water development projects
intended primarily for irrigated agriculture. While
federal funding for new water projects is expected to be
less than in the past, federal policies regarding existing projects remain an important factor in defining the
institutional environment for water transfers.
Federal authority over interstate commerce recently
has been extended to interstate water transfers. The
1982 _Sporhase_ v. _Nebraska_ decision declared that states
may regulate water use but do not own water and cannot ban
its export across state lines as this restricts interstate
commerce.(112)   Controversies over reserved rights
associated with federal and native American lands create
uncertainty for water users, and quantification of these
rights may have a profound impact on water allocation and
on transfer opportunities. Environmental policies such as
the Endangered Species Act and the Clean Water Act affect
water use and transfer in the West. Finally the federal
government's complex agricultural policies have a significant impact on incentives for water use and transfer by
the biggest water user in the Southwest, irrigated
agriculture.
Federal reserved rights associated with federal lands
were recognized in a 1963 Supreme Court case and
subsequent decisions, which established that the United
States held dormant but potentially significant water
rights in national forests and parks, military bases and

other federally managed lands.(113) The priority of a
reserved right has been determined to correspond to the
date the land reservation was established, and the
quantity of the right is that necessary to satisfy the
purpose of the land reservation. Quantification of these
rights is a major issue in western water adjudications, as
the establishment of these senior rights may undermine the
strength of existing water rights in many regions.(114)
Since legal and administrative processes to quantify
reserved rights are just getting under way in many areas,
it remains to be seen how significantly federal reserved
rights will affect market activity in the Southwest.

Native American water rights are based on federal
statutes and treaties. A succession of court decisions has
been necessary to specify the nature of Indian claims and
to facilitate the process of addressing conflicts between
Indian rights and non-Indian water users. The 1963
Supreme Court decision Arizona v. California reaffirmed
the power of the federal government to reserve water
rights for Indian reservations, rejecting state challenges
to this federal authority.(115) Legal foundations for
Indian reservation water rights were initiated much
earlier with a 1908 Supreme Court decision, Winters v.
United States.(116) In that case the court recognized
Indian water rights as senior to those of non-Indian
claimants to Montana's Milk River. Indian claims
implicitly dated back to the year the reservation was
established, even though actual diversions by Indians may
not have predated diversions by non-Indians. The Winters
decision also found that Indian rights are not subject to
forfeiture due to nonuse but set only a vague standard for
determining the quantity of reservation water rights--that
of water for reasonable needs.(117) The Arizona v.
California decision determined that the quantity of Indian
water rights should, at minimum, be sufficient to irrigate
all reservation land which it is economically and
technologically practical to irrigate. The "practicably
irrigable acreage" standard is not without ambiguities,
and quantification based on this standard is complex and
expensive, requiring irrigation plans, land and soil
surveys and crop water use projections.(118) Tribal
water rights have also been recognized for nonirrigation
uses such as stock watering, fishery maintenance and
hydroelectric power. Since these involve much lower
consumptive use, they have not generated the controversy
associated with the practicably irrigable acreage
standard. Indian water rights represent a significant

portion of high seniority rights in some areas of the
Southwest and, where transferrable to non-Indian users,
may play a significant role in southwestern water market
activity.

The effect of tribal water rights on western water
markets will be unfolding for many years as rights are
quantified and conflicts between Indian and non-Indian
claimants are resolved. Conflict resolution can be
expected to have a positive impact on water market
development as it will allow Indian and non-Indian right
holders to form secure expectations regarding their
respective access to water.   There appear to be
provisions, in some cases, for transfer of tribal water
rights to non-Indians.   Collins notes that tribal
resources cannot be sold without authorization from
Congress.   However, when tribal land is leased to non-
Indians for farming, irrigation water is included with the
lease.(119) In some cases, water transfers to non-Indians
for water use outside of reservation boundaries are
possible. The Southern Arizona Water Rights Settlement
Act, for instance, provides that the Tohono O'odham tribe
may sell or lease their water rights within the Tucson
Active Management Area.(120)

The Endangered Species Act is another route by which
federal policies have affected western water use and
transfer. For instance, a Colorado reservoir project has
been delayed due to concerns over its impact on whooping
crane habitat, and Bureau of Reclamation reservoir
management in Nevada's Truckee River Basin has been
modified to preserve an endangered fish species, to the
detriment of water supply availability for local municipal
and industrial water users.(121)   Western states are
concerned that rights to develop surface water recognized
in interstate compacts will be constrained by implementation of the Endangered Species Act. Tarlock argues that
both the Endangered Species Act and the Clean Water Act
create de facto regulatory water rights that have the
potential to generate considerable uncertainty for water
users holding state-created property rights in water.(122)

Uncertainty also exists regarding Bureau of
Reclamation policies on market transfers of water supplied
through federal projects. Wahl notes that voluntary
transfers of federally supplied water have been occurring
since the 1930s, though usually under special circumstances such as drought or for water not yet under
contract. Wahl argues, based on past Bureau decisions on
transfer requests, that the Bureau is taking a positive

view toward market transfers but is likely to make
approvals on a case-by-case basis rather than to announce
an overall policy of approving and facilitating
transfers.(123) Representatives of the U.S. Department of
Interior, the Western Governors Association and the
Western States Water Council convened meetings several
times in 1986 and 1987 to formulate policy recommendations
dealing with efficient use and transfer of federally
supplied water. These discussions indicate that clarification of policies on transfer of federally supplied water
may be forthcoming.(124)

In addition to the question of whether federal
project water can be transferred in a market setting, the
question of whether federal project conveyance facilities
may be used to transfer nonproject water in order to
facilitate market transfers is crucial. This is a key
issue in Arizona where cities and private firms in the
Phoenix area have purchased water rights in remote rural
areas from which water could only be economically
transported through the CAP aqueduct.(125) The conditions
under which excess capacity in federal conveyance
facilities will be available is an important issue that
market participants confront throughout the West. While
the Warren Act of 1911 authorizes use of federal
conveyance facilities to transfer nonproject water, there
is no consistent Bureau of Reclamation policy on use of
conveyance facilities.(126)

The federal government's extensive agricultural
policies play a key role in determining the profitability
of growing irrigated crops and the agricultural sectors'
consequent willingness to sell or lease water rights. The
Reclamation Act of 1902 authorized federal funding of
water projects to support irrigated agriculture and the
economic development of the West. About 15 percent of all
water in the West is supplied by Bureau of Reclamation
projects(127), and federal water for irrigation is heavily
subsidized, priced at less than one-fifth of its real
cost.(128) Subsidized water for agriculture distorts
water use decisions by allowing farmers to ignore the
actual cost of their water supplies. Agricultural
commodity programs were initiated in the post World War I
years in response to a dramatic drop in net farm income.
Many different programs have evolved since the 1920s, with
the goal of sustaining revenues received by farmers at
levels above that which would result from the free play of
supply and demand in domestic and world agricultural
commodity markets. These policies, combined with

subsidized water for agriculture, keep the marginal value product of water in irrigation much higher than it would otherwise be. For instance, payments to Arizona cotton farmers through various federal price support programs accounted for a large percentage of the returns to water in cotton production over the years 1983 to 1986.(129) In the absence of such programs, many farmers would be willing to sell or lease water rights at much lower prices than are currently observed in transactions involving water sales by irrigators. Irrigated agriculture is the largest consumptive user of water in the U.S. and consumes nearly 90 percent of all water in the West.(130) Irrigation is important not only because of the quantity of water it consumes but also because it was the earliest offstream water use in many areas and so irrigators hold a high proportion of senior appropriative rights. The seniority of early irrigation rights makes them attractive to urban buyers seeking additional firm supplies. Changes in federal policies that affect returns to water in irrigation could have an important impact on market activity by altering the quantity of water rights farmers are willing to transfer and the prices they would accept for their rights.

SUMMARY

Policies of the southwestern states and the federal government play a critical role in defining the institutional setting for market transfers. State water law provides a basis for market activity by defining, allocating and enforcing property rights in water. Along with their other functions, water rights determine how the risk of supply short falls are distributed among right holders. Reallocation of such risk is a primary motivation for market transfers. Beneficial use and forfeiture/abandonment provisions provide incentives for water transfers by right holders who do not exercise their water rights regularly. Policies that allow transfer of conserved water reward water conservation efforts and provide opportunities for market exchanges. State policies involving appurtenancy of water rights to land and protection of vested water rights affect the procedures that market participants must follow to obtain approval of transfers and the transaction costs incurred in implementing transfers. Area-of-origin, public interest, public trust and instream flow considerations

82

are all emerging areas of state water policy that have the
potential to affect significantly the conditions under
which transfers may occur and the costs of transferring
water in the future.

Federal policies which affect market activity were
addressed only briefly. Reserved rights associated with
federal and tribal lands, federal environmental and
agricultural policy, and management of federal water
projects all play a role in determining the nature and
extent of market activity in the West. All of the federal
issues discussed involve an element of uncertainty and
impacts on the nature and extent of market transactions
will unfold slowly as disputes over reserved rights are
resolved, and federal environmental, agricultural and
water project policies evolve.

Chapter 5 describes market development and transactions in the six southwestern states. The interplay of
federal, state and local laws and institutions is embodied
in these descriptions, which illustrate the variety of
ways in which water right holders and local water user
organizations adapt to the legal setting described in
this chapter and, through their own decisions and
policies, affect the institutional environment for market
transfers.

NOTES

1. D.W. Bromley, "The Rights of Society vs. the
Rights of Landowners," paper presented at the North
Central Regional Project III Workshop, "Policy
Institutions and Incentives for Soil Conservation." Zion,
Illinois, May 19-21, 1981.

2. T.D. Tregarthen, "Water in Colorado: Fear and
Loathing of the Marketplace." Chapter 4 in Water Rights,
ed. T.L. Anderson, San Francisco: Pacific Institute for
Public Policy Research, 1983.

3. C.W. Howe, D.R. Schurmeier and W.D. Shaw, Jr.,
"Innovative Approaches to Water Allocation: The Potential
for Water Markets." Water Resources Research 22:439-445,
April, 1986.

4. Tregarthen, op cit., p. 131-2.

5. Howe et al., op cit. See Note 3.

6. G.D. Weatherford and S.J. Shupe, "Reallocating
Water in the West." American Water Works Association
Journal 78:63-71, October, 1986.

7. Ariz. Rev. Stat. Ann. Sec. 45-180, Sec. 45-131.B and Sec. 45-141.A.

8. Ariz. Rev. Stat. Ann. Sec. 45-190.

9. Ariz. Rev. Stat. Ann. Sec. 45-602.

10. Title 23, Cal. Adm. Code, Sec. 661-66.85.

11. Cal. Water Code, Sec. 1241.

12. Cal. Constitution, Article 10, Sec. 2.

13. Colo. Rev. Stat. Sec. 37-92-102(1).

14. State of Colorado response to Western Governor's Association 1985 Questionnaire on Water Use, (hereinafter referred to as Western Governor's Association 1985 Questionnaire). p. 1-2.

15. Nev. Rev. Stat. Sec. 533.490 and Sec. 533.030.

16. Nev. Rev. Stat. Sec. 533.637.

17. Nevada response to Western Governor's Association 1985 Questionnaire, p.2.

18. N.M. Stat. Ann. Sec. 72-1-2 and Sec. 72-8-4.

19. N.M. Stat Ann. Sec. 72-12-18 and Sec. 72-5-28.

20. Utah Code Ann. Sec. 73-1-5.

21. Utah Code Ann. Sec. 73-1-3.

22. Salt River Valley Water Users' Association, v. Kavocovich, 3 Ariz. App.28, 411 p.2d201 (1966).

23. Ariz. Rev. Stat. Ann. sec. 45-472A.

24. Sever and transfer proceedings are required for surface water transfers (Ariz. Rev. Stat. Ann. Sec. 45-172). Parties wishing to transfer irrigation groundwater rights located within Active Management Areas rights to nonirrigation uses must seek ADWR approval by filing a development plan describing the planned retirement of land from irrigation and the proposed new water use and location of use. (Ariz. Rev. Stat. Ann. Sec. 45-469).

25. State of California response to Western States Water Council 1986 Questionnaire Regarding State Water Marketing and Management Initiatives, The Public Trust and the Appropriation Doctrine, (hereinafter referred to as Western States Water Council 1986 Qusetionnaire), p. 3.

26. State of Colorado response to Western Governors Association 1985 Questionnaire, p.3.

27. Nev. Rev. Stat. Sec. 533.040 and Sec. 533.370.

28. Personal communication with David N. Stone, Water Rights Division, State Engineers Office, Santa Fe, New Mexico, February, 1987.

29. State of Utah response to Western Governor's Association 1985 Questionnaire, p.3.

30. Utah Code Ann. Sec. 73-1-10 and 73-1-11.

84

31. L. Brown, B. McDonald, J. Tysseling and C.
DuMars, "Water Reallocation, Market Proficiency and
Conflicting Social Values."   Part Six in <u>Water and
Agriculture in the Western U.S.: Conservation Reallocation
and Markets,</u> ed. G.D. Weatherford.   Boulder: Westview
Press, 1982.
    32. <u>Salt River Users' Association</u> v. <u>Kavocovich</u>. See
Note 22.
    33. Cal. Water Code Sec. 1011 and Sec. 1010.
    34. State of Colorado response to Western Governors
Association 1985 Questionnaire, p. 4-5.
    35. <u>Southeastern Colorado Conservancy District</u>   v.
<u>Shelton Farms, Inc.</u> 529 p.2d 1321, Colorado, 1974.
    36. State of Nevada response to Western Governor's
Association 1985 Questionnaire, p. 4.
    37. Nev. Rev. Stat. Sec. 533.040.
    38. Personal   communication with George Benesch,
Deputy Attorney General Division of Water Resources Nevada
Department of Conservation and Natural Resources, May,
1987.
    39. Brown et al., op cit, p. 219.
    40. State of Utah response to Western Governor's
Association 1985 Questionnaire, p.4.
    41. Brown et al, op cit, p. 218.
    42. Ariz. Rev. Stat. Ann. Sec. 45-172.
    43. Ariz. Rev. Stat. Ann. Sec. 45-544 and Sec. 45-
545.
    44. Personal communications with Arizona water bro-
kers, city officials and developers, January through May,
1987.
    45. Cal. Water Code Sec. 1702 and Title 23 Cal. Adm.
Code Sec. 733.
    46. B.C. Driver, "The Effect of Western Water Law on
Water Transfers."   In <u>Water Marketing,</u> ed. S. Shupe.
Denver: University of Denver College of Law, 1986, p.2.1-
2.12.
    47. For a discussion of the uncertainties that
transfer applicants have faced, see M.M. Curie, "A Dis-
tinct Policy Which Forms a Market Within the California
State Water Project." <u>Water Resources Research</u> 21:1717-
1720, 1985. For a discussion of plans to develop transfer
approval criteria, see J.T. Markle, "Facilitating
Voluntary Water Transfers in California." Senior State
Counsel, California Water Resources Control Board.
Presentation for conference on "Western Water: Expanding
Uses/Finite Supplies," Natural Resources Law Center,
University of Colorado, School of Law, Boulder, June,

1986. A California Department of Water Resources Water Transfers Committee was formed in 1986 to develop new procedures for reviewing transfer proposals. The Costa-Isenberg Water Transfer Act of 1986 directs the Department of Water Resources to facilitate voluntary exchanges of water (California Water Code Section 480) and the department expects to issue a water transfer guide in 1988.

48. Cal. Water Code Sections 1725-1740.

49. State of Colorado response to Western States Water Council 1986 Questionnaire, p. 2.

50. Brown et al.(op cit) refer to Green v. Chaffee Ditch Co, 150 Colo. 91, 371 p. 2d 775(1962), a complicated case involving transfer of irrigation rights to the City of Fort Collins. Tregarthen (op cit) refers to Metropolitan Denver Sewage v. Farmers Reservoir and Irrigation Co., Colo. 1499 p. 2d 1190(1972) and Southeastern Colorado Water Conservancy District v. Huston, Arapahoe, Colo.79-CW-1 (1981). These cases illustrate uncertainties that can arise in implementing transfers of appropriative rights. Tregarthen also cites (p.127) an observation by Colorado Assistant Water Division Engineer Kenneth Cooper that legal costs for water hearings often exceed several hundred thousand dollars.

51. State of Nevada response to Western Governors Association 1985 Questionnaire p. 4.

52. Nev. Rev. Stat. Sec. 533.345 and personal communication with Larry Reynolds, Legal Counsel, Dept. of Conservation and Natural Resources, State of Nevada, March, 1987.

53. Personal communication with David N. Stone, Water Rights Division, State Engineer's Office, Santa Fe, New Mexico, February, 1987.

54. Utah Code Ann. Sec. 73-3-3, Sec. 73-1-10, and Sec. 73-1-11.

55. M.M. Kelso, W.E. Martin and L.E. Mack Water Supplies and Economic Growth in an Arid Environment, Tucson: Univ. of Arizona Press 1973, and R.A. Young, "Local and Regional Impacts of Water Transfers" in Water Scarcity: Impacts on Western Agriculture, eds. E.A. Engelbert and A.F. Scheuring, Berkeley: Univ. of California Press, 1984.

56. For a discussion of some of these impacts, see S.C. Nunn, H. Ingram, R. Grimes and S. Eden, "Learning the Limits: Water Management in the Colorado River Basin." Paper presented at Western Social Science Meetings, Reno, Nevada, April, 1986. Also S.L. Brown and H.M. Ingram,

Water and Poverty in the Southwest: Conflict, Opportunity and Responsibility. Tucson: University of Arizona Press, 1987.

57. Ariz. Rev. Stat. Ann. Sec. 45-472 and Sec. 45-473.

58. The City of Mesa, Arizona, for instance, paid over $100,000 to Pinal County in 1986 to compensate for the loss in the county's tax base resulting from Mesa's purchase of over 12,000 acres of farmland. Personal communication with Karl Kohlhoff, City of Mesa Water Resources Manager, December, 1986.

59. The moratorium, House Bill 2153, was introduced in January 1987, but did not pass out of committee in the spring legislative session. House Bill 2462 which addresses county bonding capacity was passed in May, but only after the most effective provisions for protecting county bonding bases were removed.

60. Ariz. Rev. Stat. Ann. Sec. 45-172(5).

61. L.J. MacDonnell, C.W. Howe, J.N. Carbridge and W.A. Ahrens. "Guidelines for Developing Area of Origin Compensation." Issued by the Natural Resources Law Center, University of Colorado, December, 1985, p.8.

62. Ibid., p.10-12.

63. L.J. MacDonnell, and C.W. Howe. "Area-of-Origin Protection In Transbasin Water Diversions: An Evaluation of Alternative Approaches." *Univ. of Colorado Law Review* 57, 1986.

64. The permits, known as "1041 permits", are authorized under House Bill 1041, passed in 1973. Information reported is based on personal communication with Charles Howe, Dept. of Economics, University of Colorado, Boulder, May, 1987.

65. Colorado response to Western Governor's Association 1985 Questionnaire, p.5.

66. Nev. Rev. Stat. Sec. 533.363.

67. MacDonnell et al., op cit, p.11-12.

68. *Middle Rio Grande Conservancy District* v. *Cox*, N.M. 13 Judicial District Court, Case No. 6745 and 7145 (appeal). The case is discussed by Brown et al., op cit, p. 230.

69. Personal communication, David N. Stone, Water Rights Division, State Engineer's Office, Santa Fe, New Mexico, February, 1987.

70. Brown et al, op cit, p. 237-239.

71. C.F. Wilkinson, "Public Interest Constraints on Water Transfers." In Water Marketing, ed. S.J. Shupe, Denver: Univ. of Denver College of Law, 1986, p.2.13 - 2.24.

72. G.D. Weatherford and S.J. Shupe, op cit. J.E. Thorson, "Public Rights at the Headwaters." American Water Works Assoc. Journal, 78:72-78, October, 1986. Driver, op cit.

73. Ariz. Rev. Stat. Ann. Sec. 45-143.

74. Arizona Game and Fish Dept. v. Arizona State Land Dept., 24 Ariz. App. 29,30-31,535 p. 2d 621 (1975) and Reinhard v. Arizona Dept. of Water Resources No. 11594, Superior Court for Cochise County, Mar. 17, (1986).

75. Wilkinson, op cit., p. 2-14. California Constitution, Article X, Sec. 2.

76. National Audubon Society v. Superior Court of Alpine County 33 Cal. 3d 419, 659 p. 2d 709, 189 Cal. Rptr. 346 (1983), cert denied, 104 S. Ct. 413 (1983). This decision, referred o as the Mono Lake case, is discussed in more detail by Wilkinson, op cit.

77. United States v. State Water Resources Control Board, 182 Cal. App. 3d 82.227 Cal. Rptr. 161(1986).

78. Colorado response to Western States' Water Council 1986 Questionnaire, p.1.

79. Nev. Rev. Stat. Sec. 533.370(3).

80. Nevada reply to Western Governors' Association 1985 Questionnaire, p. 5.

81. N.M. Stat. Ann. Sec. 72-12-3.

82. Amendments to N.M. Stat. Ann. Sec. 72-5-23 and Sec. 72-12-7.

83. Young and Norton v. Hinderlider, 15 N.M. 666, 110 p. 1045 (1910).

84. In the matter of Howard Sleeper, et al., Rio Arriba County Case No. RA 84-53(C).

85. S.J. Shupe and J.A. Folk-Williams (eds.), Water Market Update, Jan. 1987, p. 9-10. (Hereinafter referred to as Water Market Update.

86. Utah response to Western Governors' Association 1985 Questionnaire, p.3.

87. Tanner v. Bacon, 103 Utah 494, 136 p. 2d 957 (1943).

88. Utah Code Ann. Sec. 73-3-8.89.

89. Thorson, op cit., p.74; S.J. Shupe. "Emerging Forces in Western Water Law," op cit., p9.4.

90. Thorson, op cit.; Shupe, op. cit.

91. United States v. State Water Resources Control Board, 182 Cal. App 3d 82, 227 Cal. Rptr. 161 (1986).

92. Nevada response to Western States Water Council 1986 Questionnaire, p. 1.110. Also see Nev. Rev. Stat. Sec. 533.

93. The authors appreciate the input of S.J. Shupe, attorney and water resources consultant, Santa Fe, New Mexico, in clarifying this discussion of the Public Trust Doctrine.

94. M. Livingston, and T. Miller, "A Framework for Analyzing the Impact of Western Instream Water Rights on Choice Domains." Land Economics 62:306-312, August, 1986.

95. S.J. Shupe, "Emerging Forces in Western Water Law." Resource Law Notes Newsletter 2-8, Publication of the Natural Resources Law Center, University of Colorado, Boulder, 1986.

96. McClellan v. Jantzen 26 Ariz. App. 723, 547 p. 2d 494 (1976).

97. Arizona response to Western Governors' Association 1985 Questionnaire, p.6.

98. Arizona Department of Water Resources, 1987.

99. Fullerton v. State Water Resources Control Board 90 Cal. App. 3d 590, 153 Cal. Rptr. 518 (1979); California Trout, Inv. v. State Water Resources Control Board 90 Cal. App. 3d 639, 153 Cal. Rptr. 518 (1979).

100. Cal. Water Code Sec. 1243.

101. Colo. Rev. Stat. Sec. 37-92-102(3) and Sec. 37-92-103(4).

102. Colorado response to Western States Water Council 1986 Questionnaire, p 2.

103. Brown et al, op. cit. p. 235-6. Water Market Update. Vol.1, No. 3, March. 1987, p.10

104. Nevada response to Western Governor's Association 1985 Questionnaire p.5 and Western States Water Council 1986 Questionnaire, p.2.

105. The decisions by Judge McDaniel of Nevada's Elko County District Court are discussed in U.S. Water News Vol.3, No.12, June, 1987, p.4.

106. Instream flow legislation was introduced in several recent legislative sessions, including the 1987 session, but no instream flow measures were passed.

107. Reynolds v. Miranda 83 New Mexico 443 493 p.2d 409 (1972).

108. Personal communication with David N. Stone, Water Rights Division, State Engineers' Office, Santa Fe, New Mexico, February, 1987.

109. Utah Code Ann. Sec. 73-3-3, as amended in 1986 and Utah response to Western States' Water Council 1986 Questionnaire, p.2.

110. For discussions of the federal role in western water policy, see F. Trelease, "Uneasy Federalism--State Water Laws and National Water Uses." Washington Law Review 55:751(1980). Also L.J. MacDonnell, "Federal Regulatory Rights in Water." Paper presented at Natural Resources Law Center Short Course, June, 1987, University of Colorado, Boulder. And C.F. Wilkinson, "Western Water Law in Transition." University of Colorado Law Review 56:317(1985).

111. Wilkinson, op cit. See Note 110.

112. Sporhase v. Nebraska 458 U.S. 941 (1982).

113. Arizona v. California 373 U.S. 546 (1963), Cappaert v. United States 426, U.S. 128.

114. Shupe, "Emerging Forces...", op cit., p.5.

115. U.S. Repts., 373:546 (1963).

116. U.S. Repts., 208:564 (1908).

117. R.B. Collins, "Indian Reservation Water Rights," American Water Works Assoc. Journal 78:48-54.

118. H.S. Burness, et al. "The 'New' Arizona v. California; Practicably Irrigable Acreage and Economic Feasibility." Natural Resources Journal. 22:517 (1982).

119. Collins, op cit., p. 53.

120. Southern Arizona Water Rights Settlement Act of 1982, Pub. Law No. 97-293, Sec. 306(c). U.S. Statutes at Large, 96:1274 (1982).

121. Shupe, "Emerging Forces...", op cit., p.5.

122. A.D. Tarlock, "The Endangered Species Act and Western Water Rights." Land and Water Law Review 20:1-30, 1985.

123. R.W. Wahl, "Voluntary Transfers of Federally Supplied Water: Experiences of the Bureau of Reclamation." In Water Marketing, ed. S.J. Shupe, Univ. of Denver College of Law, 1986, p.4.1 - 4.24.

124. Water Market Update, Vol.1, No. 1, p.8 and No.4, p.7, January and April, 1987.

125. The Arizona cities of Phoenix, Scottsdale and Mesa, along with Phoenix area private developers, have purchased water rights in remote rural areas, hoping to use the CAP aqueduct to transport water to the Phoenix metropolitan area.

126. Warren Act of 1911, 43 United States Code Section 523-525.

127. 1969 Census of Agriculture, U.S. Dept. of Commerce, Bureau of the Census, Washington, D.C.

128. Wilkinson, "Western Water Law in Transition," op cit., p.39.

129. D. DeWalt, "Rural to Urban Water Transfers in Arizona: An Economic Analysis." M.S. Thesis, Dept. of Agricultural Economics, Univ. of Arizona, 1987.

130. Westwide Study Report on Critical Water Problems Facing the Eleven Western States. U.S. Dept. of Interior. Washington D.C., (1975).

5
Market Activity in
the Southwestern States

The study area, which covers the arid and semiarid regions of the southwestern United States, includes Arizona, southern California, Colorado, Nevada, New Mexico and Utah. Within each state one or two market areas were identified for in-depth study. These areas are shown on figure 5.1. Four basic criteria were used to select the market areas.

First, each area needed to have well-defined boundaries, established by geographical and/or institutional considerations. While most markets studied are relatively closed systems, none are absolutely closed to the transfer of water into or out of their areas. Inter-basin transfers occur in several of the markets studied.

Second, each market chosen was characterized by an economic scarcity of water resources. If water were available at minimal cost to meet all potential demand, there would be little incentive for market activity. The scarcity criterion did not limit the study to areas in which absolutely no additional water resources could be appropriated. Some market areas investigated remain open to either limited new appropriations or to the importation of additional water supplies. In each of these markets, however, newly appropriated or imported water rights are generally either restricted in quantity or purposes of use, legally difficult to obtain or prohibitively expensive to develop. Therefore, purchase of existing water rights is an attractive option to users desiring additional water.

Third, markets were selected which have a sustained history of water transfers. Locations with low levels of

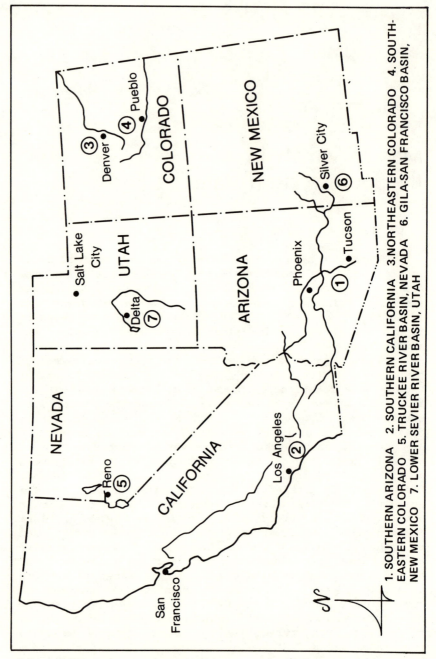

Figure 5.1
Selected Water Market Study Areas in the Southwestern U.S.

market activity were of less interest because of sporadic price data. The observation of changes in market structure and price levels over time is important in evaluating market processes.

Finally, it was important that information on market transactions should be available. Some areas were rejected because records on market transactions were too dispersed, too difficult to obtain, and/or too poorly maintained to provide meaningful information.

In many of the areas studied, public records indicate whether water rights have been transferred and often provide information regarding the parties to the transfer, the transfer date and changes in water use associated with the transfer. However, public records, with very few exceptions, do not provide information on prices. Therefore, extensive fieldwork in the study areas was necessary to obtain price data. Interviews and correspondence with water buyers and sellers, brokers, bankers, public officials and other knowledgeable market observers are the primary source of information on prices. Price levels reported are representative of the market area and time period with which they are associated, to the best of the author's knowledge. However, they are not based on a random sampling approach to price data collection. Such an approach was not possible, given the non-public and dispersed nature of sources of information on market prices.

An effort has been made to render price observations comparable over time and across market areas. All prices have been adjusted, using the Gross National Product (GNP) price deflator, to 1986 dollar values and all are reported in 1986 dollars. The comparability of price observations is affected by the characteristics of the water commodity being traded. Several conventions have been adopted to facilitate comparison of prices among various market transactions.

Water rights may be transferred in perpetuity (sold) or may be transferred temporarily (rented). Unless otherwise noted, transactions described in this study are sales rather than leases or rentals.

It is important to distinguish diversion rights and the consumptive use portion of water rights. Diversion rights refer to the maximum quantity of water that may be withdrawn from a water source. Consumptive use refers to the portion of that diversion right which is removed permanently from the hydrologic system. In many areas, only the consumptive use portion of a water right may be

transferred. That is, the historical level of return
flows occurring in the system of origin cannot be reduced
as a result of the transfer. Unless otherwise indicated,
all transfers described in this report refer to the
quantity of water the buyer is allowed to divert following
the transfer, and prices are expressed in dollars per acre
foot of diversion rights transferable to the buyer.

Water rights are quantified by flow rate or by
volume. Flow rate measures are usually expressed in cubic
feet per second, while volumetric limits are most often
measured in acre-feet per year. Unless otherwise indicated, all transfers described are expressed volumetrically, in acre-feet per year. Hydrological short-falls
and established priorities among water rights prevent most
rights from producing their maximum potential yield every
year. In addition to the maximum allowable level of
diversion, therefore, prospective buyers of water rights
are concerned with the long-term average expected yield,
the minimum possible ("firm") yield, and the variability
of the yield. Where adequate information is available,
water rights transfers are described in terms of the long-
term average yield associated with the right.

The legal treatment of return flows affects comparability of price data. For instance, holders of rights to
imported water in Colorado have not only the right to a
specific quantity that may be diverted but also the right
to use and transfer return flows from their initial
diversion and water use. In contrast, holders of rights
to native flows in Colorado do not have the privilege of
using their return flows. Rather, downstream users are
entitled to these return flows. Adequate information is
not available to characterize all water rights in terms of
acre-feet that may be used and reused. The treatment of
return flows among market areas and water rights is described in the text and prices per acre-foot of diversion
rights should be interpreted accordingly.

SOUTHERN ARIZONA

The Study Area

The Arizona market areas studied are the Tucson and
Phoenix Active Management Areas (AMAs), two of the four
AMAs created under the Arizona Groundwater Management Act
of 1980. The Phoenix AMA includes the Phoenix metropolitan area and most of Maricopa County. The Tucson AMA

includes the Tucson metropolitan area and parts of Pima, Pinal, and Santa Cruz counties. Figure 5.2 shows the AMAs along with the Central Arizona Project aqueduct and selected river systems.

Approximately 60 percent of Arizona's annual average water usage (roughly 8.2 million acre-feet) is derived from groundwater sources. The remaining 40 percent of Arizona's water is drawn from surface water sources.(1) The Salt River Project (SRP) provides substantial quantities of surface water from the Salt and Verde Rivers for users in the Phoenix AMA. Phoenix area surface water supplies are supplemented with groundwater pumping. In contrast, water users in the Tucson AMA are completely dependent upon groundwater pumping. Water supplies in both AMAs will increase as Colorado River water is delivered via the Central Arizona Project (CAP). Limited CAP deliveries began to the Phoenix area in 1985, and the project will begin serving the Tucson area in the early 1990s.

Between 85 and 90 percent of the annual water supply in Arizona is currently used by irrigated agriculture.(2) The number of irrigated acres in the state peaked in the early 1960s, and since then has been shrinking as farmland is retired for urban development. While agriculture has declined in economic importance, the nonagricultural sectors of the economy around Tucson and Phoenix are expanding at a rapid pace.(3)

Perceptions regarding the purpose of the CAP have changed as the political economy of water use in Arizona has changed. As originally conceived, the CAP was meant to be a supplemental water supply for irrigation. By the time construction of the aqueduct reached its midpoint in the early 1980s, the project had been integrated into comprehensive state plans for reducing groundwater overdraft. Recently the CAP has begun to assume an additional role as a mechanism for water transfers from agriculture to urban users. The 300-mile-long canal currently transports Colorado River water to the Phoenix area and, when completed, will convey water all the way to Tucson. The aqueduct links scattered groundwater and surface water systems where no such connection existed before. Several proposals are currently under consideration by the cities of Scottsdale, Phoenix, Mesa, and several private enterprises to use the CAP for interbasin water transfers across central Arizona.

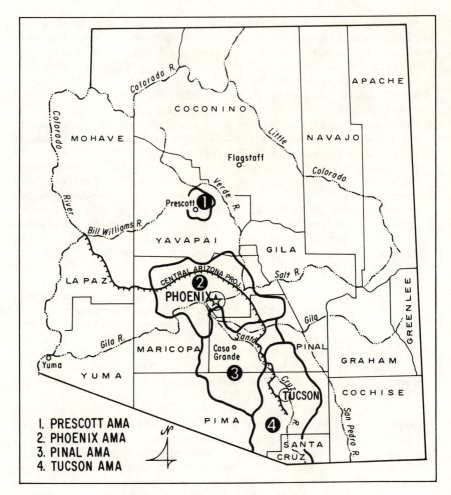

Figure 5.2   Southern Arizona

Water Rights and Institutions

Arizona has a dual system of water rights. Surface water rights were developed under the appropriation doctrine common to the western United States. Groundwater rights are managed under a permit system authorized by the Groundwater Management Act of 1980.(4)

Surface Water Rights. Before 1962, appropriative rights to surface waters were not transferable by their holder to locations other than those specified in the original granting of the right. The only exception arose when the original site was destroyed or impaired by natural calamity. In 1962 this legal constraint was removed and surface water rights became transferable to new locations, provided that the rights of existing appropriators were not impaired. However, surface water transfers continue to be hindered by institutional and hydrologic limitations and few have actually taken place.(5)

Groundwater Rights. The passage of the Groundwater Management Act of 1980 accomplished three things. First, it created a Department of Water Resources to regulate water resource development and water use in the state. Second, it explicitly defined and qualified groundwater rights in the major groundwater using areas of the state. Third, it established an agenda for groundwater management. The Act created four administrative regions, or Active Management Areas (AMAs) within the Department of Water Resources to manage groundwater rights and to establish and administer water conservation and supply augmentation programs. The objective of the water conservation and supply augmentation plans is to eliminate virtually all groundwater overdraft in Arizona by the year 2025.

Within the AMAs there are four basic classes of legally recognized groundwater rights—exempt withdrawals, grandfathered rights, service area rights, and groundwater withdrawal permits. Withdrawals of groundwater for nonirrigation uses of less than 10 acre feet per year from wells with pump capacities of not more than 35 gallons per minute, are exempt from most regulation. Individuals may continue to appropriate groundwater for exempt purposes in AMAs, so long as they conform to rules on well spacing intended to mitigate the adverse impact that a new well could have on nearby groundwater pumpers.

There are three types of grandfathered rights (GFRs): irrigation GFRs, Type I nonirrigation GFRs, and Type II nonirrigation GFRs. An irrigation GFR applies to two or more acres irrigated for the purpose of growing plants for sale or for human and animal consumption. Irrigation GFRs may be converted to nonirrigation use, but no other water right may be converted to an irrigation GFR. Irrigation GFRs are assigned only to lands irrigated during the period January 1, 1975, to January 1, 1980.

The quantity of an irrigation water right on a particular parcel of land is formulated by the local AMA on the basis of the water duty per acre, the number of grandfathered acres, and the number of water duty acres. The irrigation water duty is a measure of historical water use per acre, based on the period January 1, 1975, to January 1, 1980. The number of water duty acres is the maximum number of grandfathered irrigation acres that were irrigated during any one of those five years. Because of crop rotation practices, the number of water duty acres may be significantly less than the total number of grandfathered irrigation acres.

The maximum quantity of water that may be used per grandfathered irrigation acre is the product of the water duty and the ratio of the number of water duty acres to the number of grandfathered acres.(6) Irrigators may choose in any year to irrigate all of their grandfathered irrigation acres and spread out their water rights, or they may irrigate fewer acres and concentrate their water use. The 1980 Groundwater Management Act mandates that groundwater overdraft must decrease. As one means to accomplish this objective, irrigation water duties will be incrementally reduced over time. Since the number of grandfathered and water duty acres on any given parcel of land cannot increase, the total water available for irrigation within AMAs will gradually diminish.

Type I nonirrigation GFRs apply to farmland retired from irrigation after January 1, 1965, in anticipation of a specific nonirrigation use. Type I GFRs convey the right to pump 3 acre-feet per acre of retired irrigated acreage. A Type I right converted from a retired grandfathered irrigation right subsequent to 1980 allows a right-holder to pump the lesser of 3 acre-feet of groundwater per acre of retired irrigated land or the water duty per grandfathered irrigation acre.

Type II nonirrigation GFRs apply to nonirrigation withdrawals of groundwater occurring when the AMAs were established. Generally the quantity of water assigned to a Type II right equals the maximum amount of water withdrawn and used for nonirrigation purposes in any 1 of the 5 years before the designation date of each AMA. No new Type II rights may be granted after the designation of an AMA.

Cities, towns, private water companies, and irrigation districts have "service area rights" to withdraw and transport groundwater. Arizona's groundwater law defines the service area of a city, town, or private water company as the area of land actually served by the entity and any additional areas that contain an operating distribution system owned by the entity and used primarily for the delivery of nonirrigation water. A city, town or private water company has the right to withdraw as much groundwater from within its service area as it needs to serve the residents and landowners within the service area. The quantity of water legally available to a service area is therefore not fixed and may expand over time. However the state plans to limit the expansion of service area rights through mandatory reduction in per capita water use within each service area.

Those who are not eligible for GFRs or service area rights may obtain the right to withdraw and use groundwater for new or expanded nonirrigation purposes by applying for a temporary groundwater withdrawal permit. If certain criteria are met, the Department of Water Resources may issue such permits. Groundwater withdrawal permits specify limits on both the duration and quantity of withdrawals.

A water user wishing to acquire new or additional groundwater rights but for whom exempted groundwater rights or temporary groundwater permits are not feasible, may lease or purchase a GFR. Most permitted rights issued pursuant to the 1980 Code may be transferred. All transfers are subject to certain restrictions and must be approved by the Department of Water Resources. Temporary use permits may not be transferred.

Grandfathered irrigation and Type I nonirrigation rights are strictly appurtenant to the land to which the right is assigned. The full amount of the right is conveyed with the sale of the land. However, any quantity of water up to the limit of the right may be transported off the land to nonirrigation uses in other locations. If a Type I right has been converted from an irrigation right, the irrigated land must be permanently retired from irrigation. The number of acre-feet of water assigned to the Type I right is determined at the time of the conversion to nonirrigation use and remains fixed at that quantity for all future uses. Type I water rights may not be used for irrigation, and the right cannot be reverted to a grandfathered irrigation right.

Type II non-irrigation rights are the only ground-water rights not strictly appurtenant to a particular parcel of land. Within any given AMA, Type II rights may be transferred freely, subject only to regulations concerning the spacing and drilling of new wells.(7) Type II rights may not be used for irrigation, and rights designated for power generation or for mineral extraction are limited to those specific uses. Probably the greatest drawback to the transferability of a Type II right is its indivisibility. The law does not allow partitioning of Type II rights into smaller quantities.

Central Arizona Project Contracts. In addition to appropriated surface water rights and permitted ground-water rights, there are two other types of water rights available within AMAs--CAP water and sewage effluent. CAP water is available to municipal water service organiza-tions, water companies, and irrigation districts through service contracts with the Central Arizona Water Conservancy District (CAWCD), which serves as a liaison with the Bureau of Reclamation. Users of CAP water are divided into three classes--municipal and industrial, non-Indian agricultural, and Indian. Identified public bene-fits of the CAP include flood control, recreation, and maintenance of fish and wildlife habitat.(8)

Charges for CAP water service are structured differently according to the type of water user and the status of project construction. The "interim" period is defined as the period covering the early project years, extending from the beginning of water deliveries, which began in late 1985, to the completion of all major portions of the CAP, expected in the early 1990s. During the interim period, water users are charged for the energy cost of pumping the water, plus $10 per acre-foot for project operation and maintenance costs. Pumping costs for CAP vary between $30 and $40 per acre-foot, depending upon the distance of the recipient from the Colorado River (the farther along on the aqueduct the user is located, the higher the pumping cost).(9)

Following the completion of project construction, all water users will be charged a uniform rate of about $58 per acre-foot. This rate is set to meet the energy costs of pumping CAP water, plus maintenance costs. In addition to the costs of pumping and project operation and mainte-nance, the Bureau of Reclamation will assess certain charges to help repay the United States government for the

costs of constructing the Project. Capital construction
cost obligations are apportioned among the various types
of project beneficiaries, and repayment of these costs is
handled differently for each group. The portion of costs
attributed to the provision of public benefits are not
subject to repayment and constitute a direct transfer from
the federal government. The portion of costs allocated to
Indian reservations is repayable, but repayment is
deferred so long as the water continues to be used on
tribal reservation lands.(10)

Repayment costs are assessed directly to municipal
and non-Indian agricultural users. The portion of costs
allocated to municipal water users is repayable with
interest, amortised at a rate of 3.342 percent. Capital
repayment charges for municipal users of CAP water initially will be set at about $5 per acre-foot, increasing
gradually to as much as $40 per acre-foot in the year
2025. The portion of costs allocated to non-Indian agriculture is repayable without interest, at a flat rate of
$2 per acre-foot of water delivered.(11) Only a fraction
of the total agricultural repayment obligation is expected
to be met directly by farmers. Most of the funds are to
be collected through transferring revenues earned from the
Navajo electric generating station, which is owned by the
Bureau of Reclamation.(12)

Indian reservations and municipal water service
organizations are allocated specific quantities of project
water each year. Non-Indian agricultural and miscellaneous uses have no specific allocations guaranteed, but
instead are given prorated portions of the water supplies
remaining after all obligations to Indian and municipal
water users have been satisfied. In the event of insufficient CAP water to serve all users, the priorities of
service are as follows: First, municipal and
nonagricultural Indian users, second, Indian agricultural
users, third, non-Indian agricultural users, and fourth,
miscellaneous users.(13) Water users may not freely
transfer CAP water among themselves, although land with
CAP water service contracts may be bought and sold.
Contracts for agricultural CAP water may be converted to
municipal and industrial water service contracts at the
rate of one acre-foot per acre.(14)

Effluent. The legal status of effluent ownership,
use and transfer is not yet clear. In recent years
treated sewage effluent has begun to receive increasing
attention for its potential in securing potable water
supplies from irrigators through exchange agreements, in

satisfying Indian claims to water rights, in recharging
groundwater aquifers, and as a marketable commodity.(15)
Only small quantities of effluent have been bought and
sold in Arizona to date, but management and marketing
strategies are being actively discussed. A major unresolved question concerns whether or not effluent is
subject to regulation under state laws governing surface
water appropriation and groundwater management.(16)   A
state court has declared that effluent is neither groundwater nor surface water and is not subject to existing
state water law. The decision is currently under appeal.
If it is not reversed, then effluent will be one of least
regulated water resources in Arizona, with few legal
restrictions on its use and transfer.

<u>Water Market Activity</u>

   <u>Groundwater Transfers</u>. Water market transactions in
southern Arizona involve Type I and Type II groundwater
rights, adjudicated surface flows, and reclaimed effluent.
One of the oldest water markets in Arizona is Tucson's
ongoing acquisition of irrigated farmland in the Avra
Valley, which lies about 15 miles to the west of the city.
Tucson had contemplated developing water rights in the
valley at least since the 1940s. The city acquired parcels
of land and developed a wellfield and a transmission
system to convey Avra Valley water into the city in the
mid-1960s. Transportation of Avra Valley water into the
Tucson basin began in 1968.(17)
   In 1971 Tucson began purchasing additional land in
the Avra Valley in the vicinity of its wellfields. Over
the 8-year period from 1971 to early 1979, Tucson acquired
over 13,000 acres of irrigated land and brought farming to
an end in the southern portion of the Avra Valley. In
1979, when the passage of the new groundwater management
code was imminent, the Tucson City Council called a
moratorium on further land purchases until the legal
status of their Avra Valley acquisitions could be
clarified. Tucson ended the moratorium in 1984, and by
the close of 1986 another 7,000 acres of farmland had been
purchased and retired. The city expects to acquire the
remaining 20,000 acres of privately owned irrigated land
in the central and northern portions of the Avra Valley
over the next 10 years.(18)
   At the legal maximum of 3 acre-feet of water rights
per grandfathered irrigated acre per year, Tucson's water
right holdings in Avra Valley are in excess of 55,000

acre-feet per year. This is equal to nearly two-thirds of
annual water usage in the city. In recent years Tucson
has been pumping only between 5,000 and 6,000 acre-feet
per year from the Avra Valley wellfields. Pumpage is
expected to rise to over 15,000 acre-feet per year before
the arrival of CAP water in the early 1990's. Pumpage will
than decline to about 2,000 or 3,000 acre-feet per year,
varying as required to meet peak load demands on the
city's water system. Importation of Avra Valley water is
projected to increase again in future years as Tucson's
population continues to increase.(19)

Prices paid by Tucson for land in Avra Valley have
ranged between $1,000 and $2,000 per acre. Slightly more
than 75 percent of the total acreage Tucson has acquired
in the valley has irrigation water rights. The city spends
a total of about $150,000 per year to reduce dust and weed
problems on its retired farmlands.(20) If one assumes that
the land and improvements have no value once the
appurtenant irrigation rights have been retired for city
use and that the transferable water rights average 3 acre-
feet per acre of irrigated land per year, then purchase
prices for Avra Valley water rights have ranged between
$400 and $900 per acre-foot over the period from 1971 to
1986.

A second example of the acquisition of farmland for
the conversion of grandfathered irrigation rights to Type
I non-irrigation rights involves the City of Mesa, located
in the Phoenix AMA. In the spring of 1985, Mesa purchased
over 11,500 acres of irrigated farmland in fourteen
separate transactions. The farmlands have irrigation GFRs
which may be converted to Type I nonirrigation GFRs equal-
ing over 30,000 acre-feet per year. The farmlands lie
approximately 40 miles south of Mesa in neighboring Pinal
County within the Pinal AMA. Mesa intends to lease the
land back to farmers for 5 to 15 years, until the city is
ready to develop the water rights for municipal use. The
total cost of purchasing the 11,500 acres of land and
30,000 acre-feet of water rights was over $29 million.
Prices ranged between $1,900 and $3,000 per acre, with an
average price of about $2,600 per acre. Assuming the land
has no value without the water rights, Mesa paid an
average of about $1,000 per acre-foot of transferable
water rights.

If necessary, Mesa is willing to pipe groundwater all
the way to the city from the retired farmland. As a less
costly alternative, however, the city is seeking approval
from the Department of Water Resources for a plan to

exchange groundwater for CAP water. Under this plan, the city would pump Type I groundwater from the retired farmland into the CAP aqueduct, where it would then flow south to Tucson. In exchange, Mesa would divert an equal quantity of CAP water meant originally for Tucson at the Mesa's diversion point along the CAP aqueduct.(21)

The magnitude of Mesa's purchase has generated concerns in Pinal County about the local economic impact of the farmland sales--primarily of the effect on the county tax base and the loss of water for future development. Mesa hopes to allay these concerns by making "in lieu of tax" payments to the Pinal County government and to the two irrigation districts within which the farms are located. Over $275,000 of in-lieu payments are being paid annually. The city also will attempt to leave the local allocation of CAP water, equal to 1 acre-foot per irrigated acre, on the retired farm land for future urban and industrial development.(22)

Type II non-irrigation grandfathered rights have been bought and sold in both the Phoenix and Tucson AMAs, where nearly all the Type II rights in Arizona are concentrated. Most transfers of Type II rights have been part of real estate transactions involving land and improvements as well as water, and little can be inferred about the implicit market value of water rights in these sales. Some Type II rights have been acquired separately by individuals investing in water rights.(23) Some businesses have acquired Type II rights, perceiving them as a less costly means of getting water than hooking up to a municipal water system.(24) In 1985 and 1986, typical prices for Type II rights averaged $1,500 per acre-foot in the Phoenix AMA and slightly over $1,000 per acre-foot in the Tucson AMA.

An emerging market for Type I and Type II water rights is the leasing of water in order to create new water service areas. Under Arizona law, the service area for a water service organization is not necessarily the same as the area within which it has the legal authority to provide service. The former consists of the area physically served with water. The latter is little more than a boundary line on a piece of paper, including the actual water delivery area but conceivably extending far beyond it. Water service organizations can only withdraw groundwater from areas already currently being served. Therefore, it is difficult for a water service organization to provide water service to new locations without already having the water resources on hand. One possible solution is to lease water rights just long enough to establish water service in a new location and then to apply to the state for a service area groundwater extraction permit.(25)

Rights to pump groundwater outside of AMAs are not clearly defined or quantified and pumping appears to be limited only by the provision that other water users are not impaired. In spite of this uncertainty, several market transactions have involved groundwater outside of AMAs. One large western Arizona ranch, located in La Paz County, is expected to yield over 51,000 acre-feet of groundwater per year according to the buyer's estimates. The ranch was acquired by a Phoenix-area development firm in a series of transactions in 1985, at costs ranging from $500 to over $900 per acre-foot for the water rights. A minority interest in the ranch subsequently was sold to a third party for about $1,200 per acre-foot. The water, which the developer hopes to pump at the ranch and deliver via the CAP aqueduct, will be used for projects in the Phoenix area. In 1986 the City of Phoenix purchased 14,000 acres of farmland in the McMullen Valley in La Paz County for slightly over $30 million.(26) The city expects to export up to 30,000 acre-feet of groundwater annually from the land by the year 2005. Phoenix is also hoping to use the CAP aqueduct to transport its water from the McMullen Valley to its service area.(27)

Surface Water Transfers. Some surface water rights are also being transferred in Arizona. In the spring of 1984 the City of Scottsdale purchased the Planet Ranch, an 8,400-acre ranch in western Arizona for $12.2 million. The source of water for the Planet Ranch is the Bill Williams River. Scottsdale hopes to divert water from the Bill Williams into the CAP aqueduct for transportation to the city. Scottsdale has invested close to $4 million in improving the ranch facilities and preparing land for irrigation. Ranch operating losses are projected to total $1.5 million before the city breaks even on operating costs in 1987.(28) Adjusting for inflation, the present value of the costs associated with acquiring the Planet Ranch water rights equals about $17.7 million. If the ranch purchase yields 13,500 acre-feet of water as hoped, the cost for the water rights will be approximately $1300 per acre-foot.

Inasmuch as the water rights for the Planet Ranch are appropriated rights and are subject to beneficial use requirements, Scottsdale will need to continue using them for agricultural purposes until they can be incorporated into the city's municipal water system. The precise quantity of water rights acquired in the purchase of the Planet Ranch and the proportion of those rights that may be removed from the river for transport to Scottsdale have not yet been determined, although estimates place the quantity available for export at about 13,500 acre-feet per year. Aware of this uncertainty, Scottsdale included a clause in the purchase contract specifying adjustments in the ultimate sales price for the ranch should the water rights prove to be less than originally estimated. If the water resources turn out to be less than the expected quantity, the purchase agreement calls for a reduction in the sales price by $870 for each acre-foot of water less than 13,500.(29)

The 1,000-acre Lincoln Ranch, located along the Bill Williams River upstream from Scottsdale's Planet Ranch, was purchased by a Phoenix-area business concern for approximately $5 million. The buyer hopes to transfer between 7,000 and 7,500 acre-feet of surface water per year to the Phoenix area. Informal discussions have been carried out with the City of Scottsdale about sharing in the cost of building a 12-1/2 mile long aqueduct to transport water from the Bill Williams River to the CAP system.(30)

Effluent Transfers. Some sales of treated sewage effluent have occurred in southern Arizona. Pima County, in the Tucson AMA, has been selling up to 3,500 acre-feet per year of secondary treated sewage effluent to farmers in the Cortaro-Marana Irrigation District for several years at $5 per acre-foot. Recently the district agreed to an increase in the rate to $10 per acre-foot, beginning in 1987. Tucson city policy now encourages all large commercial water users to purchase and use effluent to the greatest extent possible.(31) New golf courses are required to irrigate with effluent. Effluent charges for commercial water users in Tucson in 1986 were $372 per acre-foot.(32)

Another example of sewage effluent marketing is an agreement signed in 1973 between the Palo Verde nuclear power station and the cities of Tempe, Phoenix, Mesa, Tolleson, Scottsdale, and Youngtown--all in the Phoenix metropolitan area. The contract includes four separate purchase options. If all are exercised, they would provide 140,000 acre-feet of effluent annually to cool the plant's reactors through the year 2040. The original price for the effluent was set at $30 per acre-foot, or 40 percent of municipal users' cost of CAP water, whichever is lower. A recent law suit challenging the agreement may force the contract to be revised.(33)   If the contract is amended, the contracted price for the effluent could be increased to equal the cost of CAP water for cities, which now is expected to be at least $300 per acre-foot.(34)

To summarize: Groundwater, surface water and effluent are being transferred through market transactions in Arizona.   Policies that define and restrict water market opportunities vary considerably, depending on the type of water right under consideration. Water is moving steadily from irrigated agriculture to nonagricultural uses as rapid population growth continues in metropolitan areas.

SOUTHERN CALIFORNIA

The Study Area

In California, as in many other western states, water resources are concentrated in one part of the state while population, industry and irrigated land are concentrated in another part of the state.   Approximately 70 percent of the state's water supplies lie north of the latitude of Sacramento, while 80 percent of the state's population, along with most irrigated agriculture and industry, lies south of that latitude.(35)   A complex system of dams, reservoirs and canals transports water south through California's San Joaquin Valley. The federal Central Valley Project (CVP), which began deliveries in 1951, extends to the southern end of the San Joaquin Valley. California appropriated funds for the State Water Project (SWP) in 1959, and the SWP's California Aqueduct transports water south through the San Joaquin Valley, over the Tehachapi Mountain range, and into the greater Los Angeles metropolitan area.   Figure 5.3 shows California's major aqueduct systems.

Southern California, defined as the region south of the Tehachapi Mountains, is characterized by a semiarid climate and a large concentrated population.   Southern California has over 50 percent of the state's population and contains the nations's third largest metropolitan area, yet receives less than 3 percent of the state's surface water runoff.   The southern part of the state imports more water than it produces locally.(36)   The southern California water industry is dominated by public districts and municipal waterworks.   The Metropolitan

108

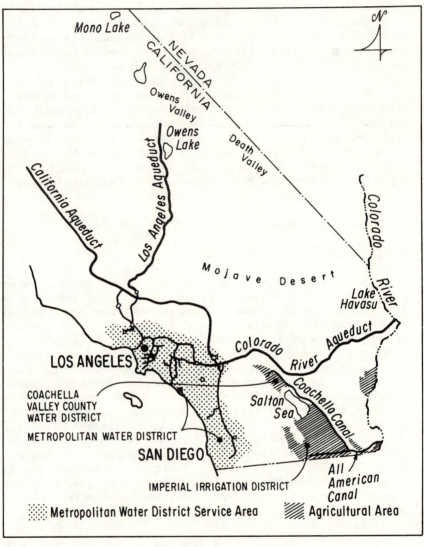

Figure 5.3 Southern California

Water District (MWD) of southern California services more than half the water users in the region. Over fifty reservoirs operate in southern California, managed by federal, state, city, and other water organizations. Irrigated agriculture continues to be an important part of southern California's economy, in spite of rapid urbanization of agricultural areas. Agriculture uses approximately 60 percent of the region's water supplies, and urban areas account for the other 40 percent of water use.(37)

Water Rights and Institutions

Approximately 55 percent of California's water supply is direct and stored surface water. Both riparian and appropriated surface water rights are recognized under state law.(38) While significant quantities of water are used under riparian law, most surface water within the state is managed under the appropriations doctrine. Since 1914, appropriative rights have been created under a license system operated by the state. Appropriative rights are sometimes held by individuals or corporations, but they are much more commonly held by public entities organized for the purpose of supplying water, such as the federal CVP, the California SWP, or local water districts. Appropriative water rights must be obtained before surface water development may be undertaken.(39)

Groundwater rights in California are typically associated with land ownership. Owners of land overlying a groundwater basin are entitled to pump water for use on that land. If the basin has surplus water, that excess may be transported for use on lands that do not overlie the aquifer. Surplus water is available when current groundwater pumping is less than the average annual recharge of the groundwater basin, so the level of current pumping and recharge determines whether an aquifer's groundwater may be used on nonoverlying sites. There is no statewide groundwater basin management statute. However, case law indicates that groundwater overdraft can be reduced by mandatory limitations on pumping by each overlying owner, through a doctrine known as "mutual prescription."(40)

The California Department of Water Resources (DWR) was created by statute in 1956 to take the responsibility for matters pertaining to water resources. In 1967, the legislature merged the functions of the State Water Rights Board and the state Water Quality Control Board into the

Water Resources Control Board (WRCB), which has jurisdiction over the nine regional water quality control boards. The WRCB exercises authority in three distinct areas-water quality, water rights, and planning and research. The Board acts in a quasi-judicial role in determining rights to surface water. Of particular concern when making water rights determinations is the prevention of waste and unreasonable use of water.

A wide array of private and public institutions exist for developing and allocating water resources. More than 3,000 different organizations supply water in the state, of which nearly 1,000 are public water districts. About 900 public districts were formed under 40 general water district acts; the remainder were individually created by the legislature under special acts.(41)

The public water districts that supply most of the water to agriculture are reclamation districts, irrigation districts, and water districts. Their primary purpose is to irrigate lands and to reclaim and protect them from overflow. These public districts are, in essence, nonprofit wholesalers of water. They may have water supply sources of their own, both surface water and groundwater, or they may contract for water developed by the federal government (e.g., the CVP) or by the state of California (e.g., the SWP). They are governed by boards of directors, may have powers of eminent domain, and have the power to sell general obligation bonds, levy water charges, and impose ad valorem taxes on landowners within the district. Most water service agencies function under appropriative water rights laws. Riparian users are typically small, and take water only for their own use.

Commercial water companies and mutual water agencies number in the hundreds. Their principal purpose is to establish rights to water use and to sell and deliver water to users. Mutual agencies sell water to members at supply costs and are thus nonprofit. Water companies sell water to customers within their service area at whatever prices the market will bear, and the profits are distributed to stockholders as with any other private company. Mutual companies are more frequently utilized in irrigation, and commercial companies are more heavily involved in serving urban customers.

The agencies and individuals participating in the water allocation system in California can be stratified into four levels. First are the courts and the Water Resources Control Board; next are the federal and state water supply agencies; then come the regional and local

water agencies. While much of the developed water initially was allocated through the federal and state water
projects, some rights are held directly by regional and
local water districts, and some are held by individual
users.(42)

Uncertainty over legal restrictions on the transfer
of water rights can make water users reluctant to consider
selling or leasing water rights. California has attempted
to reduce much of this uncertainty. It has been declared
to be the "established policy" of the state to "facilitate
the voluntary transfer of water and water rights where
consistent with the public welfare..." In recent years,
several legislative measures have been enacted to facilitate water transfers. A few of the most significant
include permitting water agencies to transfer and market
any portion of their water supplies declared "surplus" to
their "needs", permitting the transfer and marketing of
conserved or salvaged water supplies, and permitting the
use of "unused capacity" in public water conveyance
facilities for water transfers.(43)

In California, riparian surface water use and
overlying groundwater use are legally defined on the basis
of land ownership--the rights to use such water cannot be
transferred independent of the land title itself. Hence,
purchasing a piece of land with either riparian or
overlying groundwater rights is akin to purchasing the
land plus an option to use water on that land subject to
its availability, to requirements for reasonable and
beneficial use, and other restrictions discussed earlier.

The state Water Code, as amended in 1971, prohibits
districts from transferring water outside district
boundaries unless it is declared "surplus." The test of
"surplus" is strict and can rarely be met, requiring the
water to be unwanted, at any price, by any member of the
district. The enabling acts of many water districts do
not provide for reallocation of water from one member to
another once an initial allocation is made.

Appropriative rights, however, are legally transferable and can be sold independent of title to land. The
transfer must satisfy applicable provisions of water law
governing a change in the purpose of use, place of use,
and point of diversion. The WRCB may approve a transfer
if it is in the public interest and there is no injury to
other water users. In instances where the possibility for
injury to other users is unknown, the Board may authorize
a trial transfer not to exceed one year in order to judge
the effect of the transfer. The Board may modify or

revoke the trial transfer if it determines that the transfer will result in substantial injury to any water user. However, actual transfers have been limited in number and are subject to the uncertainty of WRCB approval.

Groundwater in adjudicated groundwater basins may be transferred only after a determination that a surplus exists. Surplus water may be exported from a basin if this will not result in injury to other overlying land owners.

Water Market Activity

The current system for defining and managing water rights in California presents obstacles to market allocation of water rights. Individual water users often do not own the water rights themselves--the water companies or districts do. In California, the Bureau of Reclamation and the Department of Water Resources are permittees of the State Water Resources Control Board, which has ultimate jurisdiction over water rights. Contractors of these agencies technically do not hold any permanent water rights. Instead they hold options to purchase water from the districts on terms specified in the contract. Districts, which are bound by contract to supply water, are not free to negotiate the sales of water rights or even water rentals unless they have surplus water available.

In the case of State Water Project water, any changes in contracts or in points of diversion must be approved by the director of the Department of Water Resources. Contracts for options to buy State Water Project water are generally not transactable. They cannot be bought, sold, or leased without approval of the SWP.

A series of water transfers took place within California during the 1976-77 drought, all under special circumstances. Nearly all of the transfers occurred outside of the WRCB appropriations system, and with few exceptions, the water was sold by individuals or corporations with clear title to the water rights, rather than by a water district. These sales tended to be short-term leases negotiated in response to drought conditions.(44) Many of the transfers that occurred were within the Bureau of Reclamation's Central Valley Project. The federal Emergency Drought Act, passed by Congress in 1977, granted the Secretary of the Interior the authority to establish a temporary water program for the purpose of minimizing

agricultural losses resulting from the drought. During
the program's period the Bureau purchased 46,438 acre-feet
of water at prices ranging between $20 and $87 per acre-
foot. The Bureau resold 42,533 acre-feet of water to
various buyers at a price of $53 an acre-foot plus
conveyance charges.(45) The Bureau administratively
determined the purchase and sales prices of the water.
Under the Act, the purchase price could "not confer any
undue benefit or profit to any person or persons compared
to what should have been realized if the water had been
used in the normal irrigation of crops adapted to the
area." The Bureau negotiated the purchase price by considering the seller's net income adjusted by certain
handling costs. Resale prices were restricted to cover
the actual expenditure involved in acquiring and redistributing the water. This transfer program rationed water
allocation through a buyer preference system; it resold
water at cost and therefore does not constitute a market
reallocation process.

Market exchanges and transfers take place routinely
in the Central and West Coast Basins of Los Angeles
County. The basins are shown on figure 5.4. These basins
were adjudicated in the early 1960s and groundwater use is
administered by the Department of Water Resources, which
serves as court-appointed Watermaster. Both basins
participate in groundwater replenishment programs, sea
water barrier projects, and water quality and groundwater
level monitoring. The Watermaster administers the
Exchange Pool, which facilitates transfer of water from
water users who will not use their entire allotment to
water users who desire water in excess of their current
allotment. The price charged for Exchange Pool rights is
based on a formula specified in the adjudication court
orders, not on negotiation between water users. In 1985
the Exchange Pool price was $184 per acre-foot in the
Central Basin and $69 in the West Coast Basin.(46) Prices
in the Central Basin fell to $159 per acre-foot in 1986
and to $118 per acre-foot in 1987.(47)

The Exchange Pool is not the only method of obtaining
additional pumping rights. Water users may buy, sell, and
lease groundwater rights within each basin. In the Central
Basin, water rights sales over the past two decades have
served to concentrate groundwater rights ownership,
reducing rights holders from 508 in 1966 to 194 in 1985.
Sales and leases are recorded with the Watermaster.
Summary price information shows a steady rise in average
leasing prices from $50 to more than $90 per acre-foot

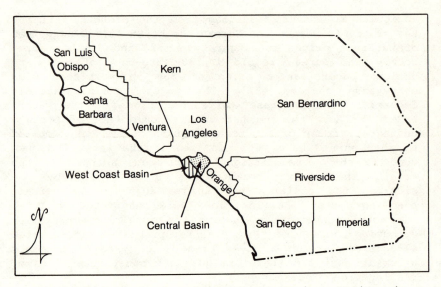

Figure 5.4   Central and West Coast Basins, California

over the period from 1964 to 1985. Privately negotiated leasing rates lie 20 to 30 percent below the Exchange Pool rates and are up to 50 percent less than MWD's water rates per acre-foot. Pumping rights, including leases, are taxed as property rights by Los Angeles County.(48)

Wahl and Davis (49) note that substantial economic incentives exist for water transfers between the federal CVP and the SWP, both of which move water south through California's San Joaquin Valley. In particular, they argue that farmers in the Westlands Water District, who are confronted with the water quality impacts of agricultural drainage on Kesterson Reservoir, would be willing to sell land and water rights to the State Water Project for prices that lie below the costs of SWP's least expensive supply development alternatives. While clear economic incentives for the transfer exist, the author points out that unresolved legal questions remain a barrier to CVP-SWP transfers, as do the high transactions costs of multi-agency negotiation over transfer conditions.

Southern California's MWD has been negotiating with Imperial Irrigation District (IID) over transfer of conserved water from IID to MWD. MWD proposes to finance conservation measures within IID in exchange for rights to use conserved water. The average cost per acre-foot for 400,000 acre-feet of conservation investments is $240 per acre-foot conserved. This represents an economically attractive source of water, relative to MWD's other supply enhancement alternatives. However, negotiations have proved complicated because of legal uncertainties, federal and state agency concerns over the proposal, and MWD and IID concerns over security of rights transferred and terms of transfer. Negotiations have been discontinued and no plans have been announced for resuming discussions between MWD and IID.(50)

MWD is currently negotiating an arrangement to conserve and use waters from the Coachella Valley Water District north of the Imperial Irrigation District. Lining a 39-mile stretch of the Coachella Canal could make an additional 25,000 to 45,000 acre-feet available for use without interfering with existing agricultural water uses. Testing of a low cost method of in-place canal lining must be completed prior to finalizing this proposal.(51)

MWD is also actively engaged in discussions with the Palo Verde Irrigation District to establish procedures permitting MWD to increase its Colorado River diversions by 100,000 acre-feet per year. MWD has offered to pay local farmers to temporarily reduce irrigated acreage or

to adopt water saving techniques (financed by MWD) in
order to increase its dry year supply. Another alternative under consideration is for MWD to pay farmers for the
option of diverting water out of agriculture when needed
for municipal use in drought years.(52)

There are numerous innovations in water management
under consideration by private and public water agencies
in California. While most of these innovations do not
constitute market transfers of water, some of them could
serve as models for the formation of water marketing
systems. An example is the proposal to form the Kern
Water Bank. In 1987, the Kern County Water Agency approved a memorandum of understanding with the state
Department of Water Resources to pursue the establishment
of the Kern Water Bank. Under the proposal, the State
Water Project would acquire a 46,000-acre parcel of land
to develop an underground water storage facility. During
years of surplus water flow, the state would store surface
water supplies in the bank and then pump and sell this
water to project participants during dry years. State
officials estimate that 1,000,000 acre-feet of water could
be stored under the site, and up to one-third of this
quantity could be pumped out and sold in any one year.(53)

To summarize: There is increasing economic and
political pressure for market transactions in California.
It is the established policy of the state of California to
encourage the voluntary transfer of water rights. The
legislature has specifically stated that transfer of water
or water rights does not, in itself, constitute evidence
of waste or unreasonable use. California legislation ex-
pressly allows water to be transferred if the water use
has been reduced or discontinued because of water conservation or the substitute use of reclaimed or waste water.
Given these developments, and current efforts to clarify
the criteria for water transfer approval by the WRCB,
market transfers of water in California are likely to
become increasingly common.

NORTHEASTERN AND SOUTHEASTERN COLORADO

The Study Areas

The market areas chosen for study in Colorado are the
Northern Colorado Water Conservancy District (NCWCD) and
the Southeastern Colorado Water Conservancy District
(SCWCD). The NCWCD includes farming areas, towns and
cities in the South Platte River basin. The principal

metropolitan centers are Boulder, Fort Collins, Greeley, Longmont, and Loveland. The SCWCD includes farming areas, towns, and cities in the Arkansas River basin. The principal metropolitan centers are Pueblo, Fountain, and Colorado Springs. Another city located outside the SCWCD in the Denver area, Aurora, has successfully purchased and won the right to transfer large quantities of water out of the Arkansas basin, and therefore is included in the discussion of SCWCD water transfers. The two market areas are shown in figures 5.5 and 5.6.

The predominant source of water in both areas is mountain stream runoff. The natural supply of surface water is supplemented with transmountain diversion projects and with groundwater pumping. Transmountain diversion water and most native stream water are of high quality, except for flows in the lower reaches of the Arkansas River, where salinity levels are significant.(54) Groundwater quality varies depending on location, but is generally poorer than that of surface flows.

Nearly all native water supplies appropriated for use below (east of) the Front Range of the Rocky Mountains are controlled by mutual stock irrigation companies, privately held irrigation companies, rural-domestic water districts, or municipal water service organizations. Some native water flows, especially in the upper reaches of the Arkansas River, are still held under individual appropriation decrees.

There are two major transmountain diversion projects in the NCWCD, the Colorado-Big Thompson Project (C-BT) and the Windy Gap Project. The C-BT was the first and largest transmountain diversion project in Colorado. Built by the Bureau of Reclamation in the late 1950s, the C-BT delivers up to 310,000 acre-feet of water per year to agricultural and municipal and industrial users throughout its service area.(55) The locally financed and newly completed Windy Gap Project, which began deliveries in 1985, promises to furnish primary rights to an additional 48,000 acre-feet of water for municipal and industrial users in the area. Return flows from the Windy Gap Project will be transferred to other water-using entities for a variety of purposes including irrigation, domestic use, and groundwater recharge.(56)

More than a dozen transmountain diversion projects have been constructed to serve the Arkansas River basin, although none approach the size of the C-BT. Most of the projects are owned in their entirety by individual municipal water service organizations. The two major

118

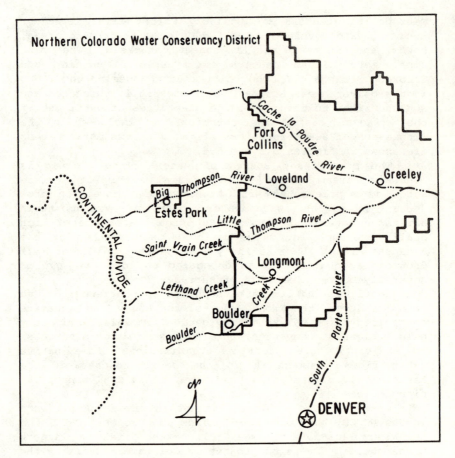

Figure 5.5   Northeastern Colorado

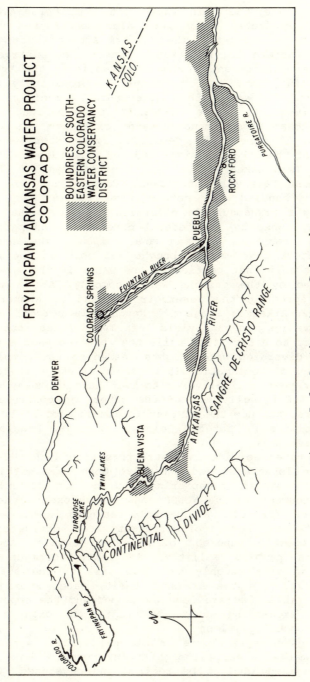

Figure 5.6 Southeastern Colorado

exceptions are the Twin Lakes and Frying Pan-Arkansas
(Fry-Ark) Projects, which were also constructed by the
Bureau of Reclamation. The Fry-Ark Project, managed by
the Southeastern Colorado Water Conservancy District, is
the largest transmountain diversion works in the Arkansas
River basin. The Fry-Ark delivers approximately 80,000
acre-feet of water to agricultural, municipal and
industrial users in the SCWCD. About 70 percent of the
water comes from transmountain diversion while the
remaining 30 percent is developed from "storable flood
waters" of the Arkansas River and its tributaries.(57)

The Twin Lakes Project is an enlargement of the old
Twin Lakes Reservoir and Canal Company system, which
originally handled only native flow waters but is now
primarily a transmountain diversion project. The system
is partly owned by the federal government and partly by
the Twin Lakes Reservoir and Canal Company. The shares of
mutual stock that may be bought and sold on the market
represent only that portion of the water in the reservoir
controlled by the private water company. All remaining
storage space in the reservoir is used to support the
Frying Pan-Arkansas Project. Roughly 10 percent of the
total average annual yield of Twin Lakes stock is
attributed to native flow while the rest represents transmountain diversion water rights deeded to the company by
the Bureau of Reclamation.(58) About 50,000 acre-feet of
water per year are delivered to Twin Lakes company stockholders. Originally all of the water was controlled by
irrigators, but now the company is almost completely owned
by the cities of Aurora, Colorado Springs, Pueblo, and
Pueblo West.(59)

The water service infrastructure within the NCWCD is
much more integrated and extensive than that within the
SCWCD. The system of capturing, storing, and distributing
water resources in the NCWCD constitutes one of the most
complex and flexible water supply networks in the western
United States. Dozens of different water service organizations operate hundreds of miles of canals, storage,
reservoirs, pumping facilities, and water treatment plants
serving an area roughly equal in size to the state of
Connecticut. In the Arkansas Basin, water storage and
delivery facilities are less developed and the opportunities for exchanging water among different organizations
are correspondingly less.

Irrigated agriculture is the predominant water user
in both market areas although urban expansion has caused
some irrigated land to be retired and developed. Growth

has brought pressure to transfer water rights out of irrigation to municipal uses. The geographical locations of
water resources, population centers, and economic activity
in each of the two areas have had a strong influence on
the ease with which transfers can be implemented. In the
NCWCD, the newer nonagricultural water users are inter-
mingled with older agricultural users. Growing urban
developments often acquire additional water rights by
expanding onto previously irrigated farmland. In contrast
to the relatively smooth transfers of water rights in the
Platte River basin, transfers in the Arkansas River basin
have often been complex and difficult. The main centers
of population growth and new economic activity in the
SCWCD are clustered about the centers of Pueblo, Colorado
Spring, and Fountain (and Aurora), which are located
upstream from most existing agricultural water users.
Transferring water rights from irrigators to urban users
does not usually involve a simple change of use within the
same general area. Water rights must instead be transferred over long distances and across jurisdictional
boundaries. Conflicts over water transfers are common and
new water development projects have been initiated as a
costly but practical alternative to the uncertainties and
difficulties involved in water rights transfers.

Water Rights and Institutions

Water rights in Colorado have been subject to the
doctrine of prior appropriation since statehood was
declared in 1876. Both surface water and tributary
groundwater are administered under the appropriations
doctrine. All appropriated rights must be put to beneficial use or risk forfeiture.(60)
The Colorado Supreme Court appoints a water judge for
each of the seven administrative water districts in
Colorado. The district water courts play the primary role
in determining water appropriations, and the merits of an
anticipated transfer of water rights. Colorado law specifies that to make a change in point of diversion or
place or purpose of use of a water right, one must bring
suit in a district water court. The purpose of this litigation is to allow the court to hear all protests to the
transfer so that no person with water rights in the area
affected by the water transfer will be injuriously
affected. Change applications are generally approved if
it can be demonstrated to the satisfaction of the water
judge that the change will not adversely impact third

parties. Changes might still be allowed in the face of third-party effects if the presumed injuries can be appropriately mitigated or compensated.

   Surface Water Rights. Surface water rights in Colorado are of two different types—streamflow and reservoir rights. Appropriated stream flows are generally specified in terms of flow rates and priority dates. Appropriators may withdraw water from the stream at specified maximum flow rates (cubic feet per second) so long as the flow rate in the stream itself is at or above some specified minimum level. The more recent the priority date, the higher is the minimum streamflow rate required to activate the right. In contrast, reservoir rights are specified in terms of acre-feet of volume. During any given year the most senior reservoir right holders may fill their reservoir(s) to the capacity of their right first, followed by the next most senior right. Reservoir rights are usually activated in periods of high streamflow (winter and spring runoff), before the beginning of the irrigation season.(61)

   Reservoir rights in Colorado are extremely important. Stream systems in Colorado are highly variable, and without a means of regulating water supplies, appropriators in Colorado could not expect to have reasonably secure water supplies unless they held very senior water right and/or a quantity of rights disproportionate to their average use patterns. Storage facilities can increase the effective volume and thereby the value of a water right. They allow users to regulate the timing and volume of releases to conform to their patterns of use. Water storage facilities also facilitate water exchanges. A good example of a water exchange that necessitates the use of reservoir space is a program developed by the City of Colorado Springs to exchange effluent for potable water. Historically, Colorado Springs had released its treated effluent into the Fountain River, where it provided a windfall gain to downstream appropriators in the Fountain and Arkansas River systems. In recent years the city has begun to exchange a portion of its return flow for a compensating quantity of water in Pueblo Reservoir (located upstream from the confluence of the Fountain and Arkansas Rivers). From Pueblo Reservoir the water is exchanged further upstream for water stored in mountain reservoirs. From these reservoirs Colorado Springs is able to draw the water to the city through its existing conveyance system.

   Water rights transfers in Colorado are often complicated by the fact that both flow rights and storage

rights may change hands in a transaction. Because of the
flexible nature of storage rights, their market value may
reflect far more than the value of the water that could be
impounded in a single filling of the right. It is not
unusual for a buyer to acquire a package of water rights
primarily for the purpose of gaining additional storage
capacity and only incidentally to increase its inventory
of water rights.

Storage rights can increase the value and usefulness
of water rights through allowing the right holder to
capture, store, and/or exchange quantities of water
several times over the course of a single season. The
storage right itself is valid for only a single filling of
a reservoir per year. Once the water has been removed,
however, the storage space may still be available for
other purposes. Users may refill their space in a reservoir with exchange water or stored water that they have
under other flow decrees. Turquoise, Spinney Mountain, and
Twin Lakes reservoirs all serve this latter purpose for
the cities of Colorado Springs and Aurora. The storage
space available in these reservoirs form essential links
in bringing water from many scattered flow rights into the
cities.

Groundwater Rights. The application of the appropriation doctrine to groundwater rights has been a slowly
evolving process. Distinctions are made between groundwaters that are tributary to a surface watercourse and
those that are not. There was little legislation
concerning groundwater in the early history of Colorado
because groundwater supplies were not extensively
developed until fairly recently. For most of the state's
history, groundwater wells were allowed to develop as if
they took water from a source of supply entirely separate
from the surface water streams. It was inevitable that as
more and more groundwater resources were developed, the
effects would begin to be felt on surface water flows.(62)

Most groundwater appropriations are junior to most
surface water appropriations and both the Arkansas and
Platte River basins are now closed to additional groundwater appropriation. Those groundwater resources that are
judged to be tributary to a surface water flow are limited
in the number of days of the month that they can operate.
If groundwater users wish to pump beyond the legal limit,
they are required to file an approved "augmentation plan"
with the state. Alternative means of augmenting stream
flows affected by groundwater pumping include acquiring
and then retiring stream flow rights, releasing stored

water into streams, or purchasing another water user's
return flow for release into streams.(63)

Transfers of appropriated rights are often difficult
in Colorado. The major problem is the uncertainty with
regard to how the water rights will be quantitatively
defined by the courts. Courts must consider multiple users
of water associated with a given set of appropriations and
related return flow patterns. Generally, it is the
consumptive use portion of the water right (i.e., the net
quantity of water historically removed from the system
under the existing appropriation) that is judged by the
water court to be the quantity transferable to a new
location and use. Water rights transfers are further complicated by the adversarial nature of water court
proceedings. Since the State Engineer is not consulted on
proposed water rights transfers, the courts call for
engineering reports from each of the contesting parties.
Both the petitioners for the water rights transfer and the
protestors are called upon to support their contentions
relating to the transfer.

In spite of these obstacles, water transfers are
common in Colorado, primarily owing to the existence of a
number of policies that can simplify the water transfer
process by reducing or eliminating the legal claims of
opposing parties. These facilitating policies include
special treatment of rights to imported water and of water
transferred within water company and public project
service areas.

Imported Water Rights. Water in one hydrologic basin
may be appropriated and "exported" for use in other
hydrologic basins. Once the transbasin diversion of water
is accomplished, users of "imported" or "foreign" water
are not subject to the return flow obligations that users
of "native" flows have to other appropriators on the
stream system. Holders of imported water rights may
transfer their water rights to any user within the decreed
area of use for the water right without liability. Court
proceedings are necessary only if an owner of transmountain water rights wishes to transfer water out of the
original area of use, or use it for a purpose not
specified in the appropriation decree.

Holders of imported water rights have dominion over
the entire right. They may use and reuse and/or sell the
water to extinction (total consumption). Suppose, for
example, that a water user owns 100 acre-feet of transmountain diversion water and can demonstrate to the satisfaction of the water court that 70 percent of the water it

uses returns to the stream system. The user may then develop the right to reuse or sell the 70 acre-feet. Suppose he sells the 70 acre-feet of return flow rights to an irrigation company downstream, which in turn can demonstrate that 30 percent of its use is return flow. The company may therefore in turn either recapture 21 acre-feet or sell it to yet another water user, and so on until the water is either abandoned or totally consumed within the system.

District water courts in the NCWCD and SCWCD have handed down opinions that essentially give transferred native flow rights the same legal status regarding return flows as imported waters. Because only the consumptive use portion of a native flow right is transferred and that portion is, by definition, the quantity of water histori- cally lost to the system, it may be presumed that no other appropriators to native stream flows have any claim to the water. Rights to native flow waters that have already been transferred are therefore rights to the entire measure of the right, and may be used, reused and/or sold to extinction. Although the implications of the rulings of these courts have not yet seen widespread application in Colorado, they may have a significant impact on the future transfer and management of water rights.(64)

Water Companies. Water companies typically control a "bundle" of different water rights, including decreed native flow rights, reservoir rights, and transmountain diversion water.(65) Company ownership of water rights can make some transfers easier because rights are appur- tenant to the company's service area as a whole and not to any specific parcel of land. All water rights managed within the company service area are legally recognized as having the same point or points of diversion (the company diversion works) and the same place of use (the company service area).

Individual water users in the company service area own a proportional interest in the company, most often represented by shares of stock. Dividends in the form of water allotments are declared on the basis of stock owner- ship rather than on land ownership. The size of the allotment varies from season to season in accordance with the hydrologic cycles of the system, but the long-term average yield and the variability of water service per share of stock generally are well known. The water stock, and the water service represented by that stock, is legally considered personal property that can be bought, sold, or rented for any desired length of time within the

company service area, without the need for proceedings
before the district water court. Transfers of water
company stock require proceedings before the water courts
only if the contemplated transfer includes a change in the
purpose of use or if the stockholder wished to transfer
water outside the company service area.

Public Project Water. Mechanisms and procedures
for allocating public project water vary substantially
within Colorado. The Fry-Ark and C-BT were both conceived
as multipurpose projects to supply supplemental water to
existing irrigated lands and growing urban centers. The
means of allocating water under each project to its users,
however, is very different.

Shortly after its creation in the late 1950s, the
governing board of directors of the SCWCD decided that the
allocation of Fry-Ark water would be fixed at 51 percent
for municipal and industrial use and 49 percent for irrigation. The allocation may be changed by the board in the
future to reflect conversion of agricultural lands to
nonagricultural use. Users of Fry-Ark water who sell
other (nonproject) water rights that they hold are not
permitted to replace those rights with Fry-Ark water.(66)

Each year the board makes a determination of how much
water will be available for distribution to eligible
project beneficiaries. It then contracts with each individual water user or water service organization in the
conservancy district that wishes to buy water. No one is
required to buy project water. The unit price for Fry-Ark
water, $8 per acre-foot, is predetermined by the board and
is the same for all users. The SCWCD holds both the
primary and return flow rights to Fry-Ark water, and no
user has the right to resell their project water to
another user. (67)

The Fry-Ark Project offers water storage programs for
its users. Users are allowed to store any unused quantities of their Fry-Ark water in project storage facilities.
Agricultural users may hold their unused water until May 1
of the following year, while municipal and industrial
users may carry their unused water over from year to
year.(68) The carry-over program is limited by project
reservoir space. SCWCD also allows agricultural users to
store their own (nonproject) decreed native flow rights
during the winter season for use in the summer.(69)
Whereas decreed flow rights in other areas of Colorado
sometimes specify a particular season of use for the right
(typically April 1 to October 1), most direct flow rights
in the Arkansas River basin may be exercised all twelve

months of the year. Large quantities of water that previously had to be released downstream unused during the winter may now be captured and stored in Pueblo Reservoir for later use. The District charges $3.20 per acre-foot of water stored, and the water may be stored until May 1 of the following year. Under the Winter Storage Program several cities and town that have storage rights in their own privately owned reservoirs may also retain their direct flow rights for use later.

The C-BT Project differs in a number of important respects from the Fry-Ark Project. Water rights allocated under the C-BT Project are deeded directly to the individuals and the water service organizations within the project service area. The NCWCD retains all rights to the return flows of project water, but each water user has the full right to purchase, sell, trade, or rent rights to the primary flows.(70) Return flows from the C-BT may be neither recaptured nor resold by C-BT users. Return flows that are not allocated by the NCWCD to its users simply remain in the river. The effect has been to firm up the water supply available under native flow appropriations on the lower reaches of the South Platte. Water users at the downstream end of the NCWCD have found little advantage in holding on to shares in a project that effectively provides them with water whether they participate directly in the project or not. Many downstream appropriators have sold most, if not all, of their C-BT rights to upstream users.(71) Unlike the Fry-Ark, the C-BT System does not allow carryover or storage privileges.(72)

Water rights to the C-BT are represented by 310,000 shares, or units. An annual fee to cover the fixed and operating costs of the project are assessed on each unit owned. The vast majority of C-BT units are held either by individual irrigators, or by municipal or domestic water service organizations. A smaller number of miscellaneous units are held by collective irrigation organizations, nontaxable entities, and manufacturing concerns.(73) The NCWCD discourages excessive speculation in C-BT water by individuals by limiting the ownership of project units to only that quantity that may be put to beneficial use on the property to which it is assigned. As a hedge against future growth and also against supply fluctuations, however, municipal and rural water service organizations are permitted to hold rights in excess of current use.

The Windy Gap Project was planned, organized, and funded locally by the cities of Boulder, Estes Park, Fort Collins, Greeley, Longmont, and Loveland. Since the

project's inception, Fort Collins has transferred its
direct interest in the project to the Platte River Power
Authority, and Estes Park has sold part of its interest to
the city of Broomfield and to the Central Weld County
Water District. Each participant in the Windy Gap Project
assumes a proportionate share of the responsibility for
the project costs, and in return has the right to a proportionate share of the water supply available for
delivery through the project. Owners of Windy Gap water
can use the primary flow and then reuse or sell the return
flow to extinction. The service area for the Windy Gap
Project includes all of the NCWCD and some additional
areas to the south.

Water Market Activity

Water markets in northeastern and southeastern
Colorado differ greatly in both the frequency and nature
of activity, and in the degree of access that the various
users have to the market. In northeastern Colorado, buyers
and sellers are often within the same water company
service area, while those in southeastern Colorado usually
are not. Users in northeastern Colorado usually can
transfer water rights simply by signing a water stock
certificate, but in southeastern Colorado nearly any major
transfer requires formal water court proceedings to change
the point of diversion and place of use of the water
rights. Northeastern Colorado has a favorable institutional environment for transferring large quantities of
water rights over wide geographical areas. The single
largest source of water in the area, the C-BT, is also the
easiest type of water to transfer. The only source of
water in southeastern Colorado that has been marketed
freely over a wide area, Twin Lakes, represents a small
portion of the water resources available to users in the
Arkansas basin. Furthermore, these water rights are now
almost impossible to buy. When Twin Lakes stock came on
the open market for nonirrigation use several years ago,
almost all of it was purchased quickly by a few large
users. Since then, virtually no shares of Twin Lakes
stock have been offered on the market.

Northeastern Colorado. Although water rights transfers have occurred in northeastern Colorado for many
years, the existing market began to assume its present
characteristics only with the completion of the C-BT
project in the last 1950s. From the beginning, the
project was intended to provide water to agriculture,

residences, and businesses in varying proportions over time. In order to ease the transfer of water rights from irrigation to nonirrigation use, the appropriation decree permitting the transfer of water from the west slope to the east slope of the Rocky Mountains stipulated that C-BT water could be used for either irrigation or nonirrigation purposes. Municipal water service organizations and rural-domestic water companies have therefore been able to acquire C-BT units from irrigators without applying to water courts to change points of diversion, places of use, or purposes of use. Moreover, they are free, whenever they choose, to rent any portion of their unused C-BT water back to irrigation users without obtaining special authorization.(74)

When the 310,000 units of the Colorado-Big Thompson Project were distributed by the NCWCD to project participants in the 1950s, nearly 85 percent were assigned to agriculture. The remaining 15 percent assigned to other uses was adequate to meet all virtually all nonagricultural demands for C-BT water and there was little pressure to reallocate supplies. Until about 1961, the market value of C-BT water was zero.(75) Purchase records of municipal water departments and rural-domestic water service organizations indicate that the market price for C-BT units became established in the early 1960s at a price of about $95 per unit. With each C-BT unit representing a long-term average yield of about 0.75 acre-feet, the average price of C-BT water was about $125 per acre-foot. Through the 1960s and 1970s, prices for C-BT water climbed at an accelerating rate. Prices reaches $220 per acre-foot in 1963, $560 by 1967, $860 by 1971, over $1,000 by 1974, $2,540 by 1977, and over $3,500 by 1980. After 1980, prices began to decline rapidly. In 1981 prices fell to below $3,000 per acre-foot, to less than $1,600 by 1983, and to about $1,000 in 1985, where they remained throughout 1986.

Many other types of water rights are transferred in the NCWCD, though C-BT units represent a significant proportion of area water supplies. Table 5.1 summarizes price data on several different water rights. Shares of stock in the North Poudre Irrigation Company are considered by many in northeastern Colorado to be the most marketable water rights in the NCWCD after the C-BT. The company's issue of 10,000 shares of stock is held by a variety of municipal and industrial, rural-domestic, and agricultural water users within a service area covering much of the northern portion of the NCWCD. The long-term

130

Table 5.1: **Representative Prices for Sales of Perpetual Water Rights in Northeastern Colorado**
(1986 dollars per acre-foot)

Year	C-BT	N. Poudre	Pleas. Valley Lake & Canal	Farmers Ditch	Anderson
1961	130				
1962	150	120			
1963	220	ND	135		
1964	370	205	130		
1965	440	280	125		145
1966	530	ND	120	150	435
1967	560	355	120	180	340
1968	600	435	115	250	455
1969	850	530	110	240	570
1970	920	545	105	235	565
1971	860	515	95	245	535
1972	860	545	95	235	510
1973	930	675	ND	225	500
1974	1,050	970		ND	500
1975	1,090	835		250	ND
1976	1,330	975		ND	ND
1977	2,540	ND		275	ND
1978	2,590	1,720		230	330
1979	3,050	1,450		230	ND
1980	3,600	670		250	580
1981	2,990	ND		225	1,005
1982	1,880	380		245	890
1983	1,600	880		265	1,075
1984	1,460			255	
1985	1,080				

Water price data were obtained from rural-domestic water districts and municipal service organizations in the area. ND indicates that no data were collected for the type of water right and year indicated.

average yield on each share of stock is just under 6 acre-feet per year. Stockholders may split their shares up into quarter-shares representing an average yield of about 1.5 acre-feet per year in order to buy and sell smaller quantities of rights. There were 9,926 shares of stock in general circulation in 1984. A substantial portion of the water rights controlled by the company consist of senior direct flow rights, reservoir rights, and C-BT units.(76) North Poudre and C-BT water rights are based on large and reliable water supplies available to many different types of users, can be transferred within an extensive geographical area, have a large number of available shares, and allow small quantities of water to be transferred in a single transaction. Typical prices for North Poudre stock have followed the historical movement of C-BT prices. On a per acre-foot basis, North Poudre water generally sells for between 60 percent and 70 percent of the going market price for C-BT water. North Poudre water sells for a lower price per acre-foot than C-BT water due to the more limited service area within which North Poudre water can be transferred without water court proceedings.

As Table 5.1 illustrates, other water rights within the NCWCD typically sell for 50 percent or less (on a per acre-foot basis) than C-BT water. Some of these water rights can be transferred to only a relatively small number of potential buyers within a limited geographical area without water court proceedings. Some provide water that is designated only for agricultural use, and their transfer to a nonirrigation use would require potentially expensive legal proceedings. In addition, many of these alternative water rights cannot be exercised for more than a few months during the spring and summer. Municipal and rural-domestic water suppliers, whose customers demand steady supplies of water throughout the year, have a limited demand for highly seasonal water rights.(77) The less flexible ditch rights, privately adjudicated water rights, small private reservoirs, and groundwater rights are rarely sold apart from the land to which they are deeded. Most often these water rights are retained for agricultural use and their market values are low.(78)

Windy Gap water has the potential to become one of the most flexible and marketable water resources in northeastern Colorado. This project is thought to be one of the causes for the downturn in water rights prices during the early 1980s. It has only recently been completed, however, and there are many uncertainties about transfer of project water. There are two main barriers to buying and selling primary rights to Windy Gap water at the present time--the high cost of participation in the project, and the system of ownership. The current annual cost to project participants, including bond debt service and operation and maintenance costs, is between $200 and $300 per acre-foot. Participants in the project hold prorated shares of bonded indebtedness in proportion to their entitlement to the water. The sale of primary Windy Gap water necessitates the transfer of an equal share of the bonded indebtedness, which can be a very complex transaction.(79) Few transfers of primary water rights in the Windy Gap Project have taken place thus far. There have been two sales by the town of Estes Park. In the summer of 1985, the town sold an interest in 100 acre-feet per year to the Central Weld County Water District for about $510 per acre-foot. In the fall of 1985 Estes Park concluded another agreement to sell 3,700 acre-feet of primary Windy Gap rights to the city of Broomfield for about $415 per acre-foot.(80)

Interest in the Windy Gap Project remains high despite the cost of the water relative to the market price for alternative water supplies in northeastern Colorado. Participants in the project believe the advantages of having Windy Gap water will prove to be worth the costs because, unlike holders of C-BT units, they own not only rights to primary flows but also the return flows. They are free to recycle their shares of Windy Gap water by selling the return flow to downstream users or by exchanging them for other water supplies.(81) Since Windy Gap is operated jointly with the C-BT and they share a common service area (the service area for Windy Gap is actually larger than and includes the NCWCD), Windy Gap will share the same market area and have many of the same market advantages that C-BT water has.

Water rights purchased from agriculture by non-irrigation users are rented back to agriculture in large quantities every year. Municipal and rural-domestic water service organizations maintain large inventories of water rights in order to protect their users against fluctuations in supply. On the average, less than half of the C-BT units owned by nonagricultural water users are actually used each year. Since the NCWCD does not carry over unused water rights to subsequent years, shareholders have an incentive to at least cover the assessment costs by renting water to other users. Irrigators are the primary renters, although in a few cases nonagricultural water service organization have also rented water.(82)

The rental market for C-BT and other types of water rights in northeastern Colorado exhibits few of the price trends observed in the purchase and sales of rights. Prices have remained low with no definite trend over time, varying between about $5 and $20 per acre-foot. With the development of the Windy Gap Project and with urbanization continuing in the NCWCD, it does not appear that rental water will become more scarce in the foreseeable future. More and more water rights have been acquired for development by municipal and rural-domestic organizations and offered for rent to agricultural users. Meanwhile irrigated acreage continues to decrease and agricultural demand for water is declining. Even in relatively dry years and even at prices that are equal to or only slightly above the cost of the annual assessment fee for their water rights, renters frequently fail to find enough takers for all of their surplus water.

Southeastern Colorado. Activity in the southeastern Colorado water market is at once much simpler and more difficult to describe than the market in northeastern Colorado. Southeastern Colorado is simpler to describe because there has been much less market activity than in the NCWCD. However, most of the important water rights transfers have necessitated extensive negotiation and litigation over controversial issues and complex details. More than a dozen different transmountain diversion projects bring a total of 200,000 acre-feet of water per year into the Arkansas River basin. Of all the transmountain diversions, however, only the 50,000 acre-feet of water provided through the Twin Lakes Reservoir and Canal Company have ever been marketed. Nearly all of the Twin Lakes stock came onto the market and was sold within a period of about 5 or 6 years in the 1970s.

Twin Lakes Reservoir and Canal Company water is marketed in the same fashion as any other mutual water stock. The only difference is that a small portion of the water rights held by the company are recognized as native flow rights, while the rest are transmountain diversion water rights. In the early 1970s the city of Aurora purchased some Twin Lakes stock, but secured a court decree to transfer only the transmountain portion of the water rights to the city, located in the South Platte basin. Before the city could transfer the native flow portion of its Twin Lakes water rights as well, the district water court would have to determine the transferable (consumptive use) portion of the native flow component of the water rights. The yield on Twin Lakes stock held by Aurora averages slightly less than the yield on other shares of Twin Lakes stock held by other parties who retain the stock within the South Platte Basin and have access to both the transmountain and native flow portions of Twin Lakes water.(83)

The approximately 45,000 shares of outstanding stock in the Twin Lakes company were all originally owned by farmers within the service area of another irrigation water provider, the Colorado Canal Company, located about 50 miles east and downstream of the City of Pueblo along the Arkansas River. Two other water service organizations located in the same general area are the Henry and Meredith reservoir companies. These four irrigation companies provide three different types of water rights-- transmountain diversion and some native flow water from Twin Lakes, native flow rights through the Colorado Canal, and reservoir rights from Henry and Meredith lakes. Most farmers owned stock in all four water companies and had their water delivered to them through the Colorado Canal system.(84)

Until about 1970, farmland in the Colorado Canal Company service area sold for about $500 per acre, including land and all water rights. In the early 1970s an investment group called the Crowley Land and Development Company (CLADCO) offered farmers in the area about $900 per acre. Despite heated local opposition, farmers in the area sold a majority of their land and water company stock to CLADCO. As a result, slightly over 60 percent of the Twin Lakes stock changed hands. Nearly all of the remaining stockholders formed a coalition that became known as the Proxy Group. CLADCO and the Proxy Group successfully obtained a decree in water court to change the purpose of use for Twin Lakes water rights from irrigation to multiple use.(85) Twin Lakes stock suddenly became one of the most flexible and valuable sources of water in the area, and nonagricultural users quickly bid up its price.

Between 1972 and 1975, CLADCO and the Proxy Group each sold large quantities of Twin Lakes water stock to the cities of Pueblo, Pueblo West, and Colorado Springs for prices ranging from about $2,300 to $2,400 per acre-foot. In 1976 another lot of Twin Lakes stock that had been transferred from CLADCO to the Aetna Group was sold in turn to the city of Colorado Springs for slightly over $2,300 per acre-foot. Only six sales of Twin Lakes stock by CLADCO, Aetna, and the Proxy Group (one to Pueblo West in 1972, two to Pueblo in 1972 and 1973, and three to

Colorado Springs in 1972 and 1976) accounted for the
transfer of over 43,000 shares, or the vast majority of
the shares of all Twin Lakes stock.

Other transfers of Twin Lakes stock for nonagricultural users occurred during the mid-1970s. Pueblo
West bought a farm with 237 shares of Twin Lakes stock in
1971, for about $1,400 per acre including all land,
improvements, and water rights. The farm is still in
operation and is continuing to use the water rights until
Pueblo West wants them. Pueblo West acquired another 117-
acre farm with Twin Lakes water rights from a real estate
development corporation, but the amount paid is unknown.
Colorado Springs bought a total of approximately 500 acre-
feet from miscellaneous owners during the summer of 1976
for an average price of over $2,000 per acre-foot. Aurora
acquired approximately 2,500 shares of Twin Lakes stock in
1973 for $2,675 per acre-foot.

Very little specific price information is available
on the sale of other shares of Twin Lakes stock. Small
quantities have reportedly been sold to homeowners in
mountain resort communities. As an alternative to purchasing less expensive but also less flexible native stream
rights and undertaking potentially lengthy and expensive
water court transfer proceedings, some individuals have
purchased shares of Twin Lakes stock for prices ranging
from $8,000 to over $10,000 per acre-foot.[86]

In 1983 and 1984, the Colorado Foundry & Iron (Cf&I)
Steel Corporation sold its storage rights in Turquoise
Reservoir to the cities of Colorado Springs, Pueblo, and
Aurora. Colorado Springs purchased 17,470 acre feet of
storage rights, plus two direct flow rights totaling about
another 4,200 acre-feet, for about $400 per acre-foot.
The city purchased the rights primarily for the reservoir
storage space, which it can use to facilitate the
exchange, storage, and delivery of water supplies developed from numerous other sources. These sources include
water from the Homestake and Blue River transmountain
diversion projects as well as various direct flow and
storage rights acquired in the Arkansas River basin.
Colorado Springs considers the 4,200 acre-feet of direct
flow rights that it acquired from CF&I unimportant, as the
rights are too junior in priority to be very
dependable.[87]

In the fall of 1986 Colorado Springs purchased 17,500
acre-feet of direct flow and storage rights in a complex
transaction involving three different water companies.
The package included land, improvements, and water rights

136

in the Henry and Meredith reservoirs and the Colorado
Canal Company. The seller, Foxley and Company, had acquired the property from CLADCO, which had purchased it
originally in order to market the shares of Twin Lakes
stock associated with the lands. Foxley sold its interest
in the companies to Colorado Springs for a total of about
$27.75 million, or slightly under $1,600 per acre-foot.
Henry and Meredith reservoir rights were valuable to
Colorado Springs not only for the deliverable quantities
of water but also for the reservoir storage space.
Colorado Springs may store unused water from some of their
direct flow water rights in the Henry and Meredith
reservoirs should there ever be insufficient storage
capacity in Pueblo Reservoir. Water stored in these
reservoirs is then available to serve downstream users who
in turn may exchange their flow rights to Colorado Springs
for water upstream in the Pueblo Reservoir.

Until recently, Colorado Springs hardly utilized its
legally reusable return flow water. A small portion of
water has been marketed to downstream users for their
groundwater augmentation plans. The price charged for the
sale of return flow in 1985 was about $235 per acre-foot.
In 1986 the price was increased to about $260 per acre-
foot. Additional small quantities of return flow have
been used for urban irrigation. Colorado Springs hopes
eventually to be able to recapture, reuse, market, or
exchange all of the return flows associated with its
transmountain diversion water supplies.(88)

The City of Fountain is a small town 10 miles south
of Colorado Springs in the Fountain Valley. Fountain
formerly obtained all of its water from the Mountain
Reservoir. The city was forced to seek an alternative
source when state health authorities ordered expensive
renovations in the water treatment system. Fountain first
considered purchasing a groundwater wellfield about 20
miles to the east in the Black Squirrel Basin, but local
opposition successfully blocked the sale. Fountain then
developed its own wellfield in another area during the
1960s. With the closing of the area to further groundwater appropriation and the passage of new groundwater
management legislation, Fountain had to acquire additional
water rights to compensate for its groundwater pumping.
Part of its legal obligations are met by releasing water
from the Mountain Reservoir. The rest is met through the
retirement of water rights associated with Fountain Valley
Mutual Irrigation Company water stock, which Fountain has
been gradually purchasing for several years. With the

completion of the Fountain Valley Pipeline in 1985,
Fountain now also has the option of purchasing Fry-Ark
water. Fountain has also considered purchasing additional
groundwater rights in the area, but the water quality is
poor and the asking price for the rights is considered too
high.(89)

The City of Pueblo is located along the Arkansas
River just below Pueblo Reservoir, about 30 miles east of
the Front Range. In addition to its participation in the
Frying Pan-Arkansas Project and its acquisition of stock
in the Twin Lakes Company, it has purchased a number of
shares of stock in other ditch companies and has constructed some water development projects of its own.
Pueblo's principal water company acquisitions in recent
years have been the purchase of storage rights in the
Otero Canal Company, the Booth-Orchard Canal Company, and
storage and flow rights in the Rocky Ford Highline Canal
Company.(90) The city also bought storage rights in
Turquoise Reservoir from CF&I Steel Corporation in
December, 1983, paying about $440 per acre-foot for 5,000
acre-feet of storage rights. Another 5,000 acre-feet of
storage rights were sold at about the same time to the
City of Aurora for the same price. Pueblo paid the City
of Aurora between $2,500 and $3,600 per acre-foot for the
right to lease up to 2,500 acre-feet of water per year
from Aurora, at a fixed charge of $3 per acre-foot.

Pueblo offers its unused reservoir and transmountain
diversion water rights for rent each year. Direct native
flow rights are not rented because their transfer to
another user, even for a season, would require proceedings before the water courts. Pueblo's Twin Lakes water
is offered for lease at a predetermined price. A recent
large surplus of rental water on the market forced them to
reduce their asking price from $18 to $10 per acre-foot.
Prices for other types of water are determined on the
basis of closed bids solicited by the city. The town of
Pueblo West, which also offers water for rent each year,
regularly trades information with Pueblo on the bids each
has received from prospective buyers. Pueblo generally
sets a floor on its rental prices and will not offer water
below that minimum price, even if as a consequence it is
left with large quantities of unrented water. The city of
Aurora regularly leases Twin Lakes water from Pueblo,
paying a unit price equal to the highest bid received by
Pueblo for its water that year.(91)

Pueblo West is a resort community located several
miles west of the city of Pueblo. Pueblo West began de-

veloping its water supply in the 1960s by drilling several groundwater wells. Most of the wells drew poor quality water, and the potable water available from the wells was of insufficient quantity to support the growing community. In the early 1970s, Pueblo West purchased shares of Twin Lakes water stock and negotiated an agreement with the SCWCD to store the water in Pueblo Reservoir. The municipality now owns enough water rights to serve a population ten times its current size. Each year the extra water is made available to whoever wants to lease it. The rental prices are determined through closed bids. Real prices since 1982 have varied from as little as $3 per acre-foot to over $30 per acre-foot. Pueblo West has never succeeded in renting all of its unused water rights. Since 1982, it has rented out as much as 1,680 acre-feet and as little as only 331 acre-feet annually.(92)

The City of Aurora, a fast-growing metropolitan center just east of Denver, concluded three major acquisition of water rights at the close of 1986. A majority interest in the Rocky Ford Ditch Company was acquired, giving the city 8,200 acre-feet of water at a cost of about $2,500 per acre-foot. Following the successful transfer of water from the Colorado Canal Company by Colorado Springs, Aurora picked up its own 5,600 acre-feet from the Colorado Canal Company, also at a cost of about $2,500 per acre foot. Finally Aurora acquired 45 percent of the outstanding shares of stock in the Busk-Ivanhoe Ditch Company, yielding about 3,000 acre-feet at a cost of $3,500 per acre-foot. The city was willing to pay a premium price for the Busk-Ivanhoe stock because they represent transmountain diversion rights, which are both legally and hydrologically easier to transfer to the South Platte Basin than are native flow and storage rights in the Arkansas River.(93)

Other examples of large blocks of water rights offered for sale in the Arkansas River basin include the Bessemer Ditch and the Huerfano-Cuchares Ditch Companies. In 1986 the Huerfano-Cuchares Ditch Company, which had been offered for $13 million, sold for about $10 million. The quantity of transferable water rights is currently under study. Historic diversions by the company have totaled about 6,800 acre-feet per year, of which perhaps half may have been used consumptively and are therefore available for transfer. In addition, Huerfano-Cuchares has an adjudicated right to 60,000 acre-feet of storage water, although the reservoir is in need of repair and at the present time cannot hold more than 35,000 acre-feet.(94)

The 10,000 shares of the Bessemer Ditch Company are being offered for $60 million, or $6,000 per share. Each share has an average yield of 3 acre-feet. It has not yet been established how much of this average yield may be transferred out of the company service area. Previous to this offer, the market price for the stock among irrigators had been between $1,200 and $1,500 per share.(95)

Prospective water rights buyers in the Arkansas basin have not forgotten the disastrous purchase of water rights by the state Game and Fish Commission in 1971. Up until that time, shares of stock in the Catlin Canal Company, with a long-term annual average yield of 4 acre-feet per share, had been selling for about $160. The Game and Fish Commission bought 2,097 shares in the company at a cost of about $320 per acre-foot, intending to transfer the water rights to a large reservoir for fish and wildlife habitat. The remaining stockholders in the Catlin Canal Company successfully opposed the transfer by arguing that their water rights would be impaired. The Game and Fish Commission appealed the decision, which was eventually upheld by the state Supreme Court. Over $2.5 million (not including court costs) was paid by the state for water rights that could not be transferred to their intended location.(96)

To summarize, market transfers of water occur in Colorado under highly diverse conditions. Appropriated water rights represented by water company stocks having a large service area and approved for multiple uses can be readily transferred. As is apparent from other types of transactions in the Northern and Southeastern Colorado Water Conservancy Districts, market transfers can also be subject to expensive, time-consuming, and complex approval procedures and litigation.

TRUCKEE RIVER BASIN, NEVADA

The Study Area

The market area studied in Nevada includes the Truckee River Basin and adjacent areas in southern Washoe County, Story County, and parts of Churchill and Lyon counties. Most of the area's population of 250,000 is concentrated in and around the twin cities of Reno and Sparks, which are located in a valley known as the Truckee Meadows. The Meadows are flanked on the west by the Sierra Nevada Mountains and on the east by the Great

Basin. Most agricultural activity is concentrated in the
Newlands Project, about 50 miles east of the Truckee
Meadows. The Newlands Project, managed by the Truckee-
Carson Irrigation District (TCID), was one of the first
irrigation projects built by the Bureau of Reclamation in
the early 1900s. These areas are shown in figure 5.7.

The Truckee River begins at Lake Tahoe in the
California Sierras, crosses the state line into Nevada,
and flows east past irrigated farms and ranchlands
surrounding the metropolitan centers of Reno and Sparks in
the Truckee Meadows. It approaches the western edge of the
TCID near the town of Fernley where the river turns north
to empty into Pyramid Lake on the Pyramid Lake Indian
Reservation.

Nevada is the driest and one of the fastest growing
states in the United States. Reno and Sparks are regional
centers of tourism and commerce and their populations are
expanding rapidly. Rights to Truckee River water are
highly controversial. Conflicts among the cities, native
Americans, fish and wildlife managers, and irrigated agriculture have continued for most of the 20th century.

An average of approximately 650,000 acre-feet of
Truckee River water is used per year in northwestern
Nevada. Roughly 50,000 acre-feet is used for municipal and
industrial purposes in the Truckee Meadows, while 300,000
acre-feet is used for irrigation.   Irrigation uses are
divided among farms in the TCID (190,000 acre-feet), and
other farms and ranches (about 105,000 acre-feet). About
300,000 acre-feet of Truckee River water flow into Pyramid
Lake.(97)   Consumptive use of the water rights along the
Truckee River has risen over time, and as a result the
quantity of water emptying into Pyramid Lake has declined.
Falling lake levels have alarmed sportsmen, conservation-
ists, and the Pyramid Lake Indian Tribe.(98)

On average, about 375,000 acre-feet of water are used
annually by TCID from rights developed on the Truckee
River and on the Carson River, which parallels the Truckee
20 miles to the south. Water taken from the Truckee River
by TCID is carried by the Truckee Canal into Lahontan
Reservoir, where it mingles with roughly an equal
quantity of water from the Carson River before its distribution over TCID's 75,000 irrigated acres. By a joint
agreement among the TCID, the state of Nevada, and the
U.S. Fish and Wildlife Service, return flows from the
Newlands Project are allowed to dissipate in marshlands to
the east of the TCID to support the Stillwater Wildlife
Refuge.

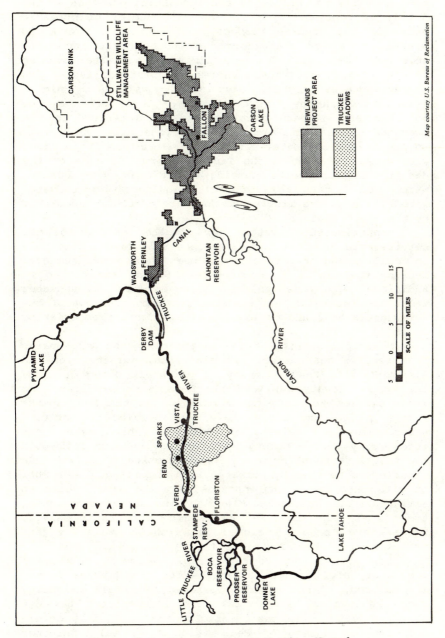

Figure 5.7   Truckee River Basin, Nevada

Approximately 10,000 acre-feet of groundwater are used annually for municipal and industrial purposes in the cities of Reno and Sparks. A small number of domestic users in the Truckee Meadows area outside of Reno and Sparks and a few irrigators use another 2,000 to 3,000 acre-feet per year. There is limited groundwater pumping in the TCID by individual users; the district itself has no groundwater rights. Groundwater quality is highly variable within the Truckee Meadows. It is poor in some southern and eastern portions of the area due to the presence of heavy metals. In some locations, quality is so low that groundwater cannot be used unless it is mixed with purer water from the Truckee River. Because of the danger that excessive pumping could draw poor quality water into the more potable aquifers, groundwater withdrawals in the Truckee Meadows are carefully regulated by the State Engineer.(99)

Nonagricultural water users located outside of the service area of water purveyors generally have had to rely on local groundwater supplies to meet their water demands. Because the basins in northwestern Nevada are closed to additional appropriation, and because exempt groundwater wells are too small and inadequate for most purposes, new water users have had to acquire water rights from existing users.

Municipal and industrial customers in the Reno-Sparks area receive gas, water, and electrical service from the Sierra Pacific Power Company, a privately owned utility. The Washoe County Public Works Department provides some water service to outlying communities in the Reno-Sparks area. A few communities have been serviced by private water companies, several of which have been taken over recently by Washoe County. Irrigators outside TCID hold individual decrees for water in the Truckee River which is distributed to them by private ditch companies. A number of ditch companies once provided Truckee River water to irrigators in the Truckee Meadows. Many of these companies are now inactive because the lands within their service areas have been developed and their water rights transferred to Sierra Pacific.(100)

Lake Tahoe and Boca Reservoir serve as area-wide regulatory and storage facilities for the Truckee River; in addition, Sierra Pacific operates two small privately owned reservoirs, Donner Lake and Independence Lake. A third facility, Stampede Reservoir, was originally developed by the Bureau of Reclamation as a multi-purpose, supplemental water supply. The water supply, however, was preempted to support fish habitat and has never been made available for municipal use. Sierra Pacific is attempting to work out a compromise solution with the federal government whereby at least some water may be made available to the company.(101)

Water Rights and Institutions

Nevada applies the appropriation doctrine to both groundwater and surface water resources.(102) The Office of the State Engineer was created in 1903 by Nevada's first comprehensive water law, which defined and protected existing rights to appropriated water. Relatively few changes in the basic water laws have occurred since 1939, when legislation declared all groundwaters not hitherto subject to the appropriation doctrine to be explicitly included. Small domestic wells were exempted from regulation. Nevada's general policy towards groundwater has been to restrict withdrawals to hydrologically safe yield levels.(103)

In the 1960s, Sierra Pacific began developing groundwater rights in the Truckee Meadows to supplement its surface water rights on the Truckee River during periods of peak demand. Rights to 48,000 acre-feet per year have been appropriated, but this is far in excess of the area's hydrologically safe yield. The State Engineer and Sierra Pacific have agreed to maintain groundwater pumping at 8,000 to 10,000 acre-feet per year while permitting as much as 12,000 acre-feet to be withdrawn under short-term critical conditions.(104)

The State Engineer has primary responsibility for distribution of all water in Nevada except federally decreed stream systems, which are administered by a Water-master appointed by the federal district court. The Truckee River is a federally adjudicated stream adminis-tered under the Orr Ditch Decree of 1944. About 29,000 acre-feet of water per year were allocated to the Sierra Pacific Power Company, over 230,000 acre-feet per year to the Newlands Project (TCID), and 177,000 acre-feet per year for irrigation on other lands. Another 30,000 acre-feet per year were designated for irrigated agriculture on the Pyramid Lake Indian Reservation.(105) The Sierra Valley Decree of 1958 confirmed the right of the Sierra Valley Water Company of California to divert an average of 10,000 acre-feet per year from the Little Truckee River. These water rights are also subject to the Orr Ditch

Decree and are administered by the federal Watermaster as part of the Truckee River system.

No water was allocated under the Orr Ditch Decree specifically for the purpose of maintaining the level of Pyramid Lake or streamflows in the Truckee River itself. The Pyramid Lake Indians, who derive benefits from fishing the lakes and rivers, have contested this omission. In recent years they have been partially successful in winning some concessions in their battle to protect lake and stream habitat for two endangered species of fish, the cui-cui and the Lahontan cut-throat trout.

The Pyramid Lake Tribe has won concessions on two fronts, and in both cases their victories have had an impact on the water rights available for other users along the system. Their first success was alteration of management objectives for Stampede Reservoir, which was built by the Bureau of Reclamation in eastern California in 1970 to aid in regulating the flow of the Truckee River. The reservoir originally was conceived as a multipurpose water project, but no water has ever been diverted from it for either irrigation or municipal and industrial uses. Since the early 1970s, the federal government has allocated all the water in the reservoir to help maintain the level of flow and the temperature of the Truckee River for fish habitat. The reservoir will continue to be used for this purpose so long as the native trout species in the Truckee River and in Pyramid Lake are considered endangered. Sierra Pacific Power Company had counted on receiving a substantial allocation of water from the reservoir. Appeals by Sierra Pacific and the State of Nevada against this decision thus far have been unsuccessful. Another success for the tribal community was a change in the operating criteria for the Truckee River system, initiated in 1985, to maintain river flow levels. Water supplies released for irrigation purposes both inside and outside of the TCID have been reduced by several tens of thousands of acre-feet per year. Conservation requirements for reducing evaporation and seepage losses are being enforced as a part of the efforts to maintain river flows.(106)

Although water rights under the Orr Ditch Decree were assigned on the basis of prior appropriation, water is distributed on a prorated basis. Minimum levels of flow in the river at selected points along the stream are maintained according to operating criteria set forth in the Truckee River Agreement of 1935 and modified in 1985.(107) The operating criteria provide for the servicing of all appropriations on the river and for the proration of all claims in the event of insufficient water supplies. Modified operating criteria are used during drought conditions. The operating criteria are ineffective only during periods of severe drought, such as occurred during a few years in the 1930s and once again for a brief period in the late 1970s. When this happens, the federal Watermaster may resort to a system of relative priorities.(108) Under these extreme conditions, the 29,000 acre-feet of water rights assigned to Sierra Pacific have priority over all irrigation rights.(109)

The State Engineer's Office oversees any prospective change in the point of diversion or place or purpose of use of any groundwater or surface water right in Nevada, including those on federally decreed streams. A water right is considered a property right and when water rights are granted they are appurtenant to a given piece of land for a specific purpose. Generally, when land is sold all water rights appurtenant to the property described in the deed automatically transfer to the new owner. However, application to the State Engineer may be made to sever the water right from the land to retain it or convey it separately.

In a federally adjudicated stream system such as the Truckee River, the State Engineer consults with the federal Watermaster on administering water rights transfers in the system under the directives of the federal decree. As long as the transfer is compatible with the operating criteria for the river, it may be approved. Water rights transfers on the Truckee River have not been limited to only the consumptive use portion of the right. Temporary water rights transfers (leases) have not been permitted on the Truckee River. The federal Watermaster has opposed leasing water rights, arguing that leasing would overly complicate the administration of the river.(110)

Water Market Activity

Market transfers of water in the general area of the Truckee River Basin have been confined mainly to the Truckee Meadows. A small number of groundwater transfers have occurred in some nearby valleys. The legality of regional water transfers involving the TCID, the Pyramid Lake Tribe, and the Stillwater Wildlife Management Area is uncertain and none have yet been attempted. These entities are nevertheless included in the discussion because their

use of water has a significant impact on the availability
of supplies in the Truckee Meadows water market.

Water rights in the TCID are difficult to transfer.
TCID is a federally funded and administered project and
ownership of water rights used on project lands by
individual water users has been unclear. Financial
obligations to the project are based on land ownership and
not water usage. There is no established procedure in the
Newlands Project for transferring project assessments with
water rights that are transferred off of project
lands.(111) The district's water supply is a mixture of
water from two different river systems each of which is
administered under its own federal decree. The relative
proportions of water from each river system have varied
from year to year with changes in relative flow levels in
each river. It is thought that any attempt to transfer
water rights outside of the TCID would create serious
legal and administrative problems for the management of
the Newlands Project.(112)

Until recently, no transfer of TCID water rights had
been permitted into, out of, or within the district.
Federal adjudication of the Carson River in 1983
established the legality of water rights transfers within,
but not into or out of, the District.(113) Over 100
proposed water rights transfers within the district have
been approved by the State Engineer. Final approval of
water rights transfers within TCID are being withheld
pending an appeal by the Pyramid Lake Tribe.(114) The
outcome of this case will have a strong bearing on whether
or not water transfers will become common in the TCID. No
price data were collected on transfer of TCID water
rights, which are exclusively surface water rights.
Groundwater rights in the Fallon area of the district are
reportedly selling for about $300 per acre-foot.(115)

Much of the market activity in this study area has
involved Sierra Pacific Power Company. Sierra Pacific
began purchasing irrigation rights to supplement its
original Truckee River appropriations in the mid-1940s,
and continued to acquire additional water rights actively
until 1979. Real prices ranged from a low of about $35
per acre-foot in 1946 to a peak of about $160 per acre-
foot in the mid-1960s. From 1966 to 1979, real price per
acre-foot for water rights fell steadily. Most of the
water rights acquisitions during the period 1946 to 1979
actually occurred between the late 1950s and 1970.

The present water market developed during the late
1970s when the U.S. Department of Interior decided not to

provide water and storage rights in the Stampede Reservoir
for municipal and industrial purposes. Sierra Pacific had
been counting on receiving between 17,000 and 34,000 acre-
feet of additional water rights and regulatory storage
space in the reservoir for a cost of about $17 per acre-
foot per year. Meanwhile, Sierra Pacific's rate of acquiring additional irrigation water rights from irrigators had
been declining as the real price offered by the company to
farmers dipped below $75 per acre-foot. Unprecedented
rates of urban growth in Reno and Sparks threatened to
outpace Sierra Pacific's capacity to serve them with
additional water. In 1978 Sierra Pacific commissioned an
independent study of its water resources and projected
demands. The report concluded that the current rates of
growth in water use in Sierra Pacific's service area would
exceed the firm yield of the company's existing water
rights inventory and would be insufficient to meet demand
within two or three years.(116)

A water crisis hit the Truckee Meadows seemingly
overnight. Holders of water rights on the Truckee River
recognized that they possessed a scarce and valuable
commodity. Landowners who had until then subdivided their
holdings indiscriminately with the water rights appurtenant began to sever the water rights from the land to
sell them separately. Sierra Pacific was reluctant to pay
the increased costs for water rights. In 1980, the
utility raised its offer price for water rights to a range
of $95 to $135 per acre-foot, based on relative water
rights priority dates. Later it raised its offer price to
$140 per acre-foot and eventually to $250. The increase,
however, was not enough to attract sufficient numbers of
sellers, who found many other buyers willing to pay over
$1,500 per acre-foot. Water rights acquisitions by Sierra
Pacific slowed to a trickle as potential sellers held out
for higher prices.

Faced with an impending water shortage, Sierra
Pacific began rationing additional water service. New
water users were put on a lengthy waiting list pending the
acquisition of sufficient water rights. The creation of
the waiting list touched off an intense political battle
between government and industry and between pro-growth and
no-growth advocates. Private developers and the cities of
Reno and Sparks accused the utility company of becoming a
self-appointed regional planning agency.(117) Environmental groups criticized the cities for trying to grow beyond
the limits of their water resource base.

Throughout the early and mid 1980s, a series of actions by Sierra Pacific, private interest groups, the state Public Service Commission, and the state, county, and local governments led to the creation of new legal and administrative processes to accommodate the pressures for a more efficient, equitable and workable system of water rights transfers in the Truckee Basin. The new system was largely in place by the spring of 1985. Under a ruling of the Public Service Commission, Sierra Pacific is required to provide water service to approved new developments within 60 days.(118) Water rights are provided by the appropriate local government (the cities of Reno or Sparks, or Washoe County) through 99-year leases.(119)

The water rights inventory of Sierra Pacific and the additional surface water rights available for purchase and transfer to municipal use in the 1980s in the Truckee Meadows and elsewhere are approximately as follows. Sierra Pacific has water rights with an average yield of roughly 79,000 acre-feet per year. This includes 29,000 acre-feet of originally adjudicated flow rights in the Truckee River, 12,000 acre-feet of groundwater, and 38,000 acre-feet of additional surface water rights acquired since 1944. Approximately 38,000 acre-feet of water rights are still used for irrigation, 28,000 acre-feet in the Truckee Meadows area and 10,000 acre-feet in Sierra Valley, California. Finally, an estimated 32,000 acre-feet of water rights formerly used for irrigation are no longer in use. These water rights are still appurtenant to lands that were incorporated into the service area of Sierra Pacific and were provided with water service without ever having the water rights severed and transferred.(120) Sierra Pacific has determined that the firm yield (the minimum yield from the water rights that could be expected under the worst drought conditions) averages about 58 percent of the long-term average yield for Truckee River water rights. Sierra Pacific's original appropriation of about 29,000 acre-feet per year, however, is given the highest priority on the river and has a firm yield of 100 percent. In accepting water rights in exchange for water service, Sierra Pacific established the following guidelines. The water rights have to produce a firm yield (defined as 58 percent of the long-term average yield) of water sufficient to meet the estimated water demand for the proposed development. The water rights must be decreed Truckee River water rights. If the new development is already within the service area of Sierra Pacific, the water right may come from either within or

from outside the service area boundaries. If the new
development is located on land that the applicant was
seeking to have annexed into Sierra Pacific's service
area, then the water right has to come from outside the
current service area boundaries. Sierra Pacific will consider accepting groundwater rights, if they have valid
permits and the groundwater is of acceptable quality.

Local governments acquire the water rights they lease
to Sierra Pacific from two different sources. Most of the
water rights are provided by developers who must dedicate
sufficient water rights to the local government jurisdiction as a precondition for project approval. Sierra
Pacific assists prospective buyers of water rights by
providing a list of potential sellers. The list is updated periodically and is available upon request from the
company. The cities are slowly acquiring additional water
rights under a special program created by state legislation regarding the disposition of the estimated 32,000
acre-feet of unused irrigation rights appurtenant to lands
served by Sierra Pacific. The cities of Reno and Sparks
and Washoe County are authorized to acquire the water
rights appurtenant to these lands by purchase or by condemnation, if necessary.(121) Water rights acquired by
the cities are "banked" by the local government until
such time as the city or county wishes to use them in
support of a particular development project.(122)

Since 1983, Washoe County has been acquiring private
water companies providing groundwater in rural areas. The
acquisitions began because of concerns regarding the poor
condition of many of the companies and potential health
problems posed by their deteriorating facilities. As a
condition for taking over the companies, the county
generally has required that the owners sell all assets and
rights of way necessary to provide water service to
existing customers, including water rights, for an amount
not to exceed the cost of the initial investment. For the
water rights the initial investment might be no more than
the cost of the filing fees for the appropriation of the
water right, a total of about $100.(123)

In one exceptional acquisition in January, 1984,
Washoe County not only acquired a water company but
purchased a quantity of water rights separately from the
other assets. The Trans Sierra Water Company had an
appropriated, but as yet undeveloped, right to pump 2,600
acre-feet of groundwater over and above what it was
already pumping to serve its existing customers. The
county was interested in acquiring the rights and entered

into negotiations with the company for their purchase.
Initially the company offered the rights for $1,500 per
acre-foot, an amount equal to the current price for
Truckee River rights. Washoe County refused the offer,
arguing that the groundwater rights were not as transferable as surface water rights, were not available for use
in the areas of high water demand, and therefore could not
be valued equally. Furthermore, the rights had not yet
been developed and were potentially subject to forfeiture.
Eventually Trans Sierra relented and sold the rights to
the County for $50 per acre-foot.(124)

Other groundwater rights in northwestern Nevada have
sold for substantial sums of money. In some isolated
groundwater basins near the Reno-Sparks area where development pressures are strong but municipal water service is
not readily available, prices have risen to unusually high
levels. In recent years, for example, groundwater rights
in the Spanish Springs and Lemon Valley areas near Reno
and Sparks have sold at prices ranging between $4,000 and
$10,000 per acre-foot.(125)

In contrast to groundwater rights, surface water
rights in northwestern Nevada are almost uniformly highly
valued, although prices still vary. High prices are
observed for large, consolidated blocks of surface water
rights appurtenant to lands located outside the existing
service area of Sierra Pacific. Somewhat lower prices are
observed for small rights appurtenant to urbanized lands
within the Reno-Sparks metropolitan area which are already
served water by Sierra Pacific. An independent water
rights appraisal conducted in 1984 listed 52 water rights
transactions occurring between 1982 and 1984, with
(nominal) prices ranging from $875 to $2,016 per acre-
foot.(126)

Larger lots of water rights tend to bring higher unit
prices than do smaller lots because of the high costs of
transacting water rights transfers in the Truckee Meadows.
Frequently it is unclear whether land subdivided from a
parcel with water rights retained any of the water right.
Lengthy and sometimes expensive title searches are often
necessary to prove ownership of water rights before they
can be transferred. According to Sierra Pacific, the total
cost for the title search, the payment of filing fees, and
other costs for transferring a water right may be $1,000
per transaction or more.(127)

A survey conducted in March, 1985, by the Public
Service Commission found that of the 32,000 acre-feet of
water rights identified as subject to local government

acquisition (by purchase or condemnation), about 16,000 acre-feet were in blocks of less than 10 acre-feet. The other 16,000 acre-feet involved blocks of 10 acre-feet or more, of which perhaps a dozen holdings were in excess of 100 acre-feet each. Of these 16,000 acre-feet of larger holdings, about 8,000 acre-feet were being retained by developers who wanted them for building projects. The remaining 8,000 acre-feet were held by owners who were willing to sell but were holding out for a higher price. Of a dozen interested sellers who were contacted with offers of $1,000 to $1,100 per acre-foot, none accepted. Four counteroffers were given ranging from $1,750 to $2,000 per acre-foot.(128)

Reno, Sparks, Washoe County, and Sierra Pacific have agreed to offer landowners $422 per acre-foot for their water rights under the local government acquisition pro- gram. The price is based on a market value for the rights of $1,500 per acre-foot, less transactions costs. Sierra Pacific leases the water rights from the cities and county for $422 per acre-foot, plus the costs to the local governments of handling the rights. When the water rights are applied towards a new development, Sierra Pacific passes its costs of acquiring the water right, plus the expenses incurred in doing the title work on the transfer, on to the new water users.(129) As of the end of 1986, this program of acquiring water rights had met with only limited success. Sparks had purchased about 50 acre-feet of rights, and Reno about 325 acre-feet. Most of the potential sellers of water rights contacted by the cities had either failed to respond or had rejected the offer. Apparently there were two reasons for the general lack of response to the program. First, many holders of water rights have resisted selling their rights in the belief that prices will rise significantly in the future. The second is that several private water brokers operating in the Truckee Meadows have been outbidding the cities. Typi- cally, the price offered by the brokers to the sellers ranges between $600 and $800 per acre-foot, less a broker- ing fee. The brokers assemble several small water rights, each one as small as an acre-foot or less, into a package for resale to a local developer. The price for these brokered packages of water rights has exceeded $2,000 per acre-foot.(130)

Sierra Pacific is actively considering various market and nonmarket alternatives for acquiring additional water rights from sources outside the Truckee Basin. The market alternatives include buying surface water rights in Sierra

152

Valley, California, and groundwater rights in the Warm
Springs and Honey Lake valleys in Nevada. Ranches in
Sierra Valley are irrigated by surface water rights from a
number of sources, including the Truckee River. Sierra
Pacific has considered purchasing land with water rights
at prices up to $2,000 per acre. Because Truckee River
water rights tend to be spread relatively thinly over many
acres, the company would have to purchase large parcels of
land from dozens of different owners to secure an adequate
supply of rights. The high cost of the water rights--in
excess of $2,000 per acre foot, not including pumping
costs--local opposition to the purchase, and uncertainty
over the legal implications of transporting water across
the state line, have diminished interest in this
particular alternative.(131)

Acquisition of distant groundwater rights appears to
be a more promising alternative. In 1986, Sierra Pacific
concluded an agreement with a landowner in the Warm Spring
Valley, located approximately 20 miles northeast of the
Truckee Meadows. Pending approval of the transfer by the
state engineer and authorization of the purchase by the
Public Service Commission, Sierra Pacific will buy 2,100
acre-feet of groundwater rights. The company also retains
an option to purchase up to an additional 700 acre-feet of
groundwater rights. The purchase price of $1,150 per
acre-foot, which is considerably less than the current
value of over $2,000 per acre-foot for Truckee River
rights, reflects the high costs of transporting and treating the groundwater relative to local surface water
supplies. Funds for purchasing the rights have been
placed in escrow pending approval of the sale and transfer. In the meantime, the seller may collect the interest
accruing on the money.(132)

A second possible source of distant groundwater is in
the Honey Lake Valley, located about 35 miles north of the
Truckee Meadows. Due to the high cost of developing this
water supply, Sierra Pacific does not expect to offer to
pay more than $500 to $600 per acre-foot. Proposed transfers of groundwater out of Honey Lake Valley have been
extremely controversial because the groundwater basin lies
partly in Nevada and partly in California. In early 1987,
the state engineer called a three-year moratorium on all
water transfers and appropriations of groundwater in the
Honey Lake Valley pending the results of a comprehensive
study of the basin's hydrological capacity.(133)

To summarize: Water prices and conditions for water
transfer vary considerably in the Truckee River Basin of

western Nevada. Sierra Pacific and the cities of Sparks and Reno are large market participants and exert some influence on water prices within their service areas. Transfers within the Basin are complicated by unresolved Indian water rights claims, separate federal decrees for management of the Truckee River and the Carson River, and ambiguities surrounding interstate transfer and transfer of water developed by Bureau of Reclamation projects.

GILA-SAN FRANCISCO BASIN, NEW MEXICO

The Study Area

The market area studied in New Mexico is the drainage basin of the Gila River, including its major tributary in New Mexico, the San Francisco River. The Gila-San Francisco Basin, a federally adjudicated basin, is located in southwestern New Mexico, bordered on the east by the Continental Divide and on the west by the State of Arizona. Most of the land area in the basin is included in the Gila National Forest and the Gila Wilderness, vast expanses of sparsely populated forest and chaparral environments at elevations ranging between 6,000 and 10,000 feet. In the southern and western portions of the basin, where most of the population and most private landholdings are concentrated, elevations are lower and forest gives way to grasslands and high desert.

The major urban center in the area is the town of Silver City with a population of about 20,000. Silver City is just outside the Gila-San Francisco Basin, south and east of the Continental Divide in the Mimbres Basin. Towns located within the Gila-San Francisco Basin are small and widely scattered. The principle settlements include Reserve and Glenwood in Catron County and Cliff and Redrock in Grant County. These areas are shown in figure 5.8.

The predominant industries in the Gila-San Francisco Basin are mining and ranching. Irrigated crop farming has been declining for many years. Since the late 1960s and early 1970s a number of vacation and retirement homes have been built in the vicinity of the Gila National Forest.

About 31,000 acre-feet of groundwater and surface water rights are held in the Gila-San Francisco Basin, roughly 6,500 acre-feet in the San Francisco portion of the basin, and 23,500 acre-feet in the Gila portion. Water rights in the San Francisco portion are used almost

154

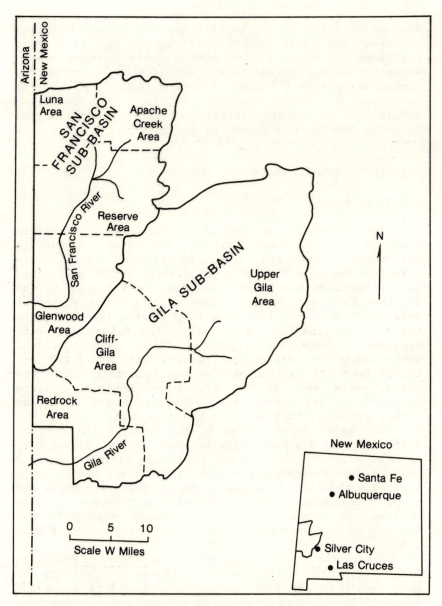

Figure 5.8   Gila-San Francisco Basin, New Mexico

exclusively for irrigation and domestic purposes. Water
rights in the Gila portion are divided up as follows.
Silver City holds over 1,300 acre-feet of water rights of
which it is permitted to export the consumptive use
portion, or about 800 acre-feet, to the Mimbres Basin.
Mining companies hold about 11,800 acre-feet of rights,
but their level of consumptive use is considered to be
high so the quantity they are permitted to pump is less
than this. The remaining 10,000 acre-feet of rights in
the Gila sub-Basin are held by households and irrigators.

Much of the water used in the Gila-San Francisco
Basin comes from surface water sources, but groundwater
pumping is also extensive. Surface water rights on the
Gila and San Francisco rivers and on tributary streams are
usually supplied by small private ditch companies. A large
block of both surface and groundwater rights is used by
the Phelps Dodge copper mine, located near the town of
Tyrone. The Boliden copper mine, which is still under
construction, will use groundwater exclusively for its
operation. Silver City and a few other small towns and
residential subdivisions operate water treatment and
distribution systems that also depend entirely upon
groundwater. Most other domestic and commercial water
users operate their own private groundwater wells.

Water Rights and Institutions

Virtually all groundwater and surface water rights in
New Mexico are subject to the legal doctrine of prior
appropriation. A comprehensive administrative water code,
passed by the territorial legislature in 1907 and adopted
by the newly constituted state government in 1912, remains
the basic surface water law of New Mexico today. Groundwater was first regulated in 1931.(134)

The State Engineer's jurisdiction includes all
surface water rights and any groundwater in declared
groundwater basins. The State Engineer designates a
particular hydrologic region to be a declared groundwater
basin when there is reason to believe that rapid development in the area might impair existing water rights. Most
important water-using areas in the state are now included
in the more than thirty declared groundwater basins. The
State Engineer's responsibilities include all matters
relating to the apportionment, transfer, and distribution
of water. The State Engineer must approve all new appropriations of water for beneficial use as well as for
changes in the place or purpose of existing uses.

Those who cannot be served by a municipal or domestic water service organization may drill a well for household use. A well that provides water for a single household and irrigates no more than a single acre of land is usually exempt from state regulation. In declared groundwater basins, however, exempt wells must be registered with the State Engineer. Exempt groundwater rights are routinely granted by the State Engineer in most parts of New Mexico (the Gila-San Francisco Basin being an exception) for indoor and for outdoor household uses such as watering gardens, small orchards and lawns; washing cars; and filling swimming pools.

Both groundwater and surface water rights can be sold or transferred. The transfer can be of both location and purpose. In some instances where surface water and groundwater resources are considered integrally related, the State Engineer may allow transfers from surface appropriations to groundwater appropriations on a limited basis. Under these circumstances, a new appropriation of groundwater may be permitted under the condition that the appropriator acquire and retire from use surface water rights in quantities sufficient to compensate for the effects of groundwater pumping.(135)

Water right owners can lease and temporarily transfer all or part of their rights for up to 10 years at a time. A major benefit of leasing water rights is that by doing so, owners can keep their water rights free from the risk of forfeiture due to nonuse, even when they have no immediate use for the water themselves. Leases may be effective immediately or may be designated for future use.(136)

In the mid 1960s, the State Engineer formally declared the Gila-San Francisco Basin following the U.S. Supreme Court's adjudication of the lower Colorado River basin in Arizona vs. California.(137) The U.S. Supreme Court divided the Gila-San Francisco Basin into two separate sub-basins, corresponding to the respective drainages of the Gila and the San Francisco Rivers, and specified the maximum quantity of water that could be consumptively used from each of the two rivers before they flowed into Arizona. The court also divided each sub-basin into a number of areas, and specified the maximum number of allowable irrigated acres within each area. There are four areas in the San Francisco sub-basin: Luna, Apache Creek, Reserve, and Glenwood. There are three areas in the Gila sub-basin: Upper Gila, Cliff-Gila, and Redrock.(138) Following the issuance of the U.S. Supreme

Court's final decree in March, 1964, the State of New
Mexico adjudicated all water rights in the basin, and the
process was completed by 1967. Finding that the total
existing water rights were somewhat less than the limit
imposed by the Supreme Court, applications for additional
appropriations were allowed to continue for a short time.
The Basin has been closed to additional appropriations
since the late 1960s.(139)

During the state adjudication proceedings in the mid-
1960s, the State Engineer identified the acres of
irrigated land, domestic households, and commercial
enterprises that were putting water to beneficial use and
had a valid claim to a water right. Commercial and industrial water rights were determined on the basis of their
historical levels of use. Irrigation water rights (per
acre) were determined on the basis of three different
measures: the maximum allowable diversion right, in any
one year, the maximum 10-year rolling average diversion
right, and the consumptive use portion of the right.
These measures vary throughout the Gila-San Francisco
Basin but are uniform within each one of the seven areas.
Domestic well rights are fixed at 3 acre-feet per year
throughout the Gila-San Francisco Basin. There is no recognized consumptive use portion to a domestic well
right.(140)

As a federally adjudicated basin, the Gila-San
Francisco faces particularly stringent controls on the
allocation, use and transfer of its water rights. Appropriation of water rights for outside domestic use is not
permitted even though this is routinely granted in closed
groundwater basins elsewhere in the State. Households with
exempt groundwater wells cannot maintain lawns, gardens,
orchards or otherwise use any water outdoors unless
additional water rights are acquired to serve that
purpose. As a result, the Gila-San Francisco has an
active market for individual household water rights.(141)

Water rights transfers are permitted within the Gila-
San Francisco Basin although they are subject to several
restrictions. Water rights are not transferable into or
out of the Gila-San Francisco Basin and are not transferable between the Gila and San Francisco sub-basins. However, quantities of water equal to the consumptive use
portion of any water right may be physically transported
into or out of the basin or from one sub-basin to the
other. Any diversion right in any quantity may be transferred within the same area. Only the consumptive use
portion of a water right may be transferred between areas

within the same sub-basin. Surface water and groundwater throughout the Gila-San Francisco Basin are considered to be interchangeable and the rights to one may be converted into the other--the point of diversion for a surface water right may be transferred to a groundwater well, and vice versa, usually without altering the quantity or priority of the right. In some cases where a surface water right is of very junior priority or is drawn from an intermittent stream, the quantity may be adjusted downwards when converted into a groundwater right.(142) Domestic well rights may be transferred anywhere within their respective sub-basins without changing the quantity of the right. Industrial water users who acquire irrigation rights are generally limited to divert no more than the consumptive use portion of the right.(143) Irrigation rights may be transferred for other purposes of use, but water rights assigned to nonirrigation purposes may not be transferred for irrigation use.

Water Market Activity

Water market activity in the Gila-San Francisco Basin has occurred since the basin was closed to additional appropriation in the mid-1960s. Thousands of acre-feet of water were transferred from irrigation to mining within the first few years, mostly in nonmarket transfers of water rights from a large ranch to a newly opened copper mine--both of which were owned by the Phelps Dodge Corporation. The ranch and its water rights had been acquired and developed by Phelps Dodge before the closing of the basin. The Phelps Dodge development holds over 11,000 acre-feet of water rights, almost half of all the water rights in the Gila sub-basin. The market for the remaining water rights has been very active. Buyers for water rights in the Gila-San Francisco Basin include other irrigation users, individual households, the town of Silver City, and a few smaller mines and commercial enterprises. The major commercial-industrial buyer of water rights since the Phelps Dodge acquisitions has been the Exxon Corporation and its successor, the Boliden Minerals Company, which acquired several hundred acre-feet of water rights in the early 1980s for a new copper mine 20 miles north of Silver City.

In 1986 Phelps Dodge announced that it had purchased Kennecott's interest in the Chino mine in the Mimbres Basin, and that it planned to phase out its mining operations at its Tyrone mine in the Gila-San Francisco

Basin. Approximately half of the over 11,000 acre-feet of water rights owned by Phelps Dodge in the Gila-San Francisco will no longer be used for mining within 10 years, and within 20 years the mine will be shut down completely, freeing up the water rights for alternative uses. The mine has considered transferring some of its rights to domestic purposes on company land that may be sold for retirement homes, but it is unlikely that all or even most of Phelps Dodge's water rights could be used for that purpose. The future of the supply and demand for water rights over the next few decades in the Gila-San Francisco basin is therefore highly uncertain.(144)

San Francisco Sub-basin. Almost all water rights in the San Francisco sub-basin are used for irrigation or domestic purposes. A few small mills and a small mine are the only commercial water users in the area. Market transfer of water rights did not begin in the San Francisco sub-basin on a significant scale until the mid to late 1970s, about 10 years after they began in the Gila sub-basin. Most transfers have been in quantities of 3 to 6 acre-feet or less. Prices for water rights in the late 1970s were about $500 per acre-foot; then prices rose to as much as $3,000 per acre-foot before leveling off. Prices have fallen below $1500 per acre-foot since 1983, when a major flood washed out many irrigated lands and a number of irrigation rights holders chose to sell their rights rather than invest in reestablishing their farms.(145)

Gila Sub-basin. A substantial portion of the water rights in the Gila sub-basin are controlled by three major entities: the Phelps Dodge Corporation, the Boliden Minerals Company, and the town of Silver City. The remaining water rights are distributed over many individual holders, mostly in quantities of less than 50 acre-feet. The most active trading has been in small quantities of rights, often 1 acre-foot or less of rights at a time. The earliest sale of water rights dates to 1966 when a parcel of water rights were sold for about $1,800 per acre-foot. Real prices for water rights increased steadily through the 1970s, reaching over $3,000 per acre-foot by 1980. Since 1980, prices have generally declined to a range of $1,100 to $2,500 per acre-foot.

Price increases in the Gila sub-basin during the late 1970s may have been attributable to the entrance of the Exxon Corporation into the water market. In 1979 and 1980, Exxon negotiated with about 25 different owners of land and water rights for the sale of as much as 1,200 acre-

feet of irrigation water rights for transfer to mining.
Roughly half of the transactions involved the sale of
water rights only, and the other half involved the sale of
land and water rights together. There appears to be no
significant difference between the prices paid for water
rights with and without the inclusion of appurtenant land.

Exxon contracted to buy the land and water rights
through 5-year, annually renewable options. Option prices
for the properties varied between about $3,300 and $6,600
per acre of land (about $2,000 to $4,000 per acre-foot of
water rights). Annual payments to keep the option
contracts current ranged from 6 percent to 10 percent of
the option price. Generally these payments were not
credited against the option price. In a few cases, a down
payment in the first option year equal to about 20 percent
of the option price substituted for annual payments. Some
options were exercised as early as 1981, but most sales
were not concluded until late in 1984. Two or three
options were cancelled. Exxon negotiated each option
contract separately. In 1982 Exxon sold most of its water
rights purchase options and other assets to the Boliden
Minerals Company.(146)

Water Leasing. Price data on five leases occurring
between 1963 and 1983 were collected, four in the Gila
sub-basin and one in the San Francisco sub-basin. Prices
ranged generally between $100 and $250 per acre-foot with
no evidence of any long-term trend either up or down.
Rental prices for water in the Gila-San Francisco Basin
appear to stand at roughly 10 percent of the market price
for the rights.

Water Rights Acquisitions by Silver City. Silver
City owns water rights in both the Mimbres and Gila-San
Francisco basins. Most of the rights were appropriated and
developed at a very low cost, but some were purchased at
high market prices. Until 1982, nearly all of the water
rights owned by Silver City were concentrated in two
groundwater wellfields: the Franks field in the Gila-San
Francisco Basin and the Woodward and Anderson fields in
the Mimbres Basin. Since 1982, groundwater rights in two
new areas in the Mimbres Basin have been acquired by the
city.(147)

Rights to develop groundwater on the Franks ranch
were acquired by contract in 1945.'(148) Silver City agreed
to pay the landowners a rent of about $3.50 (nominal
dollars, not adjusted for inflation) per acre-foot of
water pumped and transported off the ranch. The contract
had no termination date and there was no inflation

adjustment clause. The price paid for the water has not been increased since it was established in 1945. A similar contract signed in 1954 allowed Silver City to develop the Woodward field.(149) The Woodward contract was amended in 1967 to increase the nominal dollar rental price from $3.50 to about $5 per acre-foot. Silver City has the right to pump and transport about 1,500 acre-feet per year from the Woodward wellfield, approximately 800 acre-feet per year from the Franks wellfield, and an additional 400 acre-feet per year from the Anderson wells.(150)

Additional groundwater rights have been acquired by Silver City in both the Gila-San Francisco and Mimbres basins. All purchases of water rights in the Gila-San Francisco Basin have been in the Gila sub-basin. In 1981 the city purchased 78 acre-feet of water rights with a consumptive use of 43 acre-feet at a cost of about $3,000 per acre-foot of transportable (consumptive use) water. In 1984, the city purchased another 131 acre-feet of transportable water at a cost of $2,900 per acre-foot.(151) In 1985, the city acquired 32 acre-feet of transportable water for slightly more than $2,200 per acre-foot. All of these water rights were successfully transferred to the Franks wellfield, in the Cliff-Gila area, and the water is being pumped over the Continental Divide into the Mimbres Basin. There have been two recent water rights acquisitions in the Mimbres Basin. In 1982, Silver City paid about $1,500 per acre-foot for 193 acre-feet of water rights.(152) In 1985, 1,433 acre-feet of water rights were acquired for about $2,200 per acre-foot.(153)

To summarize, water rights transfer in the Gila-San Francisco Basin can usually be implemented with lower transactions costs than in many other areas studied. Silver City and the mines hold the majority of water rights in the basin, and the number of potential market participants is relatively small. The announced closing of the Phelps Dodge Mine has cast a cloud of uncertainty over the future supply and demand for water rights in the basin. Nevertheless, market sales and rentals of water rights among irrigators and between irrigation and non-irrigation water users continue to occur.

LOWER SEVIER RIVER BASIN, UTAH

The Study Area

The market area chosen for study in Utah is the Lower
Sevier River Basin of west-central Utah. The Sevier River
begins in the highland plateaus of southwestern Utah and
flows north for about 150 miles before turning south and
west for a short distance to terminate in Sevier Lake. The
study area lies within the sparsely populated, isolated,
and extremely arid Sevier Desert. Average precipitation is
less than 8 inches per year. The principal population
center is the small town of Delta, with approximately
5,000 residents. It lies in the northeastern corner of
Millard County, about 140 miles southwest of Salt Lake
City. Other small towns near Delta are Hinckley,
Sutherland, Deseret, and Oasis. Also included within the
study area are the towns of Lynndyl and Leamington,
located along the Sevier River 15 and 20 miles north of
Delta, respectively. The Lower Sevier River Basin is shown
in figure 5.9.

Approximately 50,000 acres are irrigated in the
vicinity of the northern bend of the lower Sevier River.
Agriculture, the mainstay of the local economy, is the
primary water user in the area. Alfalfa and alfalfa seed
are the major products. A significant quantity of acreage
is also devoted to barley and other small grain crops. A
major new water user in the area is the Intermountain
Power Project (IPP)--a large, coal-fired, electric power
generating facility located about 10 miles north of Delta.
Currently under construction, IPP will retain several
hundred permanent employees when it begins full-scale
operations in 1987.

Four mutual ditch companies cooperatively manage most
of the surface water supplies within the study area. The
Delta, Mellville, Abraham, and Deseret irrigation
companies are collectively known as the DMAD companies. A
fifth company, the Central Utah Irrigation Company,
distributes water out of the Sevier River upstream from
the DMAD system. The Gunnison Bend, DMAD, and Sevier
Bridge Reservoirs operate on the lower Sevier River.
Gunnison Bend, the smallest reservoir with a storage
capacity of 4,500 acre-feet, is owned exclusively by the
Abraham and Deseret Companies. The DMAD Reservoir, with a
capacity of 11,500 acre-feet, is owned by all four of the
DMAD companies. Sevier Bridge, the largest reservoir with
a storage capacity of 235,000 acre-feet, is owned jointly

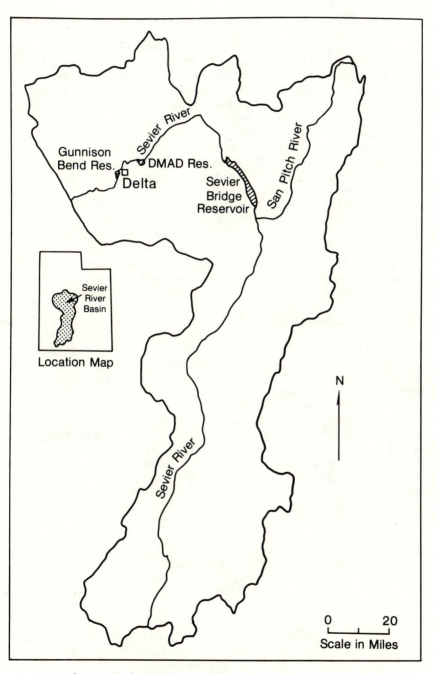

Figure 5.9 Lower Sevier River Basin, Utah

by the DMAD companies and the Central Utah Irrigation
Company. (154)

An average of about 120,000 acre-feet of water per
year are delivered through the DMAD system. Most of the
supply comes from direct flows in the Sevier River and
from storage water in the Gunnison Bend, DMAD, and Sevier
Bridge Reservoirs. Supplemental water is pumped from
several shallow groundwater wells jointly owned and
operated by the DMAD companies. Groundwater is pumped into
the river to maintain minimum flows and also to reduce
salinity levels. As much as 28,000 acre-feet of groundwater per year may be diverted into the river although the
volume pumped usually is much less. (155)

The high level of salinity in the Sevier River
prevents the water from being used for human consumption.
Groundwater quality, however, is generally good throughout
the basin. Hence, groundwater is the only source of water
for domestic, municipal and most commercial water users.
Groundwater is also used to supplement surface water
supplies for irrigation during critical periods.

Water Rights and Institutions

While Utah recognizes the prior appropriations
doctrine, absolute priorities were not implemented in Utah
because early Mormon leaders gave greater weight to
proportionate sharing of water shortages. When rights to
Utah streams were established, each claimant was assigned
proportionate shares of the flow. The shares assigned to
each canal were based on priority of appropriation--the
canals that had first diverted water and put it to use in
irrigation water were given preference over later canals--
though this principle was far from absolute. The prior
appropriations doctrine was modified considerably by the
apportionment of the variable water supply by fractions
instead of by physical volume. In this way, the effects
of drought were spread over all users instead of only the
most junior appropriators (156)

Groundwater rights and transfers are controlled carefully in the Delta-Lynndyl area. The groundwater basin
has been closed to major additional appropriations since
the late 1970s. Water rights of less than 2 acre-feet per
year for private domestic use are the only groundwater
appropriations still permitted. (157) All lands surrounding
the town of Delta and lying east and south of the Sevier
River are considered to be within a "high impact" part of
the basin. This is where most of the area's population,

growth pressures, and economic activity have been located, especially since the arrival of IPP. Groundwater rights transfers are permitted within and out of the high impact area, but no water rights can be transferred into the area from surrounding areas. The State Engineer also distinguishes between shallow and deep groundwater wells when managing water rights. The best water quality is obtained from wells drawing from deeper groundwater aquifers. Transfers of rights are not permitted between wells that draw water from different hydrologic formations in the basin. High quality groundwater within the high-impact portion of the basin is scarce and highly valued.(158)

Nearly all of the irrigation water used in Utah is distributed through organized irrigation entities, most of which were established by Mormon pioneers. The successors of these early cooperative organizations are mutual water companies and are the most common type of private irrigation company in Utah. Water rights represented by stock in a nonprofit mutual irrigation company are not appurtenant to the land upon which the water is used. Individual stockholders are not subject to state laws regulating the beneficial use of water rights. They may own as many or as few shares of water stock as they wish, regardless of whether they own sufficient land on which to use the water. A farmer who has a right to more water than he plans to use in a given season or in a given crop rotation may rent his right to a farmer who wants it. An individual may own water stock without owning any land at all and rent out the entire portfolio of water rights every year. Conversely, a farmer may own land but own no water stock and rent the desired quantity every season. The only condition on the use of the water transferred is that it be used within the service area of the mutual stock company.

Water rights represented by mutual water stock can be transferred between farmers simply by transferring the stock. The transfer of stock representing water rights does not require administrative proceedings before the State Engineer to change the point of diversion or place of use of the water. Such proceedings are required in transfers of water rights not represented by mutual company stock. Water rights not represented by stock are appurtenant to the land for which the appropriation was made, although they may be severed from the land and sold separately. The transfer of water stock outside of the service area of the mutual stock company requires filing an application before the State Engineer to request a change in the point of diversion or place of use. If such a change is not within the boundaries of the controlling irrigation company, an administrative hearing is required.

Water rights in the Lower Sevier River Basin were adjudicated under the Cox Decree of 1936.(159) Local mutual ditch companies had already been in existence for many years. Water rights were assigned to each water company on the basis of current use and not prior appropriation. The timing and distribution of proportional shares of the streamflow were specified, along with formulas for prorating water supplies to all users during drought years.

Water is allocated by the governing boards of each of the DMAD companies, who meet each spring to determine the water "credit" to be issued on each share of outstanding water stock. The size of the credit is based on projections of yields from storage and flows along the lower Sevier. Stockholders are given water accounts which function much like a bank account. Water may be withdrawn from the account at any time during the irrigation season, or deposits may be registered by transferring water from another stockholder's account. DMAD permits owners or renters of company water to carry over any part or all of their holdings to the following irrigation season, less 20 percent to account for evaporation losses. Water may not be carried over for more then a single year. This option enhances flexibility for the individual farmer although there is some risk involved in carrying over water rights. If the storage capacity of the reservoirs is reached at the beginning of the following irrigation season, all carryover accounts are erased and water credits are reissued to all stockholders based on the total available water supply.(160)

Water transfers among water users in the DMAD service areas have been common for several decades. Sales and rentals of water among shareholders within individual companies have occurred since the early 1900s. In about 1950, the DMAD governing boards instituted an agreement to permit informal seasonal transfer (rental) of water between companies. Normally, the transfer of water among different mutual stock companies would require proceedings before the State Engineer. In this case, however, the State Engineer waived the proceedings because the DMAD companies are located near the end of the Sevier River where no downstream users could be impacted by any transfer or change in use of the water in the system.(161)

Seasonal intercompany water transfers among the DMAD Companies continued without formal legal sanction until 1980. In 1980, upon approving the change application to transfer DMAD and Central Utah Company water to IPP, the State Engineer formally declared that the points of diversion and place of use for the four DMAD companies were interchangeable.(162) Multiple use permits were granted for all the water rights transferred, allowing the seasonal rental of water unused by IPP back to irrigators. The DMAD company secretary works closely with the river commissioner for the lower Sevier River to ensure that all water accounts "balance," and that the total appropriations by each of the DMAD companies does not exceed the legal limit of its prorated shares.(163)

Rentals are handled in the same fashion whether the renter wishes to transfer water to land within the same water company service or to land within the service area of another DMAD company. The prospective renter submits a form describing the requested transfer to the DMAD company secretary. Provided that sufficient water credit is left in the individual's water account for that season, the quantity of water to be rented is debited against the lessor's account and credited to the lessee's account. Water is usually rented in acre-foot units, but the parties sometimes choose to rent shares of water stock instead. Individuals renting water stock have the option to use the water in the current irrigation season, or to carry the water over into the next season.(164)

Water Market Activity

Management of the DMAD companies has been highly integrated since at least the early 1960s. Although the historical average yield per share of stock differs from one company to another, the value of the water rights represented by the stocks (on a per acre-foot basis) are virtually identical. In 1985, the price for water represented by stock in any one of the four companies was approximately $350 per acre-foot.

Water rights prices between 1974 and 1985 exhibit no trend either up or down except for a brief period between 1979 and 1982, when the introduction of the IPP to the Delta area caused a speculative boom in land and water rights. IPP paid over $2,400 per acre-foot for one large package of groundwater rights and water company stock. Prices exceeded $1,000 per acre-foot for other sales of water stock occurring at about the same time. By about

168

1982, the speculative bubble subsided and water stock
prices began to return to their former levels.

The package of 45,000 acre-feet of water rights
purchased by IPP for its power generating station was
composed of 5,400 acre-feet in groundwater rights and
39,600 acre-feet in water company stock. The stock com-
prised roughly 20 percent of all the water rights owned by
the DMAD companies and 85 percent of the rights owned by
the Central Utah Irrigation Company.(165) Many different
sellers were involved in the transfer, and most of the
water rights were sold in relatively small lots. There
were 565 individual contracts signed to purchase water
company stock, averaging about 60 acre-feet per contract.
Another 31 contracts were signed for the sale of groundwater rights with an average of 174 acre-feet per
contract.(166)

Water rights were transferred to IPP via a seller's
collective called the Joint Venture. The Joint Venture
was formed after a core group of organizers announced
IPP's interest in purchasing water rights and advertised
for a collective bargaining coalition in the local news-
papers in 1978. Anyone owning stock in the DMAD or
Central Utah companies or groundwater rights in the Delta
or Lynndyl areas was invited to participate in the sale to
IPP. Participants were allowed to offer prorated quantities of water rights for sale, established as fixed
proportions of the water rights owned by each prospective
seller.(167) Individuals were free to offer more than
their assigned quantity of water rights for sale, but they
had to find other participants who were willing to reduce
their allotment by a compensating amount. This led to the
development of an active market in sales options. Option
prices for the sale of water rights to IPP through the
Joint Venture are reported to have sold for as much as
$650 per acre-foot in the late 1970s.

Groundwater rights in Utah are not quantified
volumetrically; rather, they are specified in terms of a
flow rate. In order to determine how much groundwater
could actually be transferred to IPP, the State Engineer
had to determine the consumptive use of groundwater in the
areas where the sales were to take place. The State
Engineer issued an interlocutory order (the order is not
final, pending further hydrologic studies) stating that
the consumptive use portion of the groundwater rights in
the affected areas was only about half of the average
volume diverted.(168) IPP had specified in the negotiations that it would only pay for the volume of water that

was <u>transferable</u>, not the total volume of the rights.
Option prices for groundwater rights reportedly fell by at
least half, to about $300 per acre-foot. Nevertheless,
sufficient groundwater water rights were still offered to
complete the water rights package wanted by IPP. No final
order has yet been issued by the State Engineer. If the
interlocutory order stands, the farmers who sold groundwater rights to IPP will have to retire twice as much
irrigated acreage as they originally intended. The Joint
Venture is prepared to sue the State Engineer if the order
is upheld.(169)

IPP bought groundwater rights for two different
purposes. One was to supplement the supply of surface
water rights for its power generating operations. The
5,400 acre-feet of groundwater rights acquired for this
purpose were purchased from the Joint Venture for the same
unit acre-foot price as was paid for the water company
stock. A second bundle of groundwater rights were purchased from private individuals to create a "water bank"
for the town of Delta to support urban growth.(170) New
developments in the Delta service area must now either
provide sufficient groundwater rights to transfer to Delta
or pay a raw water fee in order to get hooked up to the
town water system. The fee, $1,000 per acre-foot, is
based on the average nominal price paid by IPP for the
water rights bank, $960 per acre-foot, plus a $40 handling
charge. As projects are built and the new users pay Delta
for withdrawals from the water bank, Delta reimburses IPP
for the cost of acquiring the rights.(171)

Real prices for groundwater rights have fallen since
1980. Excluding IPP's purchases from the Joint Venture,
prices in 1980 and 1981 ranged between $900 and $1,200
per acre-foot. Since 1982, groundwater rights located
near Delta have sold for about $700 per acre-foot.
Groundwater rights located outside of the high-impact
portion of the Delta area basin range in price from $300
to $500 per acre-foot.(172)

Shortly after its purchase of water rights, IPP
announced that it would scale back the design of the
facility from four power generating units to only two.
IPP now expects to use only about 20,000 acre-feet of its
45,000 acre-feet of water rights. The excess water rights
will be retained in anticipation of future plant expansion. Unused water supplies will be rented back each year
to individual water users in the irrigation companies.
Traditionally, water has been rented for one season at a
time in the lower Sevier basin. Since IPP has such a large

quantity of water rights that will not be used in the foreseeable future, the company is considering making arrangements for long term leases for some of the water.(173)

IPP has become the dominant renter of water in the DMAD system. The long-term impact of IPP on the water rental market may not be known for several years. In 1979, a relatively dry year, DMAD water rented for nearly $30 per acre-foot. In 1980, the year before IPP began renting water, flows in the Sevier River were high and the real price of rental water subsequently fell to less than $8 per acre-foot. During the following two years flows were closer to the average, but real rental prices only rose slightly to about $9 per acre-foot. Coinciding with the IPP purchase the Sevier River system entered upon an unprecedented wet cycle that persisted into 1985. The rental market resumed in the middle of the 1986 irrigation season, but water was still abundant, trading activity light, and rental prices low.

Water rental prices between 1948 and 1982 ranged roughly between about $7 and $75 per acre-foot. Real prices generally increased from a range of $7 to $20 per acre-foot in the late 1940s and early 1950s to a range of $20 to $75 in the mid-1950s through the mid-1960s. Since the late 1960s the rental price has declined again to a range of $8 to $25 per acre-foot. Rental prices have varied tremendously from one year to the next. Between 1953 and 1954, for instance, rental prices increased from $11 per acre-foot to $26 per acre-foot. Between 1967 and 1968, real prices fell from $50 per acre-foot to $24 per acre-foot. During the 1986 season, prices ranged between $3 and $5 per acre-foot.

A study of water rental price behavior conducted between 1946 and 1963 in the Delta area indicates that fluctuations in water rental prices are strongly related to the hydrologic cycles of the Sevier River.(174) Rental prices tend to be high in dry years when water supplies are low, and low in wet years when water supplies are high. Rental activity is busiest during the spring and summer months, and the volume of rentals varies with the total supply of water. The rental volume is lowest in very wet years because supplies are more than adequate for most stockholders and demand for additional water is low. The volume of water rented is also low in very dry years when supplies are scarce and prices are high enough to cut short demand for supplemental water. Rental activity appears to be the highest in moderately dry years when the demand for water is strong and the supply is more flexible.

To summarize: Market activity in Utah's Lower Sevier River Basin demonstrates that water rights represented by mutual water company stocks can be transferred with minimal transaction costs. The entrance of Intermountain Power Project into the market, first as a major water buyer and now as the principal lessor of water to irrigators, provides an interesting opportunity to study a large new market participant's impact on water prices and transfers. The Lower Sevier Basin market also provides an opportunity to observe both sales and rentals of groundwater and surface water.

COMPARISON OF PRICES ACROSS MARKET AREAS

Table 5.2 summarizes price data collected on purchases of perpetual water rights in the various areas studied. Price observations over time are reported in terms of 1986 dollars paid per acre-foot of long-term average yield on diversion rights acquired by the buyer. As noted earlier in this chapter, differences in the nature of the water rights being transferred prevent the prices reported from being strictly comparable with one another. For instance, the prices reported for Arizona's Avra Valley include both land and water rights since the City of Tucson is required, by Arizona law, to buy irrigated land in order to obtain irrigation water rights. Twin Lakes water rights include a right to use return flows, a privilege that does not apply to most of the other water rights listed on Table 5.2. Groundwater and surface water rights differ in some important respects. The long term dependability of groundwater rights depends on the pumping patterns and depletion rates for the aquifer from which supplies are being drawn, but there is little year-to-year variability associated with groundwater rights. The dependability of surface water rights is a function of stream flow variability, the seniority of the right and other factors.

Water rights prices are a function of the interaction between demand and supply-side forces in any given market area. Demand side forces reflect expansion and contraction of water-using activities, which in turn depend on the vitality of the regional economy; price levels for energy, minerals and agricultural commodities; population and income trends and so on. Supply side forces reflect

Table 5.2: -- Representative Prices for Sales of Perpetual Water Rights
(1986 dollars per acre-foot)

Year	Arizona Avra Valley	Arizona Type II	Colorado C-BT	Colorado Twin Lakes	Nevada[c] Truckee River	New Mexico Gila	New Mexico San Francisco	Utah[e] DMAD	Utah[e] Groundwater
1961			130		150				
1962			150		140				
1963			220		170				
1964			370		150				
1965			440		130				
1966			530		160	1,790			
1967			560		160	ND			
1968			600		150	1,300			
1969			850		140	ND			
1970			920		140	ND			
1971	430		860	1,400	130	1,630			
1972	420		860	2,400	120	ND			
1973	NT		930	2,400	120	ND			
1974	NT		1,050	ND	110	1,240		330	
1975	570		1,090	ND	100	ND		ND	
1976	570		1,330	2,300	90	1,150		300	
1977	630		2,540	ND	90	1,420	510	550	
1978	NT		2,590	ND	80	3,210	480	550	
1979	700		3,050	ND	70	2,070	440	ND	
1980	NT		3,600	11,820	ND	3,270	ND	2,440	2,440
1981	NT		2,990	10,950	ND	2,090	1,110	1,200	1,150
1982	NT		1,880	ND	470	1,780	510[f]	750	680
1983	NT		1,600	ND	1,730	1,460	ND	430	ND
1984	870	560	1,460	ND	1,570	2,520	1,460	430	740
1985	NT	920	1,080	ND	1,450	ND	1,250	350	710
1986	630	1,430	ND	ND	ND	ND	1,210	ND	ND
1987	NT	1,000	ND	8,180	1,750	1,810	1,110	ND	ND

NT indicates no transactions occured in this market during the year indicated.
ND indicates no price data was obtainable for transactions occuring during the
year indicated.
See footnotes a-e on next page

Footnotes for Table 5.2

[a]Data on the sale of Type II nonirrigation water rights were obtained from investment managers, real estate developers, attorneys and other private individuals. The market for Type II rights began to develop in 1984. Data on the City of Tucson's acquisition of Avra Valley farmland for conversion of irrigation water rights were provided by city officials. Tucson began buying Avra Valley farmland in 1971.

[b]Data on sales of C-BT units were obtained from public water districts, municipal water agencies and real estate brokers in the area.

Most price data for Twin Lakes stock were made available by the towns and cities which purchased the rights in the mid and late 1970s. Earlier sales data and estimates of recent market prices for small quantities of Twin Lakes stock were provided by local individuals knowledgeable about this water market.

[c]Summary information on water rights acquisitions and prices between 1945 and 1979 were obtained from records provided by Sierra Pacific Power Company. Data on purchases occurring since 1979 were obtained from reports filed by Sierra Pacific with the Nevada Public Service Commission and from attorneys, engineers and private individuals. Price data for transactions prior to 1979 are based on Sierra Pacific acquisitions. Other buyers did not enter this market until the 1980s.

[d]Descriptive data on water rights transfers, excluding price information, were available from records in the State Engineer's office. Price data on a sample of these transfers were collected by contacting individuals involved in the transactions. Records of water rights prices paid by Silver City and by the state of New Mexico are public information.

[e]Data on transfers of groundwater rights and ditch company water stock were collected from real estate brokers, attorneys, bankers and other private individuals in the study area. The quantity and price of water rights purchased by the Intermountain Power Project is public information.

[f]The apparent drop in the market price of water in the San Francisco sub-basin in 1982 was caused by a single large transaction at a price of less than $400 per acre-foot. Prices paid for the several small transactions observed in that year ranged from $1,200 per acre-foot to over $3,000 per acre-foot.

changes in water availability and in the costs of pumping groundwater, developing new surface water supplies, contracting for public project water and pursuing other alternatives to market acquisition of water rights. Differing demand side forces were dominant in the study areas over various periods of time--energy development in the Lower Sevier Basin in the late 1970s, rapid urbanization in central Arizona and eastern Colorado during the 1960s and 1970s, mining expansion in the Gila-San Francisco Basin during the 1970s. On the supply side, Arizona, Colorado and Utah water prices are affected by expectations of new water supplies from the Central Arizona Project, the Windy Gap Project, and the Central Utah Project, respectively. Anticipation of new water supplies can decrease incentives to bid water away from existing rights holders.

Prices tend to be lower when the predominant buyer for the water rights is irrigated agriculture, as with DMAD stock in Utah until the IPP purchase, and nonagricultural water users do not compete significantly for water with irrigators. Prices tend to be higher where expanding nonirrigation water users face institutional barriers and/or physical supply limits in seeking additional water supplies. In the Gila-San Francisco Basin of New Mexico and the Truckee Meadows in Nevada, for instance, water supplies are constrained by legal and hydrologic constraints on water supply development and water users have few alternatives to market acquisition when they desire additional water.

The interaction of shifting supply and demand for water along with the variety of institutional arrangements among the study areas cause many different types of price responses to be observed. In southern Arizona, where declining groundwater tables and high energy prices have made water resources scarcer than in many other areas studied, prices for many types of water rights remain relatively low. Institutional uncertainties involved in transferring water rights, and the existence of alternatives to water rights transfers (the primary alternative being water service from the Central Arizona Project) reduce incentives for market transfers.

Northeastern Colorado provides an example of how perceptions of water scarcity may increase water rights prices rapidly even though long-term supplies remain relatively inexpensive and abundant. A speculative boom in the mid-1970s drove real prices for water rights to unprecedented levels by the early 1980s. Widespread concern that

increasing urban water demand was quickly outstripping
supply led to sharp increases in prices, although the
gradual transfer of water rights from agricultural to
nonagricultural use continued without any major change.
Gardner and Miller(175) suggest that prices peaked at
values equal to the capitalized marginal demand for water
by municipal users. As urban growth accelerated,
agricultural right holders believed that they each had a
high probability of being able to transfer their water
rights to a municipal of industrial water users and were
no longer willing to sell at prices that reflected only
water's value in irrigation.

Shifts in demand for water rights, or the expectation
of upward shifts in demand for water, have led to rapid
water rights price changes in other market areas as well.
The impact of a large new water buyer can be observed in
Utah water prices as the Intermountain Power Project
entered the Utah market in the late 1970s. Prices in the
Gila-San Francisco Basin, which had been slowly rising for
a number of years, took a sudden turn upwards in the late
1970s when the Exxon Corporation began to acquire water
rights for its new mining operation.

It is instructive to consider not only what forces
drive water rights prices up, but what forces allow them
to fall. Water rights prices in northeastern Colorado fell
in the 1980s at least partially in response to the
impending completion of the Windy Gap Project, declining
interest rates and a faltering farm economy. In addition,
some observers believe that cities began to recognize they
had acquired adequate water rights to meet foreseeable
needs and that continued acquisition of agricultural water
rights might have undesirable effects on the regional
economy and on the maintenance of attractive agricultural
greenbelts around urban communities.(176) In Utah, the
scaling back of the IPP to one-half its planned size cut
into the speculative bubble that had risen around the
project and prices fell. The stabilization of water rights
prices in Nevada's Truckee Meadows, following price
escalation in the early 1980s, may be a signal that panic
buying of water rights has slowed since private and government organizations agreed upon a system to facilitate
an orderly transition of water rights from agricultural to
municipal use. In New Mexico's Gila-San Francisco Basin,
real prices have declined since Exxon and Boliden
completed their acquisition program and the closing of a
major mining operation has been announced.

176

Relaxing existing restrictions on market transfers could have important impacts on market prices. For instance, water rights in Denver and its suburbs sell for twice the price of C-BT units and water development costs for proposed projects in the Denver area are up to six times more per acre-foot than the going price for C-BT water. If C-BT water could be transferred outside of the Northern Colorado Water Conservancy District, its price would undoubtedly rise.(177)

In summary: Legal, economic and hydrologic considerations all affect water demand and supply and thus market price levels. Prices can fall and rise rapidly as regional market conditions change. Chapter 5 has focused on market activity, overall price levels and trends in the markets studied. Chapter 6 will discuss factors affecting the value of individual water rights and approaches to water right valuation.

NOTES

1. United States Geological Survey. 1986. National Water Survey, 1985, p. 145. Water Supply Paper 2300. Washington, D.C.

2. Ibid.

3. Maurice M. Kelso, William E. Martin, and Lawrence E. Mack. Water Supplies and Economic Growth in an Arid Environment. Tucson: University of Arizona Press, 1973. (hereinafter cited as Water Supplies).

4. Arizona Rev. Stat. Ann. Vol. 15, Title 45, Sec. 461-577.

5. Kelso, Martin, and Mack, Water Supplies.

6. For example, suppose a water duty is equal to 4 acre-feet per acre, and there are 80 water duty acres and 100 grandfathered irrigation acres. The total groundwater right is 4 acre-feet X 80 water acres = 320 acre-feet. The holder of this grandfathered irrigation groundwater rights may apply a total of up to 320 acre-feet of water on all or any portion of the 100 irrigation acres to which the right applies.

7. Ariz. Adm. Rules and Regulations, Title 12, Ch. 15, Art. 8.

8. James L.Barr, and David E. Pingry. "The Central Arizona Project: An Inquiry into its Potential Impacts." Arizona Review, Vol. 26, No. 4 (Hereinafter cited as "Central Arizona Project.")

9. "Policy for Delivery, Use, and Sale of Colorado River Water." Central Arizona Water Conservancy District, January 8, 1987. Phoenix.

10. Ibid.

11. Ibid.

12. Barr and Pingry, "Central Arizona Project."

13. U.S. Department of the Interior, Central Arizona Project. "Arizona: Water Allocations and Water Service Contracting, Record of Decision." Federal Register, Vol. 48, No. 58, March 24, 1983.

14. U.S. Department of the Interior, Bureau of Reclamation. "Subcontract Among the United States, the Central Arizona Water Conservation District, and the _____, Providing for Central Arizona Project Water Service." Phoenix, Arizona, 1983.

15. T.J. Goldammer, "Estimating Wastewater Demand by Agricultural Producers." Unpublished M.S. thesis, Department of Agricultural Economics, University of Arizona, 1986. (Hereinafter cited as "Estimating Wastewater Demand").

16. A. Tumbling T. Ranches v. City of Phoenix, et. al.,(Arizona, 1983). (Hereinafter cited as "A. Tumbling T. Ranches").

17. Goldammer, "Estimating Wastewater Demand."

18. Tucson Water. Master Plan and Ten Year Capital Improvement Program, 1987-1997, p. 17. November 5, 1986. Tucson, Arizona.

19. Ibid.

20. Personal conversation with George Parker, City Property Manager, Tucson, Arizona. 1985.

21. Personal conversation with Karl Kohlhoff, Water Resource Management Coordinator, City of Mesa, Arizona. 1986.

22. "Pinal County Farmers Selling Mesa Land for Water Rights." Arizona Farmer Stockman vol. 65, no. 8 (1986), p. 6-7.

23. Personal conversation with David Ulfers of Duco, Inc., Tucson, Arizona, 1986.

24. Personal conversation with Mike McNulty, attorney, Tucson, Arizona, 1985.

25. Personal conversation with Steve Rossi, Water Resources Specialist, Arizona Department of Water Resources, Tucson, Arizona, 1986.

26. Personal conversation with Carrol Reynolds, Project Engineer, City of Phoenix Water Department, Phoenix, Arizona, 1986.

178

27. James M. Montgomery, <u>City of Phoenix Water Resources Study, McMullen Valley</u>. Report of Consulting Engineers, Inc., Phoenix, Arizona, December, 1986.

28. Personal conversation with Leonard Dueker, Executive Assistant to the City Manager, Scottsdale, Arizona, 1985.

29. <u>Ibid</u>.

30. Dee Michaelis, and Steve Webb, "Water to Sustain Growth." <u>The Arizona Republic</u>, June 30, 1985, p. C1-C2.

31. City of Tucson Mayor and Council Resolution 11955, "Generalized Effluent Reuse Policies," July 6, 1982, Tucson, Arizona.

32. City of Tucson Ordinance No. 6411, "Schedule of Rates and Charges." April 23, 1986, Tucson, Arizona.

33. "A. Tumbling T. Ranches."

34. "Nuke Plant Will Pay Market Price". <u>U.S. Water News</u> Vol. 1, No. 12 (1985). 1985.

35. California Department of Water Resources, <u>Water for California: Outlook in 1970</u>. Bulletin 160-170, 1970. (Hereinafter cited as "Outlook in 1970").

36. L.D. Schelhorse, P. Zimmerman, J.W. Milliman, D.L. Shapiro, and L.F. Weschler, <u>The Market Structure of the Southern California Water Industry</u>. Report prepared by Copley International Corporation. La Jolla, California, for the Office of Water Resources Research, U.S. Department of the Interior, 1974.

37. California Department of Water Resources. "Outlook in 1970."

38. Clifford T. Lee, "The Transfer of Water Rights in California: Background and Issues." Governor's Commission to Review California Water Rights Law, staff paper no. 5 (1977).

39. J.C. Bliss and Samuel Imperati, "The Legal Aspects of Appropriative Water Rights Transfers in California." <u>Davis Law Journal</u>. vol. 11, p. 441.

40. David L. Jacquette and Nancy Y. Moore, <u>Efficient Water Use in California: Groundwater Use and Management</u>. Rand Corporation, 1978.

41. N.Y. Moore, H. Graubard, and R. Shishko. <u>Efficient Water Use in California: Water Rights, Water Districts, and Water Transfers</u>. Rand Corporation, 1978.

42. <u>Ibid</u>.

43. California State Assembly. AB-3491, 1982; AB-1029, 1985; and AB-2746, 1986.

44. R.W. Wahl and R.K. Davis, "Satisfying Southern California's Thirst for Water: Alternatives." In <u>Scarce Water and Institutional Change</u>, ed. Kenneth Frederick.

Resources for the Future, Inc., Washington, D.C., 1986. (Hereinafter referred to as "Southern California").

45. Ibid.

46. Robert Potter, presentation at "Buying and Selling Water in California," UCLA Extension Public Policy Conference, Santa Monica, 1986. Also personal conversation, 1986. (Hereinafter cited as "Buying and Selling Water in California.")

47. Water Market Update vol. 1, no. 3, p. 1.

48. Potter, "Buying and Selling Water in California".

49. Wahl and Davis. "Southern California."

50. Water Market Update. vol. 1, no 1, p. 2.

51. Ibid.

52. Water Market Update, March, 1987. p. 2.

53. Ibid., p. 3.

54. Don Miles, Salinity in the Arkansas Valley of Colorado. Cooperative Extension Service, Colorado State University, May, 1977.

55. Rules and Regulations accepted by resolution of the Board of Directors, Northern Colorado Water Conservancy District, December 14, 1956.

56. Andy Hollar, Six Cities Background Information. Department of Utilities, Boulder (Colorado), 1984.

57. Water Allocation Policy, as amended by Southeastern Colorado Water Conservancy District, Pueblo, Colorado, October 22, 1981.

58. Personal conversation with John Dingess, Special Council in the City Attorney's Office, Aurora, Colorado, 1985.

59. Personal conversation with Don Miles, Extension Irrigation Engineer, Cooperative Extension Service, Rocky Ford, Colorado, 1985.

60. Colo. Rev. Stat. Vol. 15, Title 37.

61. Personal conversation with Jeff Heden, Water Resources Planning Engineer, Loveland, Colorado, 1985.

62. John R. Chalmers, "Southwestern Groundwater Law." Arid Lands Resource Information Paper No. 4. University of Arizona Press, Tucson. (Hereinafter cited as "Southwestern Groundwater Law").

63. Personal conversation with Bob Jesse, Division Engineer, Colorado Department of Natural Resources, Pueblo, 1985.

64. Personal conversation with John Dingess.

65. Raymond Anderson, "The Effect of Stream Flow Variation on Production and Income of Irrigated Farms Under the Doctrine of Prior Appropriation." U.S. Department of Agriculture, Economic Research Service, 1977.

180

66. Water Allocation Policy, as amended by Southeastern Colorado Water Conservancy District, Pueblo,
Colorado, October 22, 1981.
67. Personal conversation with Charles "Tommy" Thompson, General Manager, Southeastern Colorado Water
Conservancy District, Pueblo, Colorado, 1985.
68. Ibid.
69. "Operating Plan: Winter Water Plan 1985-1986,"
Southeastern Colorado Water Conservancy District, Pueblo,
Colorado, November, 1985.
70. Repayment contract between the Bureau of Reclamation and the Northern Colorado Water Conservancy District,
Loveland, Colorado, 1938. (Hereinafter cited as "Repayment
Contract.")
71. Craig Harrison. "Colorado Water Marketing: The
Experience of a Water Broker." Presented at the annual
meetings of the Western Agricultural Economics Association, San Diego, July, 1984. (Hereinafter cited as
"Colorado Water Marketing").
72. Bureau of Reclamation, "Repayment Contract."
73. Current and historical data on annual assessments
charged to holders of C-BT units, and data on the holdings
of C-BT units by user class, are available from the
Northern Colorado Water Conservancy District office in
Loveland, Colorado.
74. C.W. Howe, D. Schurmeier, and W. Shaw, "Innovations in Water Management: An Ex-Post Analysis of the
Colorado-Big Thompson Project and the NCWCD." Unpublished
manuscript, Department of Economics, University of
Colorado, Boulder. (Hereinafter cited as "Innovations in
Water Management.")
75. Ibid.
76. Annual Report, North Poudre Irrigation Company,
Wellington, Colorado, 1984.
77. Personal conversation with Jim Rees, realtor,
Rees & Company, Fort Collins, Colorado, 1985. Mr. Rees
referred to an unpublished manuscript prepared by Harold
Menzel, called "Northeastern Colorado Irrigation Rights",
written in 1979.
78. Harrison, "Colorado Water Marketing."
79. Ibid.
80. Personal conversation with Dale Hill, City Manager, Estes Park, Colorado, 1985.
81. Personal conversation with Andy Hollar, Director
of Utilities, Boulder, Colorado, 1985.
82. Howe, et. al., "Innovations in Water Management."
83. Personal conversation with John Dingess.

84. Personal conversation with Don Miles.
85. Colorado District Court, Water Division No. 2, Case No. W-3965. Twin Lakes Reservoir and Canal Company. April 19, 1974.
86. Personal conversation with Don Miles.
87. Personal conversation with Charles Concer, City Water Resources Planner, Colorado Springs, Colorado, 1985.
88. Ibid.
89. Personal conversation with Frank Bustamento, City Manager, Fountain, Colorado, 1985.
90. Personal conversation with Roger "Bud" O'Hara, Engineering Division Manager, Board of Water Works, Pueblo, Colorado, 1985.
91. Ibid.
92. Water rental records for Twin Lakes Stock, 1982-1985, Pueblo West Metropolitan District.
93. Personal conversation with Doug Kemper, Project Engineer, Utilities Department, Aurora, Colorado, 1987.
94. Personal conversation with Arlo Beamon, Jones Healy Agency, Pueblo, Colorado, 1986.
95. Ibid.
96. Personal conversation with Frank Milenski, President, Catlin Canal Company, La Junta, Colorado, 1985.
97. Personal conversation with Gary Stone, Federal Watermaster for the Truckee and Carson Rivers, Reno, Nevada, 1985.
98. John G. McNeeley, Economic and Institutional Aspects of Water Transfers in Northwest Nevada, Agricultural Experiment Station Bulletin No. 27, University of Nevada, 1971. (Hereinafter cited as "Water Transfers").
99. Personal conversation with Rick Moser, Water Resources Engineer, Sierra Pacific Power Company, Reno, 1985.
100. McNeeley, "Water Transfers."
101. Personal conversation with Rick Moser.
102. Nev. Rev. Stat., Title 48, Chs. 533 and 534.
103. Chalmers, "Southwestern Groundwater Law."
104. Personal conversation with Rick Moser.
105. U.S. v. Orr Ditch Company, et al., U.S. District Court, Nevada, Docket A3, 1944. See also "Truckee River Agreement Between the United States of America, the Truckee-Carson Irrigation District, the Washoe County Water Conservation District, the Sierra Pacific Power Company, et. al., July, 1935. (Hereinafter cited as "Truckee River Decrees and Agreements."
106. Personal conversation with Gary Stone.
107. Truckee River Decrees and Agreements.

108. Personal conversation with Gary Stone.

109. McNeeley, "Water Transfers."

110. Personal conversation with Gary Stone.

111. Personal conversation with Lyman McConnell, Manager, Truckee-Carson Irrigation District, Fallon, Nevada, 1985.

112. Personal conversation with Gary Stone.

113. U.S. vs. Alpine Land and Reservoir Company, U.S. District Court, Nevada, Case No. D-183, 1983. Appeal Pending.

114. Ibid. Also, personal conversation with Lyman McConnell.

115. Personal conversation with Tim Holt, Engineer, Nevada Public Service Commission, Carson City, 1985.

116. Robert Firth. "Policy statement regarding expansion of Sierra Pacific Power Company's Water Service Territory." Presented to the Nevada Public Service Commission, Carson City, August 24, 1979.

117. Personal conversation with Sandy Landeck, City Property Management Specialist, Sparks, Nevada, 1985.

118. Nevada Public Service Commission. Rule 17, Docket No. 81-204 (February 8, 1982). Revised, Docket No. 84-665 (November 19, 1984).

119. City of Reno. Agenda Report No. 85-70, February 11, 1985. See also City of Sparks, Municipal Code, Section 17.12.075.

120. Personal conversation with Rick Moser.

121. Nevada State Senate Bill 323, 1983.

122. Personal conversation with Sandy Landeck.

123. Personal conversation with John Collins, Chief Sanitary Engineer for Washoe County, Reno, Nevada, 1985.

124. Ibid.

125. Personal conversation with Tim Holt.

126. Personal conversation with Louis Test, attorney, Reno, Nevada, 1985.

127. Personal conversation with Rick Moser.

128. Memorandum: Tim Holt, Engineer, Nevada Public Service Commission, Carson City, to members of the Public Service Commission, concerning the availability of water rights in the Truckee Meadows, March, 1985.

129. Personal conversation with Robert Firth, Manager of Gas and Water Engineering and Planning, Sierra Pacific Power Company, Reno, 1985.

130. Personal conversation with Sandy Landeck.

131. Sierra Pacific Power Company, Gas and Water Engineering and Planning Department, 1985-2005 Water

<u>Resource Plan</u>. Reno, 1985. Also, personal conversation with Rick Moser.

132. Personal conversation with Rick Moser.

133. <u>Ibid</u>.

134. Robert Emmet Clark, <u>New Mexico Water Resources Law</u>. University of New Mexico Press: Albuquerque, 1964.

135. Linda G.Harris, "New Mexico Water Rights." Miscellaneous Report No. 15, New Mexico Water Resources Research Institute, New Mexico State University, Las Cruces.

136. <u>Ibid</u>.

137. <u>State of Arizona</u> vs. <u>State of California</u>. U.S. Supreme Court, March 9, 1964. See also Grant County District Court, Cause Nos. 16290 and 16610, August 23, 1967.

138. <u>Ibid</u>.

139. Personal conversation with David Alison, Office of the State Engineer, Deming, New Mexico, 1985.

140. <u>Ibid</u>.

141. Personal conversation with Hilton Dickson, City Attorney, Silver City, New Mexico, 1985.

142. Personal conversation with Frank Westrick, consulting engineer, Deming, New Mexico, 1985.

143. Personal conversation with David Alison.

144. Personal conversation with Joe Smith, Division of Advanced Planning, Bureau of Reclamation, Phoenix, Arizona, 1986.

145. Personal conversation with Lamar Mahler, realtor, Reserve, New Mexico, 1987.

146. Records of water rights options contracts and transfers of title of water rights to Exxon and Boliden, excluding price data, are available from the Grant County Clerk's Office in Silver City, New Mexico.

147. Personal conversation with Thomas Shoemaker, City Engineer, Silver City, New Mexico, 1985.

148. Town of Silver City, New Mexico, "Agreement between Randolf Franks Katherine B. Franks, and Maggie Franks and the Town of Silver City," July 30, 1945.

149. Town of Silver City, New Mexico, "Agreement between Walter W. Woodward and Marvel Woodward and the Town of Silver City, February 19, 1954.

150. Memorandum: Salvador Morales, Silver City Manager, to Hilton Dickson, December 20, 1983.

151. Town of Silver City, New Mexico. "Agreement between the Exxon Corporation and the Town of Silver City," August 31, 1984.

152. Town of Silver City, New Mexico, "Agreement between Marvin C. Glenn and Ethel M. Glenn and the Town of Silver City, October 18, 1982.

153. Personal conversation with Thomas Shoemaker.

154. Personal conversation with Warren Tenney, Secretary-Manager for the DMAD companies, Delta, Utah, 1985.

155. Personal conversation with Roger Walker, Lower Sevier River Commissioner, Delta, Utah, 1985.

156. Arthur Maas and Raymond Anderson, ...And the Desert Shall Rejoice. Cambridge: MIT Press, 1978.

157. Dee C. Hansen, "Policy Statement on Underground Water Appropriation in the Delta Area, Millard County." Staff memorandum, Utah Department of Natural Resources and Energy, Division of Water Resources, Salt Lake City, November 8, 1982.

158. Personal conversation with Kirk Forbush, Assistant Area Engineer, Utah Division of Water Resources, Richfield, Utah, 1985.

159. Richlands Irrigationl Company vs. West View Irrigation Company. Fifth District Court of Utah, Case No. 843, 1936.

160. Agreement made by Delta Canal Company, Melville Irrigation Company, Deseret Irrigation Company, Central Utah Irrigation Company and Abraham Irrigation Company, (referred to as Sevier Bridge Reservoir Owners) and the Paiute Reservoir and Irrigation Company, October 18, 1938.

161. Personal conversation with N. S. Bassett, former Secretary-Manager of the DMAD companies, Delta, Utah, 1985.

162. Personal conversation with Thorpe Waddingham, attorney, Delta, Utah, 1985.

163. Personal conversation with Roger Walker.

164. Personal conversation with Warren Tenney.

165. Intermountain Power Agency, "Stock Purchase Contract," Delta, Utah, November, 1980.

166. Personal conversation with Joseph Novak, attorney for the Intermountain Power Association, Salt Lake City, Utah, 1985.

167. Joint Venture, "Joint Venture Agreement", Delta, Utah, December 27, 1979.

168. Personal conversation with Alan Neilson, groundwater rights sales coordinator for the Joint Venture, Lynndyl, Utah, 1985.

169. Ibid.

170. Intermountain Power Agency, Municipal Water Rights Acquisition Agreement. Delta, Utah, August 9, 1982.

171. Personal conversation with Neil Forster, Director of Public Works, Delta, Utah, 1985.

172. Personal conversation with Keith Taylor, attorney, Salt Lake City, 1985.

173. Personal conversation with Manuel Perez, Management Engineer for the Intermountain Power Project, Delta, Utah, 1985.

174. Clyde E. Stewart, "Operations of the Utah Rental Market, Delta Area, Utah." U.S. Department of Agriculture, Economic Research Service, 1965.

175. Richard L. Gardner and Thomas A. Miller, "Price Behavior in the Water Market of Northeastern Colorado." Water Resources Bulletin, vol. 19, (1983) p. 57-562.

176. Water Market Update, April, 1987, p. 13.

177. Ibid., p. 14.

Part Three

Water Transfers, Water Values, and Public Policy

6
Valuing Water Rights for
Public and Private Decision Making

INTRODUCTION

Information on the value of water rights is relevant in both public and private decision making. Examples of situations in which an estimate of water's value would be useful include a farmer deciding whether to sell water rights or to continue using them for irrigation, a city evaluating whether to buy senior appropriative rights to firm up their supplies, a federal agency conducting a cost benefit analysis of a water development proposal, a court assessing the monetary damages associated with impairment of a vested surface water right or an environmental organization seeking to purchase appropriative water rights for instream flow protection.

Comparison of water's value in alternative uses and locations assists public water agencies in making better decisions about management and allocation of publicly supplied water. Some water uses are competing rather than complementary (instream flow maintenance and irrigation diversions, for instance), and information on water's value in alternative uses can be used to estimate the opportunity costs of allocating water to a particular use. Public agencies often use benefit cost analysis in their agency decision making process. Information on water values can contribute to better comparisons of the benefits and costs of water-related projects and policies.

Private businesses and individuals seek to estimate the value of water rights they already own, as well as the value of rights they are considering for purchase, lease or appropriation. Individuals investing in water rights want to know what factors are likely to affect future water values. Real estate professionals, economists, engineers and attorneys are being asked more frequently to place a value on water rights. However, little material has been published on water rights appraisal and valuation approaches are far from standardized.

In this discussion, a distinction is made between private and social measures of value. Under competitive market conditions, the price negotiated between a buyer and a seller of a water right reflects the marginal value of the units of water exchanged and thus can serve as an indicator of water value for the parties involved in the transaction. A social measure of value, however, should also take into account impacts on those affected by the transaction who were not part of the price negotiation process. This could include neighboring well owners whose pumping costs are adversely affected, fishermen whose trout habitat is disrupted, or local governments that experience declining tax bases when water sales shift resources out of the local economy. Ideally, a measure of water value used by a public agency to evaluate water-related policies and projects should fully reflect potential beneficiaries' willingness to pay for incremental changes in water quantity or quality available for various uses, as well as any positive or negative third-party impacts. Market prices will seldom provide this ideal measure of social value. Private individuals are more likely to be interested in the value of water in specific uses such as irrigation or municipal water supply and market prices can often be helpful in estimating these values.

This chapter first discusses the limitations of market prices as a measure of water's value, describing market conditions which can prevent prices from accurately reflecting social water values. Readers who are interested in a practical discussion of valuing water may wish to skip to the next section in which practical considerations encountered in collecting and interpreting market data are summarized. In the following section, market and non-market approaches to valuing water rights are described, drawing on real estate appraisal techniques and approaches used by economists to value water and nonmarket resources. The chapter concludes with a brief summary of water's value in alternative uses in the Southwest.

MARKET PRICES AS MEASURES OF VALUE

This section outlines economic concepts helpful in understanding the role of market prices as measures of

value and identifies three sources of concern regarding
the use of market prices as measures of water values. The
first set of concerns are limitations emphasized in
economic theory on prices as measures of value under perfectly competitive market conditions. The second set of
concerns involve the impact of imperfect markets on prices
as measures of social value. The third set of concerns
involve practical considerations that would confront those
seeking to use market prices as measures of value.

Limitations in a Competitive Market Setting

Prices in a perfectly functioning competitive market
will reveal buyers' willingness to pay for the marginal
(the last) unit purchased. Figure 6.1 shows a hypothetical
regional demand function for water at a fixed point in
time. The negative slope reflects the fact that, in a
competitive market setting, the first quantities of water
available to a region would be applied to uses for which
the highest returns can be obtained. Additional water
would be applied to the next most profitable set of water
uses, and so on. Given a supply curve represented by S_1,
the market clearing price for water occurs at P_1. Note
that the market price lies <u>above</u> the unit value water
users would place on additional supplies if the supply
curve shifted out to S_2. Willingness to pay for additional units of water could be substantially lower than
P_1, depending on the shape of the total demand curve to
the right of Q_1. Data on current water demand, given
existing supplies, may provide little information on willingness to pay for additional supplies. As figure 6.1
illustrates, even in a perfectly competitive market, observed prices serve only as an upper limit for what
current market participants might be willing to pay for
additional supplies.

Figure 6.1 portrays water demand, supply, and market
price formation in a static framework. As population, income levels, agricultural commodity prices or production
technologies in water-using industries change, demand and
supply curves shift and new prices evolve. Prices emerging
from current demand and supply relationships and market
exchanges could either overestimate or underestimate the
marginal value of water in the future. While current price
levels do reflect buyers' and sellers' expectations
regarding future water values, the predictive power of
current market prices is limited by the imperfect ability
of market participants to anticipate shifts in water

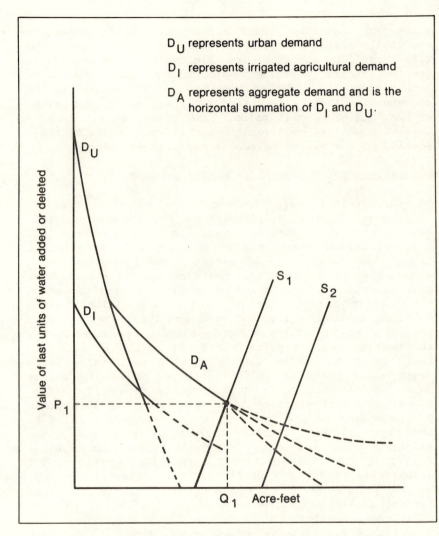

D_U represents urban demand

D_I represents irrigated agricultural demand

D_A represents aggregate demand and is the horizontal summation of D_I and D_U.

Figure 6.1   Limitations of Current Market Prices
            as Measures of Value.

supply and demand over time. The implications of imperfect information and uncertainty for prices as measures of
value are discussed below.

Imperfect Markets and Prices as Measures of Value

In a smoothly functioning competitive water market,
price is uniquely determined by convergence of buyers' and
sellers' marginal values. However, in actual market transactions, a negotiated price will lie between the buyer's
maximum willingness to pay for units of water exchanged
and the minimum amount the seller is willing to accept in
payment for water transferred. In a transfer from a farmer
to a city water supply organization, for example, the
lowest price acceptable to a farmer (the reserve price)
would be based on the marginal value product of water in
agriculture if a small proportion of his rights are sold
or the average value product if rights for the whole farm
are sold.[1]   Farmers may view water rights as an
appreciating asset and add speculative value to their
reserve price, as Gardner and Miller find in their
analysis of Colorado water market transactions.[2]
Young   notes that only a small fraction of agricultural water use is influenced by urban demands expressed
through market processes.[3]   Much irrigation water is
supplied under public project contracts and is insulated
from market pressures since the water is not readily
marketable or is not attractive to urban buyers because it
would be expensive to deliver and treat for municipal uses
compared to alternative sources of supply. Under these
circumstances, market prices will lie above the marginal
value of water in irrigation. Gardner and Miller's study
and Young's observation both imply that there is not
necessarily a close relationship between water's value in
crop production and market prices negotiated in
agricultural-to-urban water transfers. Use of market
prices to value new water supplies for irrigation would
significantly overestimate the value of the additional
water.

Many additional considerations may prevent observed
prices from representing social water values. Externalities, public goods, imperfect competition and market
restrictions, risk, uncertainty and imperfect information
were concepts introduced in Chapter 2's discussion on deviations from the competitive market model. They are
discussed in this chapter, along with equity and conflict

resolution, in the context of their implications for market water prices as measures of water values.

The first four concerns relate to the efficiency of prices generated in imperfect markets. First, if water transfers positively or negatively affect third parties and these effects (externalities) are not taken into account in market decisions, then prices will not reflect social values. Second, market prices represent the marginal value of water only to the extent that those prices represent all water uses and values. Prices are unlikely to reflect values for instream water uses, such as recreation and provision of aquatic habitat which have public good characteristics. Third, if one or more water users, suppliers or government agencies can significantly affect prices or restrict transfers (imperfect competition) then observed prices may deviate from maximum willingness to pay for additional units of water. Fourth, imperfect information regarding water availability can distort market prices, as can uncertainty regarding government programs and policies relevant to transfers.

The fifth concern involves equity and conflict resolution in water resource allocation. Prices generated in water markets inevitably reflect the prevailing income distribution and allocation of water rights. In public elections each citizen receives one vote to influence the outcome of the election. In water markets, participants "vote" with their dollars and water rights to influence the outcome of the market allocation process. Water users with more water rights and dollars have more votes in the marketplace than those with less water or money. Therefore, public agency use of market prices to measure water's value may not be consistent with distributional and conflict resolution policy objectives for a particular region. Controversies regarding native American water rights in the Southwest illustrate the need for attention to equity and conflict resolution issues.

External Effects of Market Activities. State policies that address transfer externalities were described in Chapter 4. State water transfer policies are designed primarily to protect vested water rights rather than to protect water interests not represented by vested water rights. Groups which may be affected by a water transfer but whose interests are typically not represented by vested water rights include area-of-origin residents, water-based recreationists and wildlife and environmental interests. Market prices will not reflect negative side effects of transfers unless policies require market par-

ticipants to consider those impacts in their transfer
negotiations. Therefore the legal framework governing
market transfers is critical in determining which types of
externalities are accounted for in market transactions and
which are not.

Beneficial effects of market activity on third
parties do occur. For example, transfer of Colorado-Big
Thompson units from irrigators to cities (which have lower
consumptive use and are upstream of irrigated areas) has
increased return flows for users located downstream from
the cities. In valuing incremental changes in water
availability due to public policies, the magnitude of
negative or positive externalities associated with market
activity ought to be evaluated and market prices adjusted
accordingly if they are to be used as measures of value in
public decision making.

Public Goods Characteristics of Water Resources.
Public goods are resources and commodities characterized
by non-rivalry in consumption, meaning they can simultaneously provide benefits to more than one individual. In
addition they may be characterized by non-excludability,
meaning it is difficult or impossible to exclude those who
do not pay from enjoying the benefits of the resource.
Either one of these properties pose difficulties for the
market allocation mechanism and prevent market prices from
accurately reflecting all values associated with water
resources.

If individuals cannot be excluded from enjoying a
good if they do not pay, then prices will not ration the
commodity among individuals. Prices perform their
rationing function by excluding those who are not willing
to pay the going rate. One means of financing the provision of nonexcludable goods is through voluntary payments.
For instance, public radio and wildlife habitat preservation are partially supported by voluntary donations to
nonprofit organizations. However, voluntary payments are
unlikely to represent the "buyers'" actual willingness to
pay to enjoy the good. Many individuals who do place a
positive value on the resource may be "free riders",
enjoying the good but making no payments or contributing
payments that under-represent their values. Another means
to finance the provision of nonexcludable goods is through
mandatory payments. Many nonexcludable public goods are
provided by government agencies and are financed through
tax revenues. However, the share of an individual's tax
payments that supports a particular public good is not
reflective of that individual's values for the good. Tax

payments to support nonexcludable public goods are necessarily arbitrary and unrelated to actual use and value
associated with the resource. Some authors have referred
to such payments as "forced ridership".(4) Financing of
non-excludable public goods is a choice between two
inefficient alternatives, free ridership (voluntary contributions) and forced ridership (mandatory contributions), neither of which provides information on the
values individuals actually place on the good.

Even if a public good is excludable so that a price
can be charged for use, the non-rivalry characteristic
still poses difficulties for the market process and for
use of prices as measures of value. Several users can
simultaneously derive benefits from a non-rival good but
they will generally derive differing levels of benefits
depending on their own tastes and preferences. Therefore
each ought to pay a different price at the margin, that
price which corresponds to the value they place on the
last unit of the resource consumed. Such a pricing scheme
would equate price paid with marginal benefits received
for each user, but would be difficult to implement. Individuals would have to provide information on the value
they derive from the good in order to determine the price
they should pay and would have strong incentives to under-
represent their actual values in order to reduce their
payment. To further complicate matters, any pricing
scheme for non-rival goods which excludes individuals who
experience positive benefits from use of the good is inefficient because each individual's benefits from the good
add to the total benefits generated by the good. Use of an
entry fee to exclude anyone who receives positive marginal
benefits reduces the total benefits. Payments made to
enjoy non-rival goods, like those for non-excludable
goods, are unlikely to provide useful information on
individuals' actual willingness to pay to enjoy the good.

Non-consumptive water uses are particularly likely to
have public goods characteristics. The aesthetic, environmental and recreation amenities provided by rivers, lakes
and reservoirs are non-rival in the sense that they can
simultaneously provide different kinds of benefits to many
different individuals. Prices charged for water-based
recreation, in the form of entry fees, provide little
information on the value users place on the water
resource. Instream water uses are rarely represented in
market transactions for several reasons. First, the characteristics of non-rivalry and nonexcludability make it
difficult to organize potential beneficiaries of instream

flow purchases and to raise funds with which to purchase
water rights for instream flow maintenance. Second, as
discussed in Chapter 4, many states do not allow private
organizations to hold water rights for the purpose of
maintaining instream flows. If water rights are purchased
for lake level or instream flow maintenance, the price
paid will not represent total willingness to pay by all
potential beneficiaries due to the free ridership
phenomenon and the difficulty of collecting contributions
from all who would benefit.

Consumptive water uses may also have some public good
characteristics. Irrigated fields provide an attractive
green belt around urban areas and may provide habitat for
wildlife. Use of water for landscaping in industrial
complexes, public parks and private residences may increase the value of nearby properties and provide
aesthetic benefits to neighbors and passersby. These aesthetic impacts have value although, due to the nonexcludability characteristic, it would be difficult to collect
or even measure the benefits conferred. Market prices paid
for water rights for consumptive uses--agricultural,
municipal and industrial use, will not reflect all values
generated by consumptive uses if some values are characterized by nonrivalry or nonexcludability.

Nonmarket valuation approaches have been developed in
an attempt to value public goods, including recreational
and aesthetic aspects of water resources. These will be
discussed in a subsequent section of this chapter.

Imperfect Competition. A market is imperfectly
competitive when the actions of one or more buyers or
sellers can influence market price levels. The market
areas studied differ tremendously in numbers of buyers and
sellers, relative influence of particular buyers and
sellers and frequency of transactions.

In both the Truckee River and the Lower Sevier River
Basins, large utility companies are dominant water right
holders and market participants. In the Gila-San Francisco
Basin and in the neighboring Mimbres Basin, a few large
mining companies own a significant proportion of area
water rights. It is not possible to identify precisely
the effects that dominant buyers or sellers have on
prices. In some cases, they seem to function as price
setters, giving price signals that are followed by other
market participants. Water rights prices rose temporarily
in the Sevier River Basin in response to higher than
typical prices paid by Intermountain Power Project between
1980 and 1982. Exxon's major purchases in the Gila-San

Francisco Basin during the 1970s stimulated a price increase. However, in the Truckee River Basin, efforts by Sierra Pacific in the early 1980s and recent efforts by the cities of Reno and Sparks to purchase selected water rights at reduced prices have not affected market prices noticeably.

In using market prices as measure of value, the impact of dominant buyers and sellers needs to be evaluated on a case-by-case basis. If there is a consistent and significant discrepancy between prices emerging from negotiations involving the large volume buyers and sellers and negotiations that do not involve them, then further study will be necessary to determine reasons for the discrepancies and to identify which prices (if any) are an appropriate reflection of water values.

Both the numbers of buyers and sellers and the frequency of transactions affect the quantity of price data available. A specific price may be a more reliable measure of water value if there are a large number of transactions that confirm that price as typical. In a region with sporadic market activity and price data, use of market prices should be supplemented with non-market information to estimate water values.

Imperfect competition may result not only from the presence of a dominant buyer or seller, but also from public policy. The seven market areas studied differ in the degree and nature of legal restrictions on market transfers. For instance, in Utah water rights represented by irrigation company stock are readily transferable within the service areas of the DMAD companies and need not be tied to a specific parcel of land. In contrast, transfer of surface water irrigation rights in Arizona requires a sever and transfer proceeding with the State Department of Water Resources. Neither groundwater nor surface water irrigation rights can be transferred separately from the land. Within any given market area, different water rights may be subject to different guidelines on change of ownership, purpose of use, location, and leasing. For example, Type II nonirrigation rights in Arizona may be transferred separately from land but must be sold in their entirety. Type II right holders may not sell only a portion of their right and must make an "all or nothing" decision regarding transfers. Although Arizona irrigation rights are strictly appurtenant to land, farmers may sell portions of (rather than the entire quantity of) their land and irrigation rights. As noted in

197

the description of Colorado markets, transmountain diversion water from the Colorado-Big Thompson Project is much
more transferable than transmountain diversion water from
the Frying Pan-Arkansas Project in the southeastern part
of Colorado.

These examples illustrate the fact that generaliza-
tions among areas regarding the impacts of large buyers
and sellers and legal restrictions on transfer of water
rights must be made with caution. While none of the
markets studied could be characterized as perfectly competitive, there was very little evidence on which to
assess the degree to which imperfect competition may
distort prices as measures of value. The only guideline
that can be offered is, that where possible, prices
emerging from negotiations between many buyers and sellers
should serve as a basis for valuation, rather than prices
involving a single dominant buyer or seller.

Risk, Uncertainty and Imperfect Information. All
markets studied are characterized by varying degrees of
risk, uncertainty and imperfect information on water commodities, prices and market opportunities. The efficiency
of the competitive price system and the degree to which
prices accurately represent values assumes either that
buyers and sellers can obtain accurate information on
prices and attributes of various commodities, or that
there exist perfectly functioning contingency markets to
allocate the risks associated with not having complete
information. These conditions are fulfilled for few marketable commodities and certainly do not hold for water
markets. Instead, information sources for market participants tend to be informal and incomplete, and potential
buyers and sellers face hydrological, legal and economic
uncertainties as they make market decisions.

Arizona and Utah markets provide examples of differing access to market information. The Arizona Department
of Water Resources keeps records of Type II water rights
holders, which may help potential buyers and sellers to
find one another. There is no central clearing house for
communicating bids and offers though attorneys, real
estate professionals and others who work with water
transfers share information on transactions and opportunities in an informal network. Recorded transfers are few
in number relative to other water markets. Arizona water
markets are still in the early stages of development so
that potential buyers and sellers have little experience
and historical information on which to base expectations
about water values and market transfer processes. In the

Lower Sevier Basin, irrigation company records provide
information on ownership and rental patterns, and company
offices have served as informal clearinghouses--helping
prospective buyers, sellers, and renters to contact one
another. Historical records on the hydrologic cycle of
the river system and operating criteria for storage and
release in Sevier Basin reservoirs give water users a
basis on which to form expectations about future water
availability and market price levels.

Hydrologic uncertainty is inevitable in areas dependent on surface water since supplies cannot be accurately
estimated each year until winter snowpacks are studied to
predict spring runoff and river flows. This uncertainty
is mitigated to varying degrees by storage facilities and
inter-basin diversion projects. One of the principal
objectives of the Colorado-Big Thompson Project is to
reduce uncertainty associated with erratic and seasonal
surface water flow. Uncertainty affects groundwater
markets when there is incomplete knowledge on aquifer
capacity, rates of groundwater overdraft, and other
factors that affect expectations regarding the long-term
availability and expense of pumping groundwater.

Hydrologic uncertainty affects how much individuals
are willing to pay for a water right. Senior surface water
rights generally sell for higher prices than junior
surface water rights that are more vulnerable to seasonal
and year-to-year variations in flow. For example, the
Sierra Pacific Power Company made price offers for Truckee
River water rights based on their priority dates--with the
most junior rights valued 25 percent less than the most
senior rights.(5)

Uncertainty regarding future water demand and the
vitality of regional economies and water-using industries
is inevitable and affects price levels. Water prices rose
sharply in the Lower Sevier Basin with expectations that
Intermountain Power Project's new power plant would bring
increased population and increased water demand. Prices
dropped off when the power plant and development boom
turned out to be much smaller than anticipated. The short-
run marginal value of water to irrigators rises and falls
with crop prices. The interest of mining firms and other
industries in acquiring water rights fluctuates with the
profitability of those industries. Economic uncertainty
affects market prices because prices reflect economic
expectations and conditions. With respect to valuing
water, this implies that one needs to be aware of economic
trends that influence market prices. A short-run rise in

prices due to expectations that a new industry may enter
the area would not be a good indicator of water values
until prices stabilize after expectations either are or
are not realized. In contrast, a long-term price effect
due to stagnation of a water-using industry (copper mining
in parts of the Southwest, for example) should be taken
into account when estimating water values in the affected
region.

Equity and Conflict Resolution. Allocation of water
to a specific area or group of water users may have
political value in resolving water resource conflicts,
above and beyond measurable economic value generated by
new supplies. Both the Central Arizona and the Central
Utah Projects are viewed by some observers as strategies
for resolving conflicts among water users rather than as
economically defensible water supply augmentation measures. The Central Arizona Project and Colorado's Animas
La Plata Project play a key role in resolving native
American water claims. Supply development and water reallocation undertaken for the purpose of providing water to
tribes have conflict resolution value from several
perspectives. First they are an attempt to address the
failure of past policies to recognize tribal water rights
and thus have value from an equity perspective. Second,
unresolved native American claims create significant uncertainties for non-Indian water right holders, the quantity and priority of whose rights may be affected by implementation of tribal rights, as discussed in Chapter 4.
Clarification of tribal water rights will benefit non-
Indian right holders by allowing them to form secure
expectations regarding their access to water in light of
tribal rights, reducing the uncertainty associated with
their rights. These types of conflict resolution values
are not reflected in market prices for water rights and
are difficult to incorporate in economic evaluations of
water projects and water transfers. They are, however,
reflected in political negotiations that determine which
projects and transfers are implemented and which are not.

Water transfers often are a lower cost alternative
for providing water to a particular area or group of water
users, compared to new supply development. However,
policies that encourage market transfers from one sector
to another (agriculture to cities, for instance) may
involve political and social costs as income, employment,
and tax base shift when water moves from one sector to
another. Public agencies sometimes go ahead with supply
enhancement projects when market transfers would be a

lower cost alternative. In these situations it could be inferred that those making decisions perceive the social and political costs of water transfers as "too high" and consider the conflict resolution provided by a supply development project to be worth the "price"--the costs of supply augmentation in excess of the less costly transfer alternative. Market prices will not reflect the political conflicts associated with water transfers and, where these are a serious concern, they need to be addressed separately from a conventional cost benefit analysis of water transfer proposals.

To summarize, there are several potential problems in considering water market prices as measures of value. First, in an ideal market the observed price represents market participants' willingness to pay for the marginal unit of water currently available and provides little information about future water values and values of those who do not participate in market transactions. Second, market activities may generate externalities--impacts of water use and transfer poorly reflected in market prices. Third, many water uses have public good characteristics and market prices poorly measure water values in these uses. Fourth, observed prices may be influenced to varying degrees by imperfect competition and by legal, hydrologic and economic uncertainties. Finally, market prices will not reflect the value of conflict resolution provided by proposed water projects or the political conflicts associated with proposed water transfers. Equity and conflict resolution impacts require and deserve separate attention in water policy evaluation.

Practical Considerations in Using Market Prices

Assuming that there are no a priori reasons to suppose that market prices are not an appropriate measure of water values, what practical problems are encountered in using market prices to value water?

The diversity of institutional and economic settings in which market activities occur affects the practicality of using prices as measures of value. First, prices emerging in one market setting will not necessarily be relevant to water values in a different area. Second, even within the same market region, prices observed for one type of water right do not necessarily convey useful information about the value of a different type of water right. This underscores the importance of identifying the legal and economic conditions which influence market

activity. If market prices are used to establish the
value of a water right or of new water supplies they
should be prices that emerge from transactions involving
water rights that resemble the rights being valued.

Another difficulty involves identification and description of the various water "commodities" in the area
of study. There are many different types of water rights
with different legal and economic characteristics and
degrees of transferability in the regions analyzed in this
research. Careful study of state water law and local water
management institutions is necessary to define and differ-
entiate these commodities.

Gathering information about market prices is a time-
consuming task. Transactions must be identified from
records of state engineers or water agencies. Such records
rarely include price data, so contact must be made with
market participants or knowledgeable observers to learn
about prices associated with specific transactions. Much
effort may be needed to uncover a representative price,
though in some active market areas the prevailing price
for a certain type of water right is a matter of common
knowledge.   As noted in Chapter 3, more formal information services are evolving to provide data on market
transactions and prices.

Another practical problem involves deciding which
market prices are most appropriate for valuing specific
water rights or water supplies. In each market region,
there are many prices for water arising from various types
of transactions. In the Lower Sevier Basin, prices emerge
from rental and sales of irrigation company stocks and
occasional purchases of surface or groundwater not represented by company stocks. In Arizona, water prices arise
from sales of Type II nonirrigation rights and purchases
of farmland with appurtenant irrigation rights. Prices
vary seasonally and from year to year, as supply and
demand for water fluctuates. Which, if any, of these
prices are appropriate for valuing water? In general,
prices should be selected that most closely reflect the
conditions under which the water right or increased supplies being valued will be made available and the uses to
which the water can be applied. The price selected should
correspond to the season and the use for which the
additional water will be available. For instance, additional supplies or rights that can be used in the dry,
high-demand months will naturally have more value than the
same volume of water made available in high flow and low
demand seasons.

Every market studied is influenced to some degree by one or more of the five market imperfections discussed earlier. In addition, practical considerations in collecting and interpreting price data affect every market to varying degrees. One of the implications of this research is that observed prices, even where they are easily discoverable, should not be used as measures of value until price formation processes and market characteristics have been thoroughly studied. Such an analysis will typically find that observed prices deviate from an ideal measure of water value, suggesting that market information be supplemented by other nonmarket valuation approaches.

APPROACHES TO VALUING WATER RIGHTS

This discussion of valuation is divided into three sections. First, preliminary issues that must be addressed in water rights valuation are outlined. Second, adaptation of real estate appraisal concepts and techniques for appraising water rights are discussed. Third, nonmarket valuation approaches are described, followed by brief summaries of their application in valuing water in agricultural, municipal, industrial and nonconsumptive uses, and for valuing water quality.

Preliminary Issues in Valuing Water Rights

As is apparent from the preceding discussion, market prices may not provide relevant or appropriate measures of value and one can rarely rely on recent market prices alone to value a particular water right. Typically, valuation will involve substantial preliminary research, of which collecting data on recent market prices is only one part. A preliminary investigation involves hydrologic, legal and economic factors.

Water right valuation can be conceptualized as a two stage process. First, the characteristics of the right being appraised must be thoroughly identified and described. All characteristics which may affect the value of the right to its current owner and to potential buyers and lessors need to be evaluated. These characteristics may include long-term average and minimum (firm) yield of the right, quality of the water source and associated treatment costs for various uses, legal issues affecting the security of the right, and location of current use and costs of transferring water for an alternative location and/or use. The second step involves assessing market conditions that affect current and future water demand and supply.

Ross (6) emphasizes the importance of quantifying the historic yield of a water right and of estimating future long term average yields. He recommends converting flow rates into acre-feet per year to provide a common denominator of yield for valuation, and recommends examination of historic diversion records and consultation with experienced water resource professionals to estimate long term average yield, annual variations in yield and firm yield. The latter two characterizations of yield are of prime interest to municipal water buyers who want to know what minimum yield they can rely on in dry years. Fischer and Fischer (7) emphasize the importance of clarifying contingencies and ambiguities in water rights titles and investigating any competing claims on surface and groundwater resources associated with the right. As noted in Chapter 4, ambiguities and competing claims may come not only from other current users of the stream system or aquifer but also from federal and tribal reserved rights and evolving interpretations of the Public Trust Doctrine and of public interest language in state water codes.

Since water values are a function of supply and demand conditions, valuation must include investigation of the current cost and availability of alternatives to market transfers for satisfying water supply objectives. Are there major changes expected in regional water supplies that would affect the cost of supply alternatives? The demand side of the market also needs to be analyzed. What economic returns does water generate in alternative uses? Is demand for additional water increasing or decreasing in various sectors? Do population, income and employment trends provide any clues regarding future demand? Have water prices been based on use values for water or is there an element of speculation in the market? What expectations prevail related to regional economic growth or recession? Do these expectations affect buyer's and sellers' market decisions?

Careful hydrologic, legal and economic research is a necessary first step in valuing water rights, regardless of the valuation approaches that are taken. The expertise required may necessitate the input of engineers, hydrologists, attorneys, economists, appraisers and other professionals who are knowledgeable about the local market, water policy and hydrological, legal and economic conditions.

One final preliminary issue needs to be mentioned.
There are many different definitions of value and the
valuation process requires a clear understanding of the
type of value being estimated. The difference between
social and private values has already been addressed. A
public agency may want to value water rights in such a way
that all external and public goods values associated with
a water right or new supplies are incorporated. Private
firms most likely will wish to evaluate only the third
party impacts that they are required by law to consider.
Various types of value referred to in the real estate pro-
fession include market value, value in use, assessed
value, insurable value, and investment value. Of these,
market value serves as the basis for most appraisals.
Several variations on the definition of market value are
in circulation. For instance, the American Institute of
Real Estate Appraisers defines market value as "the most
probable price in cash, terms equivalent to cash, or in
other precisely revealed terms, for which the appraised
property will sell in a competitive market under all conditions requisite to fair sale, with the buyer and seller
each acting prudently, knowledgeably and for self-interest
and assuming that neither is under undue duress".(8) An
example of a prominent definition evolving from case law
is that provided by the California Supreme Court in an
eminent domain case. The court defined market value as
"the highest price in terms of money which a property will
bring in a competitive and open market under all conditions requisite to a fair sale, the buyer and seller each
acting prudently, knowledgeably and assuming the price is
not affected by undue stimulus."(9) While the first
definition emphasizes probable price and the second emphasizes highest price, in practice the same valuation
techniques are applied and the definitions are essentially
the same. An alternative concept of value may be relevant
in some water rights appraisals. Value in use is based
upon the productivity of an economic good to its owner or
user and is a valid substitute for market value when the
use of the good is so specialized that it has no
demonstrable market.(10) Since different concepts of
value can generate different dollar estimates, attention
needs to be given to choosing the concept of value most
suited to the purpose of the valuation and the uses that
will be made of the value estimated.

Real Estate Appraisal Approaches (11)

A number of techniques for water rights valuation
are being developed and applied in the western states.
These include sales comparisons, income capitalization,
analysis of land value differentials between parcels with
and without water, and alternative development cost
analyses.

Highest and Best Use of Transferable Water Rights
(12). Appraisals based on market value require determination of highest and best use to serve as a basis for
valuation. Highest and best use in property appraisals is
defined as the reasonable and probable use of the property
that generates the highest present value as of the
appraisal date.(13) Determining the highest and best use
of water rights can be complicated relative to making such
a determination in real estate appraisals. Water, unlike
land, not only can be applied to new uses but can often be
transferred to different locations, thereby providing a
large potential for alternative water uses and locations
that generate higher economic returns.

Determination of the highest and best use in water
rights appraisals involve questions of legal, engineering,
and economic feasibility. Proposed water transfers to
higher valued uses may encounter legal restrictions. The
feasibility of a transfer may be governed by engineering
constraints imposed by water conveyance facilities and
other physical limitations. Identification of the highest
and best use must also consider local water supply and
demand conditions. For instance, in some areas of the
West, there are more willing sellers (typically farmers
facing low commodity prices) than buyers (i.e. expanding
municipalities and industries). In such cases, appraisal
of an irrigation water right based on urban water values
as the highest and best use would fail to account for the
fact that urban buyers will purchase only a select portion
of available irrigation rights.

An appraiser must consider all the characteristics of
the water right which affect the costs of legally transferring and physically delivering the water to a higher
valued use. In order to evaluate the likelihood of the
subject property being transferred to a new use and location, transfer costs must be compared to the costs of
alternative water supplies available to potential buyers.
If alternative water sources are more expensive and thus
less attractive to buyers than transferring the appraised

water right, appraisal of the right based on a higher-valued use may be realistic.

Appraisals of irrigation rights in rural areas require assessment of the likelihood that water rights will be transferred to urban uses. In Arizona, for instance, over the last several years, Phoenix-area city governments and private businesses have purchased over 100,000 acres of farmland to acquire an estimated 300,000 acre-feet of water rights. In this market, one of the most important factors influencing the attractiveness of a specific water right to urban buyers is the cost of transporting water from its current location to Phoenix. Buyers are hoping to use the Central Arizona Project aqueduct to avoid the costs of developing their own conveyance system, and water rights appurtenant to property adjacent to the canal are in high demand. Agricultural properties located in the vicinity of the aqueduct with an estimated 100,000 acre feet of groundwater rights were purchased in 1985 and 1986 for prices ranging from $500 to $1,200 per acre foot. Specific locational patterns of water rights acquisition are emerging. Arizona law provides that an exporter of groundwater may be liable for damages imposed on other water users in the basin of origin. Hoping to avoid conflicts with other water users in the area of origin, some urban purchasers are seeking to buy out all other water rights in the basins from which they intend to export water. Thus, location in a basin where urban acquisitions have already occurred increases the chances of a specific water right being purchased for export to urban areas. In addition to these locational considerations, the attractiveness of a surface water irrigation right is influenced by its priority date, historic variability in yield and the adequacy of evidence on historical beneficial use of the right.

Analysis of the highest and best use of a water right may indicate that agriculture is an interim water use and that eventual transfer to urban use is highly probable. In making appraisals under these situations, the holding period during which the water right will remain in agriculture must be estimated and the discounted value of net returns to water in agriculture during the interim period must be calculated. Next, the value of the water in urban use during the post-conversion period (discounted back to present value) needs to be estimated and added to the sum in order to realistically appraise an agricultural water right in transition to municipal or industrial use.(14) Estimation of the holding period requires knowledge of the

rate at which water rights are being transferred in the
area around the subject property and the supply and demand
forces affecting the rate of transfer. Information on net
returns to water in agricultural uses can often be
obtained from agricultural extension specialists or county
agents, or can be inferred from comparable sales data on
water transfers between irrigators.

If an appraiser determines that an immediate transfer
to a new use and/or location is a) legally and technically
feasible, b) probable given demand and supply for water
rights in the new location and c) generates the highest
present value, then the final estimate should be based on
the new use and/or location using the sales comparison or
income capitalization approach.

Sales Comparison.(15) The sales comparison approach
involves comparison of the subject property with similar
properties which have been sold recently. Prices generated
for comparables suggest a range within which the value of
the subject property should fall. Since even similar
properties may differ in financing and other conditions of
the sale, location, and other characteristics, dollar
adjustments typically are made to the sale price of
comparables to reflect differences between comparables and
the subject property.

Market prices convey specific information on the
value to the buyer and seller of the right being transferred at the time and location of the transfer. The
negotiated price must be less than the buyer's assessment
of the capitalized net returns expected from acquiring the
water rights, including their contribution to the surplus
productivity of land and other investments. The negotiated
price must also be greater than the seller's estimate of
the capitalized net returns that would have been received
by continuing to hold the right. If these conditions are
not met, economic incentive to implement the transfer is
absent and a market transaction will not occur.
Challenges in applying price information from specific
transactions to water rights held by other users, in other
locations and time periods involve evaluation of
comparables and the need for adjustments of comparable
sale prices to reflect the characteristics of the subject
property.

In many areas sales of water rights occur sporadi-
cally, often involve the same buyers (a few municipalities, developers or power companies, for instance) and
represent water rights with varying legal and hydrologic

and characteristics. Under these circumstances, information on the degree to which the buyer or seller and water
right characteristics affect sale prices is needed in
order to adjust sales prices of comparables to represent
the value of the subject property. Analysis of water
market prices from the seven market areas in this study
indicate that priority date, water quality, legal
restrictions on transfer and the buyer's intended use
(irrigation versus urban development, for instance) can
all significantly affect sales prices for water rights.
For instance, water rights in New Mexico's Gila-San
Francisco Basin with priority dates preceding 1930 generally sell for about $300 more per acre-foot than
comparable rights with later priority dates. Those water
rights located in the more economically developed Gila
sub-basin sell for at least $1,000 per acre foot more than
comparable rights located in the less developed San
Francisco sub-basin. (In the Gila-San Francisco Basin,
water rights cannot be conveyed across sub-basin
boundaries.)(16) When price and transaction data are
available, such analyses can indicate the adjustments
needed in applying the comparable sales approach.

Transactions involving both land and water cannot be
ignored where they are a significant portion of water
market activity--as in Arizona. However, only transactions
in which water acquisition is a primary, not an
incidental, motivation should be used as comparables for
water rights appraisals and so information on buyers'
motivations is crucial. Many land purchases by Arizona
cities and developers are solely for the purpose of
acquiring water rights. Mandatory land acquisition is
incidental to the buyer and the price paid can correctly
be attributed to the water rights. In some transactions,
however, especially when irrigated land is adjacent to an
urban area, the buyer plans to develop the land and
further investigation is necessary to separate the total
purchase price into a value for land and a value for water
rights. The quantity of water acquired by buying irrigated land often exceeds the quantity needed to support
development on the land acquired. Some portion of the
water may be used at other locations, if state laws and
access to conveyance facilities permit. In these situations the water rights have value both for on-site
development projects and for off-site uses.

A recent application of the sales comparison approach
to valuing water rights in irrigated agriculture is
described in a subsequent section of this chapter.(17)

Given the complexities involved in using the sales comparison approach, use of other techniques such as income capitalization, land value differential analysis and development cost estimation is recommended in establishing a defensible final estimate of value.

Income Capitalization. The income capitalization approach involves analysis of the stream of net benefits a property will generate over time and conversion of this net benefit stream into a value estimate. It is based on the principle that a relationship exists between annual net returns attributable to property and the price that property can command in the market place.

The income capitalization approach is useful for valuing water rights being used in an activity where annual net returns attributable to the water rights can be identified and quantified. However, water is combined with other inputs in most activities and it may be difficult to separate out the contribution of water to net returns. For instance, irrigated crops are produced using not only water but also land, agricultural chemicals, labor, field equipment and management capabilities. In urban real estate development, water rights are combined with land and improvements to produce developed property. In recreation areas, water in streams and lakes combines with vegetation, fish and wildlife and other environmental amenities to provide recreation benefits.

Techniques have been developed to separate out the contribution of water in some uses. The land value differential approach is one such technique and is discussed below. The residual method has been used to evaluate the contribution of water to net returns in irrigated agriculture and this approach is discussed later in this chapter. Inferential and contingent valuation techniques can be used to focus on the value of water in recreation and these will also be discussed in a later section.

Capitalization of rental income for a particular type of property is a technique used by appraisers to value real estate. However water rental prices, like sale prices, often are influenced by forces other than economic costs and returns. Cities and utility companies, for instance, tend to hold a much larger portfolio of water rights than are needed in a typical year, as a hedge against drought and rapid growth of water demand in their service areas. They often rent unused water to irrigators at nominal rates to cover their fixed costs of owning water rights. These types of rentals account for a large proportion of rental activity in many areas, yet the rental rates are unrelated to market prices for water rights. Comparison of rental and sale prices in several states indicates that capitalized rental prices do not consistently, or even typically, approach representative sale prices. Therefore capitalization of water rental rates to estimate the value of a water right may not be a reliable technique.

Analysis of Land Value Differentials. One approach that may be useful in valuing agricultural water rights is to compare the values of agricultural land or other income producing property with and without water rights. Ross (18), for instance, suggests that comparison of market data on the price of dry land as combined with irrigated land may be used to establish a price differential that represents the increased productivity attributable to the water rights. Ross cautions that the validity and accuracy of this technique depends on the quantity and reliability of market sales data available. Hartman and Anderson (19) analyzed dry land and irrigated farm sales data in northeastern Colorado during the period 1955 to 1960 and concluded that water rights had a value of about $30 per acre foot (in 1960 dollars). This estimate was two to three times higher than the price at which Colorado-Big Thompson water rights were selling during the same period and in the same area, indicating a discrepancy between values suggested by the sales comparison and the land value differentiation approach. The authors attribute this discrepancy to the fact that the C-BT market was just developing and did not represent an area-wide market at the time their study was conducted. Crouter (20) analyzed farmland sales in northeastern Colorado's Weld County during 1970 and established a statistically significant relationship between farmland sale prices and the quantity of water rights associated with the farm parcel.

Examination of land value differentials is a useful approach in areas where parcels with and without water rights are sold routinely so that data are available with which to conduct an analysis. The approach would be of limited value in Arizona, for instance, because nearly all cropland is irrigated and is sold with water rights. Where dry land and irrigated crop production coexist, the potential for applying the land differential method is much greater.

Development Cost or Least-Cost Alternative. The development cost approach estimates the current cost of reproducing or replacing real estate improvements. In the case of water rights it would require estimation of the least-cost alternative for creating a water supply similar in legal and hydrologic terms to the subject property water right. This approach is based upon the assumption that the costs of alternatives to market acquisition of water rights, such as constructing facilities and services to create a new water supply, are related to the price an organization seeking new supplies would be willing to pay for an existing right in a market transaction.(21) This is a valid assumption only if there is evidence that water users in the area actually have been paying or could afford to pay development costs at the levels estimated to obtain water supplies. In the absence of such evidence, there is no reason to believe there would be any prospective buyers for water rights priced at development cost.

An estimate of value must be related to market demand. Development costs are a realistic measure of value only if there is reason to believe water rights would actually be demanded at the development cost price. In general the development cost alternative is considered a technique of last resort since it is not necessarily related to willingness to pay for water rights or to net benefits generated by additional water supplies.(22) At best it serves as an upper limit on water rights values. The least-cost alternative approach is used in valuing water for industrial processes and hydropower production. Applications of this approach are described in a subsequent section of this chapter.

Economists' Approaches to Valuation

Economists often are asked to determine the value of a particular set of resources or the costs and benefits associated with changes in resource availability, quality and price. A number of market and nonmarket valuation techniques have been developed. Nonmarket valuation, in particular, is an evolving specialty within economics and is a response to policymakers' and the public's desire to consider the value of nonmarketed amenities when making resource management decisions.

Producer and Consumer Surplus. For commodities traded routinely in a market setting, a market demand curve can be estimated showing the quantities of the good that would be purchased at various prices. Figure 6.2 shows a hypothetical market demand curve for water, with P_1 indicating the initial market clearing price and Q_1 showing the quantity demanded at this price. The triangular area above the market price and below the

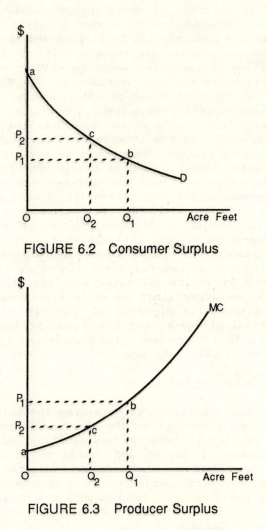

FIGURE 6.2 Consumer Surplus

FIGURE 6.3 Producer Surplus

demand curve (area abP_1 in figure 6.2) is an estimate of the net benefits generated by Q_1 units of water being purchased at price P_1. It is called consumer surplus and represents the total dollar amount consumers would be willing to pay for Q_1 (area $OabQ_1$ in figure 6.2) minus what they actually must pay for Q_1 (area OP_1bQ_1). If the market price rose to P_2 and all other factors relevant to demand remained unchanged, then quantity demanded would decline to Q_2. The area representing consumer surplus would then be P_2ac and the loss in benefits due to the price increase would be the decrease in consumer surplus, area P_1P_2cb. Change in consumer surplus is not an ideal benefit measure because it does not fully account for the fact that changes in prices involve changes in the real purchasing power of consumers. However, it is a widely used measure of the benefits and costs to consumers associated with changes in the price, quantity or quality of market goods and guidelines have been developed to adjust consumer surplus estimates to give a more precise measure of change in well-being.(23) The consumer surplus approach is useful in valuing water when a demand curve for water can be estimated. Consumer surplus also provides the conceptual foundation for many of the nonmarket valuation approaches that have been developed.

The concept of producer surplus is used to measure changes in the well-being of suppliers of a commodity. The concept is illustrated in Figure 6.3 where MC represents the marginal cost (supply) curve of the producer, the costs of supplying an additional unit of the commodity. Just as a demand curve represents willingness-to-pay by consumers, a marginal cost curve represents willingness-to-sell by producers. It measures the minimum price that a firm can accept for the productivity supplies and still cover its marginal costs of production. Producer surplus is the area above the marginal cost curve and below the market price, shown as aP_1b in Figure 6.3, for a market price of P_1. It is a surplus in that it represents revenues received above and beyond the costs of production. If the market price were to fall to P_2, the negative impact on producers could be measured by the change in producer surplus, shown on the graph as P_1P_2bc. Producer surplus is also referred to as economic rent, the net returns to inputs used in production. Producer surplus can be used to value changes in water supplies when marginal cost functions for a water-using production activity can be estimated. Producer surplus provides a conceptual foundation for valuing water rights based on the net returns generated by water as an input in a production process.

Nonmarket Valuation. Nonmarket valuation approaches can be divided into two categories--inferential valuation and contingent valuation techniques. Inferential approaches use data on actual purchase and consumption of marketed goods and services to infer the value of a nonmarket resource. The travel cost method, for instance, uses data on money and time costs incurred to enjoy a recreation experience to infer the value of that recreation experience. This method has been applied widely in valuing outdoor recreation sites and is used routinely in cost-benefit analyses by many public agencies. Another inferential approach, hedonic pricing, analyzes prices for market goods, usually real estate, to infer the value of nonmarket amenities that affect market prices. For instance, statistical analysis of sale prices for similar homes with and without lake front access could provide information on the additional amount home buyers are willing to pay for lake front amenities and this information might be useful to policymakers deciding whether it is worthwhile to protect and preserve lake environments.

Inferential approaches can be used only when a defensible case can be made that expenditures for market goods, such as homes and travel-related items, are somehow linked to the value of the nonmarket amenity being valued. Contingent valuation does not require this conceptual linkage between market prices and a nonmarket resource. Instead of drawing on data describing actual market choices that indirectly are related to the good being studied, the researcher elicits information on the value of the amenity directly by creating a hypothetical or experimental situation in which individuals reveal the values they place on the good. The values reported are contingent upon the situation created by the researcher to elicit values. Contingent valuation techniques include survey questionnaires on values, iterative bidding, creation of temporary experimental markets in which money actually changes hands and other methods of eliciting value information. The theoretical and applied literature on contingent valuation is growing rapidly as new techniques are developed. Contingent valuation has been used to value environmental amenities, including instream recreation opportunities and water quality improvements. Applications of this method to valuing water resources are described in the next section.

A thorough discussion of the complexities involved in nonmarket valuation methods and the advantages and limitations of various approaches is beyond the scope of this book. Readers wanting to learn more are referred to Anderson and Bishop and the extensive list of references they provide.(24)

Valuing Water In Alternative Uses

The water values reported in this section are drawn from a variety of sources but this discussion owes a great deal to Gibbons' recently published work, The Economic Value of Water, which reviews a large number of studies on water values in alternative uses.(25) All values in the present work are reported in 1986 dollars using the Gross National Product index. This is done to facilitate comparability with water market price data reported in 1986 dollars at the end of Chapter 5. When making comparisons, readers need to keep in mind that the values reported in this section are, unless otherwise noted, on a per acre-foot per year basis. In order to compare annual values to the value of a water right, which provides access to water year after year, the present value of the perpetual stream of annual values must be calculated.

Water Values in Irrigated Agriculture. Several approaches have been taken to estimate the value of water in irrigated agriculture. Because the prices that farmers pay for irrigation water typically do not vary significantly in any one region, direct estimation of a water demand function based on quantities of water used at various price levels generally is not possible. Instead, a programming approach based on a representative farm budget often is used to identify annual total crop revenues and input costs. Total revenues generated by irrigated crop production minus all non-water production costs gives a residual that indicates the maximum amount the producer could pay for water and still break even. This amount, divided by the quantity of water applied in production, represents the maximum average willingness to pay per acre-foot per year (the average value product) for the quantity of water currently being applied. The farm budget approach can also be used to identify willingness to pay for additional units of water (marginal value product) by estimating the contribution to total revenues minus all non-water production costs that would be generated by applying one more unit of water. Average and marginal value products calculated from annual farm bud-

216

gets generate water values for a single year. To estimate
the amount a farmer would pay for perpetual access to
additional water, i.e. a water right, it is necessary to
calculate the present value of a perpetual stream of
annual average or marginal value products.

Young and Gray (26) describe the farm budget residual
method for assigning a value to water and caution that the
validity of the estimates depend on how fully the following assumptions are satisfied. All non-water factors must
be paid according to their marginal value productivities,
as would occur in a perfectly competitive market for agricultural inputs. If there are other inputs that are
unpriced, not competitively priced or not employed to the
point where their price equals their marginal value
product then the residual method will generate inaccurate
estimates of water values. The farm budget residual
approach has been applied widely to impute a value to
water in irrigation. A few examples of studies in the
southwestern states are summarized here.

Kelso et al.(27) applied linear programming to 150
representative farm budget scenarios for various areas in
Arizona to develop marginal value functions for irrigation
water. The resulting annual values, as summarized by
Gibbons (28) range from $4 per acre foot for grain sorghum
to $221 per acre foot for cotton. These represent the
maximum a farmer could pay for water and still cover all
other variable costs of production. A study of the Salt
River area of Arizona by Martin and Snider (29) indicates
short-run marginal values ranging from $31 per acre-foot
for grain sorghum to $157 for lettuce to over $1200 for
dry onions, reported by Gibbons.(30) Bush and Martin (31)
found that the short-run marginal value product for water
in growing cotton, alfalfa and wheat in 3 central Arizona
counties ranged from $36 for alfalfa to $124 for cotton in
1984.

Shumway (32) used the farm budget residual approach
with linear programming to derive values for irrigation
water on the west side of the San Joaquin Valley ranging
from $20 per-acre foot for safflower to over $53 for
melons, as summarized by Gibbons.(33) Young (34) suggests
that 80 percent of irrigation water values in the West
are below $53 per acre-foot, with higher-valued uses for
specialty crops accounting for less than 20 percent of
agricultural water use. Gisser et al.(35) applied a
linear programming model to agricultural production in the
Four Corners Area, including the Navajo Irrigation Project

and estimated marginal values for water assuming 10 percent cutbacks in agricultural water availability due to
competition for water from electric power plants. Value
estimates ranged from $4 to $27 per acre-foot. Gollehon et
al.(36) examine the marginal value of irrigation water in
eleven Rocky Mountain sub-regions given a 20 percent
reduction in irrigation water availability. They found
marginal values greater than $20 per acre-foot in two
regions, between $10 and $20 per acre-foot for four
regions, and values below $10 an acre-foot for the remain-
ing regions.

Another approach taken to estimating water values in
irrigation involves estimation of the relationship between
water applications and crop yields (the crop-water production function) through controlled experiments in which all
other inputs are held constant and varying amounts of
water are applied. The marginal physical productivity of
water for each incremental application is thus estimated
and the marginal value of each increment is simply the
marginal physical product times crop price. Studies spon-
sored by the U.S. Department of Agriculture resulted in
crop-water production function estimates for Arizona, New
Mexico and California, and other states not covered in
this book.(37) Marginal values were calculated at 10 percent reductions from yield-maximizing water levels, at
average irrigation efficiencies on medium textured soils
and using 1980 national average crop prices. The marginal
values thus derived ranged from less than $20 per acre-
foot for grain sorghum in Arizona to $520 for tomatoes in
California. Due to lack of experimental data on crop
yield responses to imcremental water applications, this
approach has not been as widely applied as the farm-budget
residual method.

Hartman and Anderson (38) and Crouter (39), in
separate studies several decades apart, applied the
hedonic pricing approach to infer a value for irrigation
water from farmland sales data. Hartman and Anderson's
1962 study indicated average values of around $30 an acre-
foot in 1960 dollars, which is equivalent to $111 in 1986
dollars. Crouter's study did not generate an estimate of
value in dollars per acre-foot but did indicate that
marginal water values were related to other attributes of
the farm property, such as soil quality and location.

Thompson (40) applied a combination of the sales comparison and the land value differential approaches to
appraise the market value of water rights held by an Idaho
rancher. While the water rights are not located in the

study area for this publication, the valuation approach is interesting and applicable to southwestern water rights. Water rights may not be sold separately from land in the Idaho basin in which the ranch was located so the appraiser analyzed recent sales of irrigated land, dry land, homesites and recreation lands to determine the different market values associated with different types of properties. The appraiser determined the highest and best use of the subject property with all of its existing water rights to be a combination of homesites, recreation land, irrigated pasture and range land. The prospective water right purchaser wanted the rancher's most senior water rights, rights which are essential to mid and late summer irrigation on the ranch. The appraiser determined the highest and best use of ranch property without water rights available for the last half of the summer irrigation season and found that over 1,700 acres of irrigated land would have to be converted to dry range. The difference between the "with" and "without" value estimate is the value of the water rights to the rancher and provides an estimate of the minimal price that would be acceptable for his senior water rights. The analysis did not derive a water value on a per acre-foot basis because the water rights being purchased were of several different priority dates and were decreed in terms of flow rates (cubic feet per second), making it difficult to estimate a value per acre-foot.(41) The analysis indicated the total value of the 2,282 acre ranch would be reduced by $768,515 if the water rights were removed.

As is evident from this brief summary of studies in the Southwest, a variety of approaches have been applied to valuing water in agricultural uses and a wide range of values have been reported. As emphasized by Bush and Martin (42), crop prices received by farmers are the dominant factor in determining the marginal value of water in irrigation. Changes in energy costs of pumping and pumping lifts also play an important role in determining how much farmers are willing to pay for water rights.

Water Values in Municipal Uses. City governments, municipal water purveyors and urban developers are major water buyers in the southwestern states even though municipal use of water accounts for less than 10 percent of total consumptive water use in the U.S.(43) Municipal water demand for current and future use is a key force in southwestern water markets. Municipal water values reflect multiple water uses by urban dwellers, with different values associated with different uses. Water

used for indoor purposes such as drinking, cooking and
bathing is thought to be the most highly valued and to be
the least responsive to price changes. Water used outdoors for landscape watering and swimming pools is somewhat less highly valued, though Young and Gray (44)
suggest that the value urban residents place on water for
irrigating lawns is around $172 per acre-foot. This value
is above the marginal value of water in irrigating most
crops and below Young and Gray's estimate of water's value
for indoor uses of $305. Municipal water use also includes
nonresidential uses for commercial and industrial estab-
lishments, and public buildings and grounds. Residential
uses, however, generally account for the largest fraction
of municipal water use.(45) Some analyses have differen-
tiated between summer and winter urban water demand.
Outdoor uses make up a large proportion of water requirements in the summer and a minimal proportion in the winter
so that two separate demand relationships are needed to
reflect seasonal changes in the nature of water demand and
its responsiveness to price changes.

There have been many studies on urban water demand
and price elasticity. This discussion will summarize a
few studies that apply to the southwestern states. Price
elasticity of demand measures the percentage change in
quantity of water demanded in response to a 1 percent
change in price. Price elasticities are negative,
reflecting the inverse relationship between price and
quantity demanded. Price elasticities lying between 0 and
-1.0 are considered inelastic because quantity demanded
does not decrease proportionally in response to a price
increase. Elasticities below -1.0 are considered elastic
because the proportional decline in quantity demand is
greater than the proportion of the price increase. Howe
and Lineaweaver (46), in a cross-sectional study of U.S.
cities, report a average price elasticity of -0.23 for all
cities studied, with -1.57 for summer water use in eastern
cities and -0.70 for summer use in western cities. Their
finding of more elastic demand in summer supports the
notion that much of summer demand is for less highly
valued outdoor uses which will be curtailed in response
to a price increase. Gardner and Schick (47) report an
elasticity of -0.77 for urban households in northern Utah.
Young (48) reports a decrease in price elasticity from
-0.62 for the years 1946-1965 to -0.41 for the 1965-1971
period in Tucson, Arizona. Foster and Beattie's study (49)
of 218 U.S. cities estimated a price elasticity of -0.36

for Southwestern cities. Billings and Agthe's 1980 study
(50) estimated Tucson's price elasticity at -0.39 to
-0.63, depending on the statistical model used. Martin et
al. estimated price elasticity of demand in Tucson at
-0.26 for the years 1976-1979.(51)

While price elasticity estimates indicate how water
consumption patterns will change in response to price
changes, they do not provide information on urban water
users' willingness to pay for additional units of water.
Estimates of willingness to pay require estimates of quantity demanded over a wide range of observed prices. In
general water rates to urban residents do not change much
in real terms (that is, they rise at about the inflation
rate) so the opportunity to observe how quantity demanded
changes over a substantial price range is rare. Gibbons
(52) suggests, using data on Tucson water consumption,
that marginal water values in that city given a 10 percent
reduction in water availability would be about $109 per
acre-foot in the winter and $37 per acre-foot in the
summer.

Young (53) notes that values for raw water and values
for treated water delivered to residences are not directly
comparable since quite different water commodities are
involved. Martin and Thomas (54) find that demand for raw
water accounts for only about 12 percent of demand for
delivered potable water in Tucson. It is the municipal
demand for raw water that should be compared to water
values in irrigation and other uses, not what urban
consumers actually pay or are willing to pay for treated
delivered water. The prices summarized at the end of
Chapter 5 give an indication of the market value of rights
to raw water and are not comparable to the value of
treated water delivered to end users.

To summarize, the vast majority of municipal demand
studies have focused on the responsiveness of quantity
demanded to changes in price, not on marginal water
values. Lack of price variation makes it difficult to
reliably estimate urban demand curves that could be used
to value additional water supplies. Prices paid for delivered water by urban consumers do not shed much light on
how much a city water purveyor might be willing to pay
for additional rights to untreated surface or groundwater.
In addition, municipal buyers purchase water rights as a
hedge against drought, to encourage economic growth and
for other reasons unrelated to current and short term
future water use.

Water Values In Industrial Uses. Industrial processes require water for many different purposes although
industrial use accounts for only 9 percent of U.S. water
consumption.(55) The largest share of industrial water
withdrawals are used for cooling and condensation
processes. For instance, up to 74 per cent of water
withdrawn for petroleum refining is used in cooling.(56)
Cooling processes generally consume only a small
proportion of water withdrawn. Steam electric generation,
for instance, accounted for 26.5 percent of total
freshwater withdrawals in the U.S. in 1975, but for only
1.3 percent of total consumptive use. (57) Other industrial processes have a high consumptive use. The minerals
industry accounts for 2.1 percent of both total U.S.
freshwater withdrawals and consumption.(58) Overall, however, industrial processes have a much lower consumptive
use than either irrigation or municipal water uses.(59)
     Gibbons (60) notes that water quality issues are
important to industrial water values for several reasons.
First, different uses require different minimal quality
levels. Water used in food processing and beverage industries must meet very strict standards while cooling
processes often can use brackish water or treated
effluent. Second, industrial processes typically result
in some water quality degradation and costs of complying
with water quality regulations can affect the net value of
water to industry. Reuse also plays a role in industrial
water values as industrial users often can respond to
increased water costs by recycling water several times
through the industrial process.
     In general, water costs are a small proportion of
overall production or processing costs and there is little
empirical data with which to estimate industrial water
demand functions. The studies which have been done
indicate that industrial water demand is quite inelastic.
Gibbons (61) summarizes the literature on industrial water
values and notes that, due to lack of better ways to
estimate value, industrial values have been equated with
the industry's cost of recycling water. This approach is
based upon the assumption that an industrial user would
pay no more for additional water supplies than what it
would cost to treat and reuse water already being used in
the industrial process. This least-cost alternative
approach, as noted earlier, serves only as an upper bound
on the value of additional water.
     Young and Gray (62) estimated the cost of shifting
from once-through water use to recycling water using evap-

orative cooling processes at $8-13 per acre-foot of water recycled, for the electric power generating sector. Russell estimated these costs at $7 for the electric power sector and $15 per acre-foot of water recycled for cooling in petroleum refineries.(63) Since many power plants and refineries have already adopted recycling with evaporative cooling methods, further recycling would have to rely on more sophisticated technologies which are very expensive. For instance, demineralization and dry cooling recycling systems would only be economically rational at new water supply costs of $800 to $1700 per acre-foot.(64) Additional water recycling for cotton textile finishing would become economical given costs of $177 per acre-foot for new water supplies and demineralization would only be economically rational if the industry faced costs of $836 per acre-foot for new water. A study of water recycling in meat packing operations indicates that existing reuse operations have a marginal cost of from $436 to $608 per acre-foot recycled.(65)

In summary, water costs are a small proportion of industrial production costs and industrial users may be able to absorb substantial price increases without significantly increasing their costs of production. Anderson and Keith (66) found that a $200 per acre-foot increase in the price of water would increase costs of electricity production in coal-fired plants by only 1-2 percent. Many industrial users can begin to recycle, or to increase recycling, of their current water supplies and would compare additional recycling costs to market prices for water rights in order to decide whether to acquire additional water rights or to implement additional recycling. Information on recycling costs provides an upper limit to industry's willingness to pay for additional water.

Water Values in Non-Consumptive Uses. Navigation, hydropower, recreation, aesthetic and wildlife-related values for water in lakes and streams are all based on non-consumptive water uses. The authors were unable to find any evidence regarding the value of navigation in southwestern surface water systems, and studies of waterway transportation in other parts of the U.S. suggest river transportation is often not cost-effective compared to land based transportation systems.(67) Seasonal and annual variations in flow and competition with offstream consumptive uses suggest that navigation may not be a current or potential instream use of much economic consequence in the Southwest. Therefore, navigation values are not discussed.

The Southwest's contribution to U.S. hydropower production is dwarfed by the Pacific Northwest which contains nearly half of the developed hydropower capacity in the U.S.(68) However there are some important hydroelectric plants along the Colorado River system including Glen Canyon, Parker and Hoover dams. Like industrial water values, the value of water in producing hydroelectric power can be estimated by a least-cost alternative approach. Gibbons examined the cost savings possible with hydroelectric power as compared to the alternatives of coal-fired steam generating plants (the next least costly method) and gas-turbine electric plants (a more costly technology). For the Colorado River hydroelectric system, the shortrun cost savings provided by hydropower compared to coal-fired steam generating plants are $31 per acre-foot and are $76 per acre-foot when compared to gas-turbine electric plants.(69) These are the additional costs of replacing lost hydropower production due to an acre-foot decrease in flow with a more expensive source of electricity, and can be thought of as shortrun marginal values. As Gibbons notes, there are reliability, facility longevity and environmental quality advantages of hydropower compared to other electricity producing methods. These values are not incorporated into the marginal value estimates cited. Federal evaluations of hydropower facilities typically assign a 5-10 percent credit above cost-savings to hydropower generation to account for its other advantages over other methods.(70)

Water-based recreation is an important part of many Southwesterners' leisure activities and water-related recreation opportunities draw visitors and tourism dollars to the Southwest. Since there is little direct market evidence on willingness to pay for recreational opportunities, a variety of nonmarket valuation approaches have been applied to outdoor recreation.(71) However, most recreation studies focus on the value of the recreation activity (hunting, fishing, boating) or the value of a particular site, rather than the specific contribution of the water resource to recreation values. A few studies have focused specifically on water values related to recreation in the Southwest and several are reviewed here.

Daubert and Young (72) used a contingent valuation approach to examine the contribution of stream flows to recreation benefits for recreationists on Colorado's Cache la Poudre River. They found the value of an additional acre-foot of flow for fishing to be $21 during low flow periods and the marginal value of an additional acre-foot

for shoreline recreation to be $15 during low river flows.
Marginal values dropped to zero at higher flow levels
suggesting that minimum flow maintenance is of value to
recreationists rather than additional increments to already adequate flows.   Walsh et al. (73) investigated
marginal flow values at nine sites along Colorado mountain
streams and found that flow levels of 35 percent of
maximum stream flow were optimal for recreation.   Using
contingent valuation techniques, marginal flow values at
the 35 percent flow level were estimated to be $21 per
acre-foot for fishing, $5 for kayaking and $4 for rafting.
Walsh, Aukerman and Milton (74) estimate that leaving
water in high mountain Colorado reservoirs for an additional two weeks in August is worth $48 per acre-foot in
additional recreation benefits during that peak recreation
period.   Amirfathi et al.(75) used a combination of travel
cost and contingent valuation methods to estimate marginal
water values in recreation on a river in northern Utah.
They found that the marginal value was zero until flows
dropped to 50 percent of peak levels and that marginal
values reached a maximum of $80 per acre-foot when flows
were 20-25 percent of peak levels.   Ward (76) examined the
relationship between stream flow levels, recreation use
levels and travel costs incurred by recreationists on New
Mexico's Rio Chama to infer a value of $16 to $20 per
acre-foot released in the summer recreation season,
assuming optimal augmentation of stream flows during low
flow periods.   When natural summer flow levels are 20 to
50 percent of normal levels and varying quantities of
water are available from other sources to augment low
natural instream flows, instream values for recreation
range from $881 to $1040 dollars per acre-foot consumed
through evaporative losses attributable to reservoir
releases.   Consistent with other studies, Ward found that
marginal values fall dramatically for high flow periods
and when stored water is available to augment natural flow
levels.   Ward's results suggest a significant economic
payoff in augmenting stream flows in low flow years, even
though augmentation would reduce water availability for
other basin uses.
     Loomis (77) provides an overview of the various
methods that have been applied to measure the economic
value of instream flows, citing studies relying on the
travel cost method and on contingent valuation. He argues
convincingly, based on the studies cited, that dollar
values of instream flows can be measured so as to be

comparable to the value of water in offstream uses such as irrigation.

Few studies have estimated the value of improved stream flows for fish and wildlife habitat in the southwestern states. One study places the average value of stream flow in California's Trinity River at $31 per acre-foot for fish hatchery operations.(78) Water to facilitate salmon spawning in California's Trinity River has been valued at $53 per acre-foot.(79) The wildlife valuation literature recognizes many different values associated with wildlife and fish species. These include "user" values for recreational and commercial hunting and fishing, wildlife sightings (birdwatching, for instance) and photography. Non-user values are also of several types. Those associated with preserving a species and its habitat so that one has the option to enjoy them in the future are termed "option values". Willingness to pay for preservation so that one's heirs can benefit is termed "bequest value" and values generated simply by knowing a species or a unique site will continue to exist are termed "existence values".(80) Non-user values are not associated with an actual visit to wildlife habitat and are particularly difficult to estimate. Non-user values apply not only to wildlife species whose survival may be linked to water resources but also to natural environments, such as wilderness areas, whose aesthetic characteristics are dependent on water. The little empirical evidence that exists suggests non-user values can be sizable, especially for unique sites.(81) Recognizing that potentially significant but hard-to-measure non-user values are associated with water in lakes and streams, measurable values for water in recreation uses should be regarded as a lower bound or a minimum estimate of the actual values generated by maintaining instream flows and lake levels.

<u>Water Values and Water Quality</u>. Water quality affects the range of uses to which water can be put, the cost of treating water for specific uses and water's value in those uses. There is some anecdotal evidence in the seven market areas studied that lower quality water resources command a lower price in the market place than higher quality water resources. Along the East Slope of the Colorado Rockies where groundwater often contains heavy metals, surface water is the preferred water source and market activity focuses on surface water rights. However, price differentials between groundwater rights and surface water rights cannot be attributed entirely or even primarily to quality differences because appropriative

groundwater rights also typically are junior to surface
water rights. No surface water has been transferred from
irrigation to municipal uses in Utah's Lower Sevier River
Basin because of the high salinity of the river water.
The market value of groundwater, which is of a quality
level suited to a variety of municipal, industrial and
agricultural uses, is consequently higher than the market
value of Sevier River rights which are used primarily for
irrigation and power plant cooling. In general, evidence
from the markets studied on water prices and water quality
is sparse and incidental but does support the notion that
higher quality water sources are more highly valued.

Greenley, Walsh and Young (82) examine the economic
benefits of improved water quality associated with outdoor
recreation. They review a number of studies which estimate the recreational benefits associated with improved
water quality, only one of which was for a site in the
Southwest. Walsh et al.(83) found, using a contingent
valuation approach, that visitors to Colorado's Rocky
Mountain National Park were willing to pay about $5 more
in entrance fees per recreation day to avoid a decrease in
water quality for recreation activities. Greenley, Walsh
and Young found that households in Colorado's South Platte
Basin were willing to pay an average of $92 in additional
sales taxes annually to improve water quality in the basin
for recreation.(84) Given recreation use patterns by these
households, this amounts to an average of $6.10 per recre-
ation day. This study also examined option, existence
and bequest values associated with preserving natural
riparian ecosystems in the basin. In addition to the
recreation values reported, households in the South Platte
Basin reported an average willingness to pay $108 annually
in additional sales taxes for preservation related to
bequest and existence values, and $39 annually to
preserve water quality so that water-based recreation will
remain a viable option in the future.(85)

Following the least-cost alternative approach used to
value water in industrial uses, willingness to pay for
water of varying quality can be related to the costs of
treating water to bring it up to the standards required
for a specific use. Treatment costs may serve as an upper
bound for industrial and municipal users' willingness to
pay for higher quality versus lower quality water
supplies. Irrigators may also be responsive to varying
levels of water quality though there is little evidence on
variations in willingness to pay for irrigation water due
to quality differentials. Boster and Martin (86) found

that net returns to central Arizona farmers may be reduced
when Central Arizona Project (CAP) water becomes available, partially due to negative effects of salinity on
crop yields. It follows that farmers may be willing to
pay less to receive CAP water than to pump high quality
groundwater and this may explain why some irrigation
districts have not opted to contract for CAP water.

Values associated with differences in water quality
can be conceptualized as damages avoided. In the case of
agriculture, damages avoided by using a higher quality
source are the reduced crop yields and increased production costs associated with using poor quality water. The
damage avoided approach could be applied to other water
users as well. Industrial users who utilize water high in
total dissolved solids face higher operation and maintenance costs and shorter lifetime for equipment.(87) The
value of better quality water could be estimated by
evaluating costs avoided by switching from lower quality
to higher quality sources.

There is little empirical evidence on the relationship between water quality and water values. However,
analysis of the costs of treating water to improve quality
and of damages avoided by using higher quality water can
provide a rough idea of the amount a water user might be
willing to pay to acquire higher quality water.
Contingent valuation has provided useful estimates of the
impact that changes in water quality have on values
generated by water based recreation and of existence,
bequest and option values associated with water quality.

SUMMARY AND IMPLICATIONS FOR VALUING WATER RIGHTS

Many different types of public and private decisions
require an estimate of water's value in alternative uses.
Market prices, even where easily identified, seldom will
provide an ideal measure of value due to imperfections in
markets for water rights. Therefore, market prices should
be supplemented with other measures of value using one or
more valuation approaches. In addition to the market-
based sales comparison approach, real estate appraisal
techniques such as income capitalization, analysis of land
value differentials, and estimation of development costs
can be applied to value water rights. Consumer and producer surplus concepts can be used to value water when
demand and marginal cost functions have been estimated for
a particular water use. Inferential and contingent valua-

228

tion techniques do not rely on market price data and have been applied to valuing water for instream uses. A review of studies that estimate the value of water in alternative uses in the Southwest indicates that a wide variety of valuation approaches are being applied and that defensible values can be derived for use in public and private water resource decisions.

NOTES

1. Marginal value product measures the economic returns sacrificed by deleting a unit of water from the crop production activity in which water generates the lowest returns (the "marginal" crop). Average value product measures the economic returns sacrificed by removing water from the whole farm operation and thus accounts for the returns to water for all of the various irrigation crops produced. Average value product will exceed marginal value product for farms growing several crops with differing returns to water.

2. R.L. Gardner, and T.A. Miller, "Price Behavior in the Water Market of Northeastern Colorado." Water Resources Bulletin 19:557-562, 1983.

3. R.A. Young, "Why Are There so Few Transactions Between Water Users?" American Journal of Agricultural Economics 68:1143-1151, 1986.

4. E. Brubaker, "Free Ride, Free Revelation or Golden Rule?" Journal of Law and Economics 58:147-161, 1975.

5. Personal conversation with Sandy Landeck, City Property Management Specialist, Sparks, Nevada, 1985.

6. J.F. Ross, "Valuation of Water Rights for Acquisition, Condemnation and Taxation Purposes." Rocky Mountain Mineral Law Institute Vol.30, 563-593, 1984.

7. W. Fischer and W.R. Fischer, "Title and Valuation of Water Rights." Rocky Mountain Mineral Law Institute Vol.30: 16-1-16-35, 1984.

8. American Institute of Real Estate Appraisers, The Appraisal of Real Estate, 8th edition. Chicago: AIREA, 1983, p.33.

9. California Supreme Court. Sacramento Railroad Company v. Heilbron, 156 Calif. 408-409, 104 p.979-980, 1909.

10. American Institute of Real Estate Appraisers, Real Estate Terminology. Chicago: AIREA, 1981.

11. The authors appreciate suggestions for this discussion of real estate valuation approaches provided by R.E. Dietrich, MAI, of the appraisal firm Burke, Hansen, Homan located in Tucson, Arizona.

12. Sections of this discussion are adapted from B.C. Saliba, "Highest and Best Use in Water Rights Appraisals," Water Market Update Vol.1 No.2, February, 1987.

13. American Institute of Real Estate Appraisers, The Appraisal of Rural Property. Chicago: AIREA, 1983, p. 19.

14. Net returns to water that will be received in some future year can be converted to present values through a process known as "discounting." The formula used for discounting is:

$$PV = NR(t) \; / \; [(1 + r)^t]$$

Where PV represents the present value of a net return to be received in year t, designated NR(t), discounted using an interest rate r.

15. Parts of this discussion are adapted from "The Comparable Sales Approach," Water Market Update Vol.1, No. 1, January, 1987.

16. D.B. Bush and B.C. Saliba, in "Commodity Identification and Price Behavior in Western Water Markets," paper presented at American Agricultural Association Annual meetings, Reno, Nevada, August, 1986. These estimates of value differentials associated with characteristics of water rights are based on statistical analysis of 98 transactions in the Gila-San Francisco Basin.

17. C.K. Thompson. "Busterback Ranch: Valuing Water Rights in a Scenic Easement Area," Appraisal Journal, April, 1987.

18. Ross, op. cit.

19. L. Hartman and R. Anderson. "Estimating the Value of Irrigation Water From Farm Sales Data in Northeast Colorado." Journal of Farm Economics 44:207-213, 1962.

20. J.P. Crouter. "An Examination of an Implicit Water Rights Market Using Hedonic Estimation." Unpublished PhD dissertation, University of Illinois, 1982.

21. Ross, op.cit.

22. A. Randall, Resource Economics, second edition. New York: John Wiley and Sons, 1987.

23. G.D. Anderson and R.C. Bishop, "The Valuation Problem." Chapter 3 in Natural Resource Economics, ed. D.W. Bromley, Boston: Kluwer-Nijhoff Publishing, 1986, p.89-90. See also the discussions on this chapter that follow by Rick Freeman and Kenneth McConnell.

24. Anderson and Bishop. Ibid.

230

25. D.C. Gibbons, <u>The Economic Value of Water</u>. Washington, D.C. Resources for the Future, 1986.

26. R.A. Young and S.L. Gray, "Input-Output Models, Economic Surplus, and the Evaluation of State or Regional Water Plans." <u>Water Resources Research</u> 21:1819-1823, December, 1985.

27. M.M. Kelso, W.E. Martin, and L.E. Mack, <u>Water Supplies and Economic Growth in an Arid Environment</u> Tucson: University of Arizona Press, 1973.

28. Gibbons, op. cit.,23-44.

29. W.E. Martin and G.B. Snider, "Valuation of Water and Forage From the Salt-Verde Basin of Arizona." Report to the U.S. Forest Service, 1979.

30. Gibbons, op. cit., p.23-44.

31. D.B. Bush and W.E. Martin, "Potential Costs and Benefits to Arizona Agriculture of the Central Arizona Project." Technical Bulletin No. 254, University of Arizona College of Agriculture, January, 1986.

32. C.R. Shumway, "Derived Demand for Irrigation Water: The California Aqueduct." <u>Southern Journal of Agricultural Economics</u> 5:195-200, 1973 (December).

33. Gibbons, op. cit., p.23-44.

34. R.A. Young, "Direct and Indirect Regional Impacts of Competition for Irrigation Water." In <u>Water Scarcity: Impacts on Western Agriculture</u> ed. E.A. Engelbert, Berkeley: University of California Press, 1984.

35. M. Gisser, R.R. Lansford, W.D. Gorman, B.T. Creel and M. Evans, "Water Tradeoffs Between Electric Energy and Agriculture in the Four Corners Area." <u>Water Resources Research</u> 15:529-538, June, 1979.

36. N.R. Gollehon, et al., "Impacts on Irrigated Agriculture For Energy Development in the Rocky Mountain Region." <u>Southwestern Review of Management and Economics</u> 1:35-60, Spring, 1987.

37. Gibbons provides a detailed description of these studies along with a tabular summary of the marginal value estimates and references to the individual studies, op. cit., pp.31-34.

38. Hartman and Anderson, op. cit.

39. Crouter, op. cit.

40. Thompson, op. cit.

41. Difficulties involved in comparing the value of rights expressed in flow rates (cubic feet per second) and rights expressed in volumetric terms (acre-feet per year) were discussed in the early part of Chapter 5.

42. Bush and Martin, op. cit.

43. Gibbons, op. cit., p.7.

44. R.A. Young and S.L. Gray, Economic Value of Water: Concepts and Empirical Estimates, Technical Report U.S. National Water Commission, National Technical Information Service, PB210356, March 1972. Updated figures (cited in the text in 1986 dollars) on Young and Grays earlier work are provided in R.A. Young, 1984 in Engelbert's Water Scarcity, op. cit.

45. Gibbons, op. cit.,p.8.

46. C.W. Howe and F.B. Lineaweaver, "The Impact of Price on Residential Water Demand and Its Relationship to System Design and Price Structure." Water Resources Research 3:13-32, 1967.

47. B.D. Gardner and S.H. Schick, "Factors Affecting Consumption of Urban Household Water in Northern Utah." Agricultural Experiment Station Bulletin No. 449, Utah State University, Logan, Utah, 1964.

48. R.A. Young, "Price Elasticity of Demand for Municipal Water: A Case Study of Tucson, Arizona." Water Resources Research 9:1068-1072, August 1973.

49. B.R. Beattie and H.S. Foster, "Can Prices Tame the Inflationary Tiger?" Journal of American Water Works Association 72:441-445, August, 1980.

50. R.B. Billings and D.E. Agthe, "Price Elasticities for Water: A Case of Increasing Block Rates." Land Economics, 56:73-84, February, 1980.

51. W.E. Martin,H.M. Ingram, N.K. Laney and A.H. Griffin, Saving Water in a Desert City. Washington DC: Resources For the Future, 1984.

52. Gibbons, op. cit., p.18.

53. Young, op. cit.

54. W.E. Martin and J.F. Thomas, "Policy Relevance in Studies of Urban Residential Water Demand." Water Resources Research, Vol. 23: p. 1735-1741, 1987.

55. U.S.Water Resources Council. The Nation's Water Resources 1975-2000, Vol.1. Washington DC: U.S. Government Printing Office, December 1978, p.29.

56. T.H. Stevens and R.J. Kalter, "Forecasting Industrial Water Utilization in the Petroleum Refining Sector: An Overview," Water Resources Bulletin 11:156, 1975.

57. The Nation's Water Resources 1975-2000, Op. Cit., Vol.3 Appendix II, p.40.

58. Ibid.

59. Gibbons, op cit., p. 45.

60. Ibid, p.46-47.

61. Ibid. 47-55.

62. Young and Gray, op. cit.

232

63. C.S. Russell, "Industrial Water Use." Report to the National Water Commission, Sec. 2, 1970.

64. K.L. Kollar, R. Brewer and H. McAulty, "An Analysis of Price/Cost Sensitivity of Water Use in Selected Manufacturing Industries." Bureau of Domestic Commerce Staff Study, Water Resources Council, 1976, p.8-18.

65. J. Kane and R. Osantowski, "An Evaluation for Water Reuse Using Advanced Waste Treatment at a Meat Packing Plant." Proceedings of the 38th Industrial Waste Conference, 1981, p. 617-624.

66. J.C. Anderson and J.E. Keith, "Energy and the Colorado River." Natural Resources Journal, 17:157-168, April, 1977.

67. Young and Gray, op. cit., p.258-275; Gibbons, op. cit., p. 74-85.

68. Federal Energy Regulatory Commission, Hydroelectric Power Resources of the United States, p. Vii-Xiii.

69. Gibbons, op. cit.,p.94.

70. U.S. Dept of Energy, Hydroelectric Power Evaluation Washington, D.C.: U.S. Government Printing Office, 1979, p.3-6.

71. Water Resources Research published a collection of papers on valuing water-based recreation in its May 1987 issue (Vol.23, No. 5, p. 931-967) and these papers provide a current overview of valuation approaches.

72. J.T. Daubert and R.A. Young, "Economic Benefits From Instream Flow in a Colorado Mountain Stream." Colorado Water Resources Research Institute Completion Report No. 91. Fort Collins, Colorado State University, June, 1979.

73. R.G. Walsh, R.K. Ericson, D.J. Arosteguy and M.P. Hansen, "An Empirical Application of a Model For Estimating the Recreation Value of Instream Flow." Colorado Water Resources Research Institute Completion Report No.101, Fort Collins, Colorado State University, October, 1980.

74. R.G. Walsh, R. Auckerman and R. Milton, "Measuring Benefits and the Economic Value of Water in Recreation on High Country Reservoirs." Colorado Water Resources Research Institute Completion Report No.101, Fort Collins, Colorado State University, September, 1980.

75. P. Amirfathi, R. Narayanan, B. Bishop and D. Larson, "A Methodology for Estimating Instream Flow Uses For Recreation." Logan, Utah Water Research Laboratory at Utah State University, 1984.

76. F.A. Ward, "Economics of Water Allocation to Instream Uses in a Fully Appropriated River Basin: Evidence From a New Mexico Wild River." Water Resources Research 23:381-392, March 1987.

77. J. Loomis, "The Economic Value of Instream Flow: Methodology and Benefit Estimates for Optimum Flows." Journal of Environmental Management, 24:169-179, 1987.

78. A. Bush, "Is the Trinity River Dying?" Instream Flow Needs Vol.2, American Fisheries Society, 1976, p.12.

79. F.H. Bollman, "A Simple Comparison of Values: Salmon and Low Value Irrigation Crops." Paper from the Association of California Water Agencies, 1979, p.12.

80. The different concepts of value that serve as a basis for valuing wildlife and natural environments are discussed in more detail by B. Madariago and K. McConnell in "Exploring Existence Value," Water Resources Research, 23:936-942, May, 1987.

81. R.G. Walsh, J.B. Loomis, and R.A. Gilman, "Valuing Option, Existence and Bequest Demands for Wilderness." Land Economics Vol.60, Feb. 1984, p.14-29.

82. D.A. Greenley, R.G. Walsh and R.A. Young, Economic Benefits of Improved Water Quality: Public Perceptions of Option and Preservation Values. Boulder: Westview Press, 1982.,

83. R.G. Walsh, R.K. Ericson, J.R. McKean and R.A. Young, Recreation Benefits of Water Quality, Rocky Mountain National Park, South Platte River Basin, Colorado. Technical Report No.12, Colorado Water Resources Research Institute, Fort Collins, Colorado State University, May, 1978.

84. Greenley, Walsh and Young, op. cit., p.65.

85. Greenley, Walsh and Young, op. cit., 70-71.

86. M.A. Boster and W.E. Martin, "Economic Analysis of the Conjunctive Use of Surface and Groundwater of Differing Prices and Qualities: A Coming Problem for Arizona Agriculture." University of Arizona College of Agriculture, Technical Bulletin No.235, 1978.

87. Gibbons, op. cit., p.46.

7
Water Markets and Public Policy—
Do Markets "Work"?

Market transfers are already an important water allocation mechanism in some areas of the Southwest and are likely to become more widespread and more frequent in the future. Much of the policy-oriented literature on water markets focuses on the potential for market activity, estimation of benefits from market formation, and institutional arrangements conducive to market development.(1) This focus on potential and hypothetical markets needs to be balanced by evaluation of markets that are already functioning. There have been few attempts to evaluate market-oriented approaches to water allocation based on the experience of regions with active markets. Nearly every western state is considering the role that markets ought to play in allocating water and the degree to which market transfers should be encouraged or restricted. Evaluation of existing markets could provide useful information to policymakers weighing the advantages and disadvantages of market processes.

This chapter develops criteria for evaluating market allocation of water rights and applies them to assess market performance. Lack of data on third-party costs and benefits associated with transfers was the primary limitation encountered. The chapter concludes with recommendations for evaluating market outcomes when limited information is available, for further research on water allocation processes, and for development of policies that encourage efficient allocation of water while accounting for opportunity costs related to market transfers.

It is argued that markets appear to be relatively efficient in allocating water rights among those who use water for purposes recognized as beneficial uses in state water codes, purposes for which water rights can be

236

granted, such as agricultural, municipal and industrial uses.(2) The opportunity costs of water transfers and third party effects involving these uses generally are reflected in market decisions and prices. However, instream flow, water quality and other values that are not typically represented by vested water rights are poorly accounted for in the markets evaluated. Modifications in transfer approval criteria and procedures would be required to ensure that these other values are accounted for when market transactions are being considered. Such changes would raise the costs incurred by the parties to a market transfer and prevent some transfers that are otherwise economically beneficial from occurring. However if changes are not made, costs are also incurred because transfers will be implemented for which the costs outweigh the benefits. Pervasive trade-offs exist between the benefits of protecting third-party and public interests and the costs of doing so. The present research suggests that policy makers need to devise transfer policies that strike a balance between transaction costs imposed on market participants to protect third-party and public interests and the benefits foregone when these interests are neglected in market transfer processes. However, there is little data on transaction costs and opportunity costs associated with market transfers. Further research is needed to provide policy makers with information needed to weigh trade-offs and to formulate policies that avoid either of two pitfalls. "Over-regulation" of transfers means that some of the gains associated with market transactions are sacrificed, too few transfers are occurring and the costs imposed by regulation are too high. "Under-regulation" of transfers means that significant external impacts of transfers are ignored as transfer decisions are being made, and transfers may occur that are not economically beneficial.

Chapter 5's description of market activities clearly indicates that water is being transferred through market processes in many areas. How well are existing markets working? Howe, Schurmeier and Shaw(3) argue that the greatest opportunities for increased efficiency lie in inter-district and interstate markets since localized markets have been active for many years in the West. How could the inference that local markets are relatively efficient be tested? This leads to a more basic question-- how should market performance in general be evaluated? Buyers and sellers will only consummate transactions that each party perceives to be in its own best interests.

Buyers and sellers have strong incentives to carefully
consider those costs and benefits which affect them
directly. Evaluation of market performance from a public
policy perspective should focus on the benefits and costs
of market activities that are not typically considered by
the buyer and seller. In this discussion, "private" benefits and costs shall be those that buyers and sellers
consider when determining whether to go ahead with a
transfer. "Social" benefits and costs shall include
private benefits and costs plus impacts not necessarily
considered by buyers and sellers, such as effects on
neighboring water users, on water quality, and on riparian
environments. State policies and transfer approval
procedures can broaden the range of impacts that buyers
and sellers must consider, narrowing the gap between
private and social net benefits.

A thorough evaluation of market processes should
address two related questions. First, do increased
returns to water use and any other benefits associated
with market transfers outweigh the social costs of market
activities? And second, are there alternative water
allocation processes that would yield greater net social
benefits? A few studies have addressed the first
question, estimating potential gains and costs for
specific transfer proposals.(4) However, estimation of
the private, administrative and third-party costs of
market versus nonmarket allocation processes requires
information that may be costly to obtain or that may not
exist because alternative allocation processes have not
been tried. Recognizing these limitations, this research
evaluates market performance using available data on
market transactions. While this approach cannot determine
whether market processes are more or less efficient than
alternative allocation processes, it can determine whether
markets are behaving in a manner consistent with
efficient market performance and whether market activity
is evolving in the right direction.

WHAT CHARACTERIZES AN EFFICIENT MARKET?

Chapter 2 began by reviewing characteristics desirable in a water allocation process. Trelease, Ciriacy-
Wantrup, Hartman and Seastone, and more recently, Brown et
al., Young, and Howe, Schurmeier and Shaw each summarize
desirable characteristics of water allocation mechanisms.
One desirable characteristic, the focus of this

238

discussion, is economic efficiency.(5) A particular water
allocation X is efficient relative to some other
allocation Y if those who benefit in a transfer of water
from allocation Y to allocation X would be able to fully
compensate those who lose water, income or something else
of value as a result of the transfer. More simply,
benefits from the reallocation must outweigh all costs.

An often cited prerequisite for an efficient market
is property rights that are completely specified, exclusive, enforced, comprehensive and transferable.(6) When
property rights are completely specified, exclusive, and
enforced, water users have a secure basis on which to make
long-term investment decisions. If all values associated
with water are encompassed in property rights, then transfer participants will consider all of the impacts
associated with a transfer. As a result, market prices
will reflect social values and right holders will be faced
with the full opportunity costs of their water use and
transfer decisions. Transferability ensures that marginal
values for water (net of transfer costs) are equal for
various water uses by allowing water rights to be transferred whenever a transfer would generate positive net
benefits.(7)   Completely specified, enforceable and
transferable property rights are the ideal institutional
conditions for efficient market performance. What would a
market operating under these conditions look like? What
are some observable indications that a market is functioning efficiently?

In an efficient market, water will transfer from
lower-valued to higher-valued uses when differences in
water values at the margin are large enough to make it
worthwhile to undertake a market transaction.(8) As a
result, in markets where transfers do not involve substantial transaction costs, water values at the margin will be
similar for agricultural, industrial, municipal and other
uses, and prices paid by different water users will consequently be similar. If market prices vary significantly
within a particular area and time period, further investigation is necessary. Price discrepancies may indicate
that the market is not performing efficiently, that
transfers are not occurring in response to differences in
water's value across uses and locations. Prices may also
differ due to transaction costs and differences in water
right characteristics.

In markets where transaction costs are high relative
to the value of water, differences in marginal water
values across alternative uses and locations will persist.

Transaction costs are incurred in searching for trading
partners; in identifying legal and hydrologic characteristics of water rights (priority date, return flow
obligations, etc); in negotiating price, financing arrangements and other terms of transfer; and in satisfying
state laws and transfer approval procedures.(9) Transaction costs affect the level of market activity because
buyers will not undertake a transfer unless returns to
water in their intended use outweigh both the price paid
to the seller and all transaction costs borne by the
purchaser. Sellers will not agree to a transfer unless
the price they receive compensates them for returns
foregone in transferring water rights plus any transaction
costs they incur. Although transaction costs prevent
market transfers from equating marginal water values and
affect the level of trading that can be profitably undertaken by buyers and sellers, high transaction costs are
not always an indicator of market inefficiency. Some
transaction costs stem from public policies designed to
make sure various transfer impacts are considered.
Policies to protect third-party and public interests
impose transaction costs on market participants in the
form of transfer restrictions, water court hearings, and
other approval procedures.

Transaction costs are one reason why there may be
price differences within a water market at any particular
moment. Prices will also differ, even in an efficient
market, due to differences among water rights. Water
rights are heterogeneous, each consisting of a different
bundle of legal and hydrologic characteristics which
affect the value of the right and its price in a market
setting. Buyers will be willing to pay differing amounts
for water rights depending on their current location of
use and the costs of conveying them to a new point of use.
Reliability of water supplies, water quality, and the
location, season and purpose of use for which the right
may be exercised have been shown to influence water right
prices in specific market areas.(10) Price differences
attributable to differences in water right characteristics
are not an indicator of market inefficiency.

If water right holders are to be confronted with the
full opportunity costs (11) of their water use and
transfer decisions, then market prices must incorporate
water quality, instream flow, and other public interest
values. The opportunity cost criterion requires that
third-party impacts be accounted for in buyers' and
sellers' market transfer decisions. In practice this

means that procedures must exist to identify and value impacts, perhaps by including affected parties in the bargaining process or requiring compensation once a transfer has occurred and external effects become evident. State and local governments, environmental groups, and other water interests must have input in the market process and the legal ability to bid for water rights on the same terms as agriculture, industry, and cities. If market participants were forced to recognize all water values and third-party impacts, only transfers for which social benefits exceed social costs would be consummated. However, it must be kept in mind that policies seeking to uphold the opportunity cost criterion for efficiency can make water right transfers more complicated and costly, thus trading off one aspect of efficiency for another.

ARE EXISTING WATER MARKETS EFFICIENT?

The markets described in Chapter 5 are evaluated based on four efficiency criteria, using information on transfer policies, market prices and transactions from each area. The first two criteria examine transfer patterns, marginal water values and market prices to determine whether water is being allocated efficiently among water uses. Efficiency also requires that buyers and sellers be faced with the full opportunity costs of their water transfer decisions. Opportunity cost considerations are addressed in the second two criteria which evaluate how well markets account for third-party impacts on other water users and how well markets account for environmental impacts of transfers. The evaluation is preliminary because complete information needed to assess market efficiency is not available, as noted earlier. The analysis is intended to explore ways in which existing markets can be evaluated using available information and to highlight trade-offs between market transfers, opportunity costs and transaction costs. As was done in previous chapters, market prices are reported in 1986 dollars per acre-foot of water transferable to the buyer, using the Gross National Product price deflator.

1. Are market processes moving water to higher valued uses?

Market transfers occur because the buyer expects the private benefits of the transfer to outweigh the price

paid to the seller plus any costs the buyer incurs in
implementing the transfer; so the answer to the question,
"Are market processes moving water to higher valued uses?"
will nearly always be positive. Within agriculture, water
is moving from lower to higher value crop production
activities in each area studied. In Arizona, for instance,
the proportion of the state's irrigated acreage planted in
alfalfa and small grains has declined by nearly 50 percent
since 1970 and acreage in crops with higher returns to
water (fruit and nut crops, vegetables and cotton) has
increased proportionally.(12) However, shifts in agricultural water use generally represent individual farmers'
responses to changes in crop prices and input costs and do
not typically involve market transfers of water rights
from one irrigator to another. While intra-agricultural
transfers occur in each of the areas studied, water
transfers out of agriculture to municipal and industrial
uses are the primary way in which water is moving to
higher value uses. For instance, in the Gila-San Francisco
Basin well over half of the water rights in the Gila sub-
basin have been transferred out of agriculture into nonirrigation uses since the 1960s. The Intermountain Power
Project's purchase of irrigation rights for power plant
operations transferred over 20 percent of existing surface
water irrigation rights in Utah's Lower Sevier Basin out
of agricultural ownership, although about half of this
water is being rented back to irrigators.(13) In all areas
studied, agriculture is the dominant water seller and
industries or municipalities are the principal buyers so
that transfer patterns clearly indicate a movement from
lower to higher valued uses.

2. Are marginal water values and market prices similar across water-using sectors?

Two approaches are taken to address this question,
the second requiring less information than the first.
Where agricultural and municipal water demand schedules
have been estimated, marginal water values at the existing
quantities allocated to each sector can be compared
directly to one another and to market prices. Marginal
value information is available for only two of the
markets studied, Arizona and northeastern Colorado. For
the other markets, market price data are analyzed for
transactions occurring within the same time period to
determine whether price differences are due to differences

in water right characteristics or are attributable to
market inefficiency.

Comparison of Tucson municipal demand for raw water
and the value of water in southern Arizona agriculture
suggests that marginal values are similar, falling in the
range of $35 to $40 per acre-foot.(14)   Tucson has been
paying an average of $600 to $900 per acre-foot of
transferable water rights   to purchase and retire
irrigated Avra Valley land so that water can be
transferred to city use.(15)   Nonirrigation groundwater
rights typically sell for around $600 to $1,000 per acre-
foot in the Tucson area.(16)   These prices for urban
purchase of water rights are consistent with capitalization of   annual agricultural marginal-use values.

The evidence indicates that market prices in the
Tucson area are consistent with marginal water values in
both irrigation and municipal uses, suggesting that water
is being allocated efficiently   between the two sectors.
This may seem surprising, given that institutional
conditions in Arizona do not appear ideal for efficient
market allocation. However, the requirement that irrigated
land be purchased to obtain irrigation water rights is
less burdensome than one might expect.   Since there is no
dryland crop production in southern Arizona and no new
acreage in the Tucson area may be irrigated, rural land
from which water rights have been transferred has little
value and   adds little to the total water purchase price.
Transferability of Type II non-irrigation groundwater
rights is also constrained, but a market for these rights
has developed. Arizona statutes prohibit Type II nonirrigation groundwater rights from being fractured, so
that a right holder must make an "all or nothing" decision
to sell.   In addition, rights currently used for mining
and electrical power generation can only be transferred
for those specific purposes.(17)   However, these
restrictions have not prevented the development of an
active market for Type II rights.   These facts support
Howe, Schurmeier and Shaws' argument (18) that only a
portion of an area's water rights need be readily
transferable for markets to perform their function of
moving water when there are net gains to be captured by
doing so.

Phoenix area municipalities and developers have been
buying agricultural land and water rights for $800 to
$1,300 per acre-foot of transferable water rights. These
prices are higher than the capitalized value of water in
irrigation and are also higher than prices paid for water

rights in the Tucson area for several reasons. First, the Phoenix metropolitan area is growing more rapidly than is Tucson. Urban real estate values are significantly higher in the Phoenix area, suggesting that willingness to pay for water rights to support development is also higher. Approval of new developments around Phoenix and Tucson is contingent upon demonstration that long term water supplies are available to support the development (the assured one 100-year water supply provision in the 1980 Groundwater Management Act).(19) Nunn (20) notes that this requirement gives a water right value as a "license to develop" in addition to its value in agricultural and municipal uses. Indeed, many Phoenix-area developers purchase groundwater rights to satisfy the assured water supply requirement with no intention of exercising the rights to provide water so long as alternative sources (municipal water service, for instance) are available at a lower cost than would be incurred in drilling new wells and pumping at the development site.(21) Second, the city of Tucson is the principal buyer of irrigation rights in the Tucson area. In the Phoenix area several city governments and private businesses have been acquiring water rights. The presence of more than one large buyer might be contributing to higher water rights prices near Phoenix. Third, water rights currently may not be trans- ferred from the Tucson to the Phoenix area, preventing marginal values from being equated across the two urban areas. Surface water transfers may be possible when the Central Arizona Project aqueduct (which will connect Phoenix and Tucson) is completed, although the conditions under which the aqueduct may be available to facilitate market transfers have not yet been determined. Under cur- rent law, groundwater rights may not be transferred out of their AMA of origin.

Gardner and Miller (22) studied the relationship between agricultural water values and market prices for Colorado-Big Thompson (C-BT) water rights. They found that variations in the real price of C-BT units from 1961 to 1969 could be explained almost entirely by fluctuations in water's marginal value in irrigation. However, during the next decade real market prices rose sharply, approaching municipal and industrial marginal water values and exceeding capitalized agricultural values. As indicated in the price tables in Chapter 5, C-BT prices peaked at approximately $3,600 per acre-foot in 1980, after varying between $130 and $900 per acre-foot through the 1960s, and between $860 and $1,500 per acre-foot in the early-to-mid

1970s. Gardner and Miller concluded that, as urban growth
in the area accelerated, agricultural water sellers began
to incorporate urban water values into their price negotiations and were no longer willing to sell at prices that
reflected only water's value in irrigation. By 1980, the
marginal value of water in municipal uses was almost
fully capitalized into market prices.

In the Northern Colorado Water Conservancy District,
large price differentials exist among water rights traded
within the district during the same time period. These
price differentials appear to be attributable to differences in water right flexibility. In general, the more
limited the purpose and area of use and the smaller the
service area within which the right can be transferred
without water court proceedings, the lower the price a
particular water right will command. C-BT water rights
generally command the highest price per acre-foot due to
the large area over which C-BT units can be transferred
and the supply reliability provided by the delivery
and storage infrastructure of the C-BT project. Records on
C-BT sales over the past two decades indicate a relatively
small price dispersion across transactions occurring
during the same time period. As indicated in Chapter 5,
water rights transferable over smaller service areas or
limited to irrigation use sell for 20 to 80 percent less
than the market price for C-BT water. Different limitations on the geographic area over which particular rights
may be transferred and the purposes for which rights may
be exercised result in persistent price differentials. It
is not clear that these limitations result in inefficiency
within the NCWCD, however, since some water rights are
transferable throughout the district and for multiple uses
and these flexible rights allow beneficial transfers to
occur.

In Utah's Lower Sevier Basin, New Mexico's Gila-San
Francisco Basin, and Nevada's Truckee Meadows, nonagricultural buyers entering each market have paid significantly
higher prices than were observed in previous transfers.
Transfers in the Sevier River Basin during the 1970s
typically involved seasonal rentals and some permanent
transfers among irrigators, with prices for permanent
transfers ranging from $300 to $600 per acre-foot. In
1980, however, Intermountain Power Project paid $2,400 per
acre-foot for a large parcel of ground and surface-water
rights (about 45,000 acre-feet) for its power plant
operations. Following the IPP purchase, market prices
returned to slightly above their previous levels, so that

water rights were selling for $350 to $750 per acre-foot
during 1982-1985.(23)

Limits on geographic flexibility of water rights in
the Lower Sevier Basin market create price differentials
for groundwater rights. Groundwater rights in designated
high-impact groundwater zones, within which pumping cannot
be increased, sell for $300 to $700 per acre-foot more, in
1986 dollars, than comparable groundwater rights located
outside such zones.(24)

In the late 1970s and early 1980s the Exxon
Corporation negotiated water transfer agreements with
about 25 water rights holders in New Mexico's Gila sub-
basin to obtain water for mining operations. During this
same period Silver City was purchasing water rights to
support city growth. Prices, in 1986 dollars, rose to
around $3,300 per acre-foot of water rights transferable
to the buyer, a 100 percent increase over price levels
before the Exxon negotiations. Price levels dropped to
around $1,500 per acre-foot in the early 1980s, possibly
because mining operations were no longer seeking
additional water rights.(25)

In the Truckee Meadows, Sierra Pacific Power Company,
a municipal water service provider, was the dominant
nonagricultural water buyer in the 1960s and 1970s,
paying prices of $70 to $160 per acre-foot. In the mid-
1970s urban growth in Reno and Sparks threatened to outpace Sierra Pacific's capacity to provide additional
water. This prompted the creation of new policies to
facilitate faster and easier water rights transfers in the
Truckee Meadows. Under these new policies, prices rose to
over $1,500 per acre-foot and have remained at these
higher levels.

The Phoenix, Colorado-Big Thompson, Lower Sevier
Basin, Gila Basin and Truckee Meadows markets demonstrate
that market prices do not simply reflect water values in
the marginal water use. Markets also reflect expectations of economic growth or decline, and expected changes
in future water values. Discrepancies between capitalized marginal use values and market prices are not
necessarily an indication of poor market performance.
Brown et al.(26) conclude that markets in which price
levels adjust to changing expectations and new supply and
demand conditions are more proficient than markets which
do not reflect changing conditions.

City managers and water suppliers desire to insulate
water users from drought and unanticipated shortfalls in
water availability and to plan for community growth. These

objectives are a primary impetus for water right purchases. Many public and private water purveyors hold water
right inventories far in excess of what is needed to
satisfy current water users in a typical year. An important component of water rights' values lies in their role
in mitigating risk of supply shortfalls and providing a
base for economic growth. Discrepancies between water's
current value in alternative uses and market prices
indicate that risk control and planning for growth are
important forces in western water transfers.

3. <u>Do markets account for impacts on third-party water
right holders?</u>

All western state laws stipulate that third-party
water users with a perfected water right may not be
injured as a result of a water transfer. Howe, Schurmeier
and Shaw (27) note that water law on third-party impacts
is asymmetric in that it addresses third-party losses but
does not consider third-party benefits. As a result,
external social benefits are ignored and some socially
beneficial transfers may not take place. Implementation of
policies that protect water users against transfer impacts
differs greatly from state to state, and within states
there is variation in the nature of protection afforded to
different types of water rights. For instance, Young,
Daubert and Morel-Seytoux(28) describe the development of
institutions which cause Colorado buyers and sellers to
account for impacts of groundwater transfers on surface
water rights in their market negotiations. In Arizona, on
the other hand, groundwater and surface water are treated
as separate systems and the impacts that changes in
groundwater pumping might have on surface water rights
are not considered in groundwater transfer procedures. A
surface water right holder who believes his rights are
impaired by a groundwater transfer must initiate
litigation to protect his claim.(29)

Nearly all states protect surface water return flows
in some manner. Colorado, Nevada, New Mexico, and Utah
protect them by restricting the quantity of water that may
be transferred to correspond to historic consumptive use
rather than the historic quantity diverted.(30) The
burden of demonstrating that existing rights will not be
impaired by a transfer is distributed differently in
various states. In most states the applicant for a
transfer bears this burden, though state water agencies
generally also bear some of the costs of developing and

examining evidence on injury to vested rights. In California, a party challenging a transfer of an appropriative right with a priority date preceding 1914 bears the burden of demonstrating injury,(31) as does an Arizona water right holder injured by groundwater transfers.(32)

Statistical analysis of market prices in New Mexico's Gila-San Francisco Basin indicates that significant discrepancies exist between prices paid for water rights in the Gila versus the San Francisco sub-basins. There has been an average price differential of over $1,000 per acre-foot based on price data from 1966 through 1985, with the higher prices paid in the Gila sub-basin where most development has been occurring.(33) Transfers between the two sub-basins have not been permitted in order to protect water users in Arizona by assuring Arizona a portion of each river's flow.(34) This transfer restriction appears to impede this market's ability to equate marginal water values across sub-basins.

In many areas, approval procedures designed to protect third-party right holders are a major cost of implementing a water transaction and these costs may be large enough to make it unprofitable to implement other- wise economically beneficial transfers. While economic efficiency requires that all opportunity costs of a transfer be accounted for in market decisions, there are trade-offs between policies to protect third parties and policies to promote water right transferability. Transac- tion costs imposed by policies to protect third parties prevent marginal values from being equated, and transfer restrictions prevent water from moving to higher-valued uses and locations. Howe, Schurmeier and Shaw (35) describe these trade-offs in Colorado water markets. Holders of rights to transmountain diversion water (such as Colorado-Big Thompson units) need not take into account the impact of water right transfers on return flows. As a result, transaction costs are lower and transfers are more easily implemented but the value of return flows to down- stream users is not accounted for. In contrast, holders of rights to native flows must recognize return flow impacts of transfers and follow water court recommenda- tions to mitigate detrimental impacts or compensate those affected. While efficiency requires that return flow values be recognized, the adversarial water-court process may impose high costs on buyers and sellers to account for small losses to third parties--another example of pervasive trade-offs between transaction costs and opportunity costs of market processes and policies.

4. Do markets reflect environmental values?

Water transfers may have several different types environmental impacts. Interbasin transfers often require construction of conveyance or storage facilities, disrupting wildlife habitat, plant life and aesthetics in the construction areas. Environmental concerns regarding these types of transfers are usually addressed through the environmental impact assessment process, negotiation, litigation and other nonmarket processes. The effects are felt in the market place, however, as transfer proponents weigh the costs of responding to environmental concerns with the benefits of the proposed transfer. Transfers which do not involve construction still may affect environmental quality by altering instream flow levels or water quality. Transfers which involve retirement of irrigated lands may be environmentally disruptive if the lands are not managed so as to prevent dust, weeds and insects from becoming a problem. Environmental impacts may be a significant cost associated with water transfers. Can the market process account for these costs and reflect values associated with environmental quality?

Instream Flows. Several western states recognize instream flow maintenance for recreation and wildlife as a beneficial use, and, in a few states, public agencies acquire water rights for the purpose of maintaining instream flows.(36) However, individuals wishing to protect stream flow levels do not have access to markets on the same terms as farmers, cities and industry. Only a few western states, including Arizona, allow a private party to hold a water right for the purpose of maintaining instream flows for recreation, wildlife habitat or aesthetic purposes.(37) Even if these restrictions were abolished, instream flows have public good characteristics (38) which make it difficult to translate collective values for instream flows into dollars to bid for water rights in the market place. Failure to account for instream flow values can result in inefficient water allocation. Daubert and Young's research (39) on instream values in northern Colorado suggests that benefits generated by water resources could be enhanced in their study area by altering timing of water storage and releases to enhance instream flows during the fall recreation season. Recreational benefits associated with

stream flows could be increased without decreasing water
availability for irrigation, implying that payments to
persuade irrigation right holders to alter water
management practices in favor of recreation need not be
large in this particular study area. Markets could do a
better job of reflecting instream flow values if state
laws permitted appropriation, purchase and seasonal
leasing of rights for instream flow maintenance by both
public and private organizations.

Water Quality. Transfers can affect water
quality, but water quality impacts are not readily
accounted for in transfer approval procedures which were
designed primarily to protect the quantity of water
available to third party water right holders. Precedent
has been established in some courts, based on the Public
Trust Doctrine, to restrict water transfers due to water
quality considerations.(40) Many state laws permit
transfers to be rejected if they are not in the public
interest--though the public interest typically is ill-
defined.(41) In the absence of policies that require
assessment of water quality impacts before a transfer can
be implemented, buyers and sellers have little incentive
to consider such impacts when negotiating a market
transaction.

Arizona's 1986 environmental quality law will affect
market transfers for groundwater recharge. Transfers of
municipal effluent to support recharge projects could
become an important part of Arizona water markets, given
recent legislation clarifying rights to recharge and
recover water.(42) However, Arizona's 1986 Environmental
Quality Act stipulates that recharge activities may not
degrade the quality of the receiving aquifer.(43) Pre-
recharge treatment costs for projects located over potable
aquifers will be high, and buyers' willingness to pay for
effluent to recharge, consequently, will be lower. This
law forces potential buyers to consider water quality
impacts when making market transfer decisions for
recharge projects, but precludes trade-offs between the
value of recharging effluent for future use and the value
of maintaining aquifers at existing levels of water
quality. An alternative approach would be to require
treatment of water upon recovery for a specific use rather
than treatment before recharge. However, this approach
would shift any costs of recharge-related degradation from
the recharging organization to the organization recovering
water for use and also would shift treatment costs from
the recharge period to the recovery period.

In general, water quality impacts are not routinely
considered in transfer approval procedures and the burden
of raising the question of adverse impacts is left to
parties who may be affected. Howe, Schurmeier and Shaw
(44) argue that property rights in water are not
comprehensively defined unless assurances regarding water
quality are incorporated into the definition of a water
right. However, the more comprehensive the definition of
water rights and the more protection afforded to water
quality, the greater the transaction costs for potential
buyers and sellers.

Retirement of Agricultural Lands. In areas where
urban interests have purchased and retired irrigated lands
so that water may be transferred to municipal uses,
concerns have arisen over the environmental impact of
abandoned farmland. Dust, weeds and insects can
proliferate on retired lands, creating a nuisance to
neighboring property owners. Colorado Front-Range municipalities have purchased water rights from farmers in the
Arkansas River Basin and these transfers involve the
retirement of over 10,000 acres of irrigated lands.
Front-range cities and area-of-origin representatives are
negotiating over a revegetation program to restore retired
lands for livestock grazing and wildlife habitat.
Municipal representatives estimate the costs of such a
program could exceed $200 per acre.(45) The fate of irri-
gated land retired as a result of rural-to-urban water
transfers has also generated much controversy in Arizona,
where over 10,000 acres have already been retired in Avra
Valley and thousands of additional acres will be retired
elsewhere as recent transfers are implemented. The state
legislature enacted a bill in 1987 requiring that tumble-
weeds and other noxious plants be controlled by owners of
irrigated land retired as a part of a water transfer.(46)

Water markets can partially account for the environmental impacts of transfers if environmental interests
have input into the market process. This input could take
several forms. Environmental values could be incorporated
by direct participation in market transactions if private
and public agencies can purchase water rights for instream
flow maintenance and protection of riparian ecosystems.
Environmental values can also be incorporated if public
policies require transferors to bear costs associated with
environmental impacts of transfers. Examples include
requiring buyers to control pests and dust on retired
agricultural lands, or requiring mitigation in the form of
money and minimum stream flows to protect fish and

wildlife.(47) Such requirements raise transaction costs
for market participants but also force buyers and sellers
to consider the environmental consequences of transfer
decisions.

WHAT ABOUT EQUITY CONCERNS?

Economic efficiency frequently is criticized as a
criterion upon which to base water policy because efficiency is concerned primarily with the magnitudes of
benefits and costs, not who receives the benefits and who
bears the costs. It is argued here that careful application of the efficiency criterion (requiring that transfers
only be implemented if benefits outweigh all costs) would
address some, though not all, equity concerns. In principle, policies that cause third-party impacts, instream
flow values and water quality considerations to be
accounted for in market decisions can protect the interests of those typically under-represented in the market
place. The problem is that such policies themselves are
expensive to formulate and implement and these costs must
be weighed against the value of what the policies might
seek to accomplish. Since valuation of instream flows,
water quality changes and environmental degradation is
more difficult than valuation of water in consumptive uses
such as irrigation and municipal supply, there is an
information imbalance and a tendency to favor water uses
with easily documented values. This information imbalance
does not, by itself, imply that markets are disadvanta-
geous compared to other allocation mechanisms since it is
not unique to market transfer processes. Valuation difficulties will confound any allocation process in which
water values in alternative uses must be weighed against
one another.

Who Benefits From Market Transactions?

Markets redistribute water rights and wealth through
voluntary transfers between buyers and sellers. However,
who reaps the benefits of market transactions is a
function of the existing allocation of water rights and
bargaining power. Markets, as noted earlier, require
assignment of property rights in water to provide the
starting point from which transfer negotiations can
commence. The initial assignment of water rights
determines who must pay to obtain water rights and who

receives payments in return for selling rights. For instance, in many areas of the West irrigators have high priority surface water rights based on early diversions of water for irrigation. New users desiring senior water rights must bid them away from farmers. If initial water allocations had gone instead to state fish and game departments or tribal and city governments, this would have resulted in an entirely different set of high priority right holders, a different set of sellers and a different distribution of benefits from market transfers.

This connection between the existing allocation of water rights and the distribution of market benefits received much attention in Hawaii as the Hawaiian legislature worked to formulate a state water code.(48) While some have argued that a market-oriented approach would facilitate efficient use of Hawaii's ground and surface water resources (49), others note that large sugar companies historically have been the principal water users and would be in a very favorable position if transferable rights were assigned based on historic water use patterns. Therefore, some have argued that water rights should be renewable at the discretion of an administrative agency, rather than perpetual, so that allocation of rights can be altered as political and social values regarding alternative water uses change over time. Market processes, because they are predicated on some initial distribution of water rights, cannot resolve these equity issues. Rather, markets reflect and reinforce the existing distribution of water rights and wealth. Those who have water rights can benefit from markets by participating as sellers. Those who have money with which to purchase rights can benefit from markets by participating as buyers. Those who have neither water rights nor money cannot participate in the market process and are not likely to share in the benefit it generates.

Area-of-Origin Concerns

The heart of equity concerns with markets lies in the tension between individual and collective interests. Conflicts arise between the autonomy of individual right holders to lease or sell water to the highest bidder and collective preferences for predictability and stability in water allocation. Individual farmers have an incentive to negotiate satisfactory prices for their water rights on their own behalf, but have little incentive to consider community impacts associated with water transfers out of a rural area.

Transfer impacts on economic activity and local government fiscal capacity in the basin of origin raise complicated equity issues. In most states, water transfers that involve purchase of farmland by a city government remove that land from the local tax base. California is an exception, having amended its constitution to allow local government taxation of land owned by another local government.(50) Arizona, as noted in Chapter 4, passed legislation allowing voluntary payments by municipal landowners in lieu of property taxes to taxing jurisdictions in the area of origin.(51)

Regardless of whether land is purchased along with water rights, water transfers generally involve a change in water using activities in the area of origin, typically a reduction in irrigated acreage. These changes have spillover effects on local businesses. Local agricultural equipment dealers and seed and fertilizer suppliers, for instance, may do a lower volume of business. There is little consensus regarding whether or how public policy should be concerned with these spillover effects on local governments and businesses. MacDonnell et al.(52) pose the question in the following manner:

"Why should the export of water be treated differently from the export of any natural resource?...Local areas are not compensated for the removal of coal or ores beyond the royalties paid directly to resource owners...Why is water viewed differently?"

The authors go on to argue that water exports are different because, while exports of timber or minerals provide a continuing source of local jobs, income and tax base, water exports typically do not. In addition, they point out the when area-of-origin interests are injured by a transfer intended to benefit others—a transfer over which the area of origin had little control—it seems reasonable that the area of origin should be compensated so as to be no worse off than before the transfer. Their equity argument for area-of-origin compensation is reinforced by an efficiency argument. Efficiency requires that only transfers for which the benefits exceed the costs should occur. Public policies that cause transferors to count the costs imposed on the area of origin by requiring compensatory payments can help to ensure that only efficient transfers are implemented. MacDonnell et al. caution that compensation must be limited to the actual damages imposed and that the process of identifying

injured parties and determining a fair level of compensation is difficult and expensive. This underscores the
trade-offs which arise whenever public policies regarding
water transfers are considered. New policies can protect
values that would otherwise be neglected in market decisions, yet at the same time they impose costs on market
participants and increase costs incurred by public
agencies implementing water transfer policies.

Representing Collective Values

    Market decisions, by their very nature, involve
individuals making choices in their own best interest and
they do not readily accommodate collective preferences.
However, some interest groups and communities have
organized to express their collective values and to
influence market outcomes. For instance, communities on
Colorado's West Slope negotiated payment of over $10
million for construction of water projects in the basin of
origin as a condition for the Windy Gap Project, which
will deliver about 54,000 acre-feet annually over the
Continental Divide to the East Slope.(53) In response to
Intermountain Power Project's plans for a major water
purchase, local irrigators formed a group to represent
potential sellers and negotiated guidelines which ensured
that rights holders all had an equal opportunity to sell a
portion of their water rights, that all sellers would
receive the same price and that IPP would negotiate with
interested irrigators as a group so that collective
interests could be considered.(54)
    Collective action can also serve as a vehicle for
representing environmental values in a market setting.
The Nature Conservancy and other groups have purchased
instream flow rights to maintain riparian environments in
Arizona, Hawaii, Colorado and other western states.(55)
However, as noted in Chapter 6, instream flows have public
good characteristics. They create widespread benefits
from which those who do not contribute to purchase of
rights for instream flow maintenance cannot easily be
excluded. "Free-rider" problems and the difficulty of
collecting money to enhance environmental quality through
water right purchases, prevent environmental interests
from being able to compete in the market for water rights
on an equal basis with profit-making enterprises, and with
organizations such as city governments and utilities, who
can fund the cost of water rights acquisition through
taxes, bonds and service charges.

The equity concerns of those who have something with
which to bargain--money, water rights, political power and
legal power--can be reflected in market decisions. Those
who have little with which to bargain can have little
influence on market outcomes.

SUMMARY AND IMPLICATIONS

Water markets are functioning throughout the West
where economic incentives for water transfers outweigh
costs associated with market transactions. Examination of
market prices and transfer patterns in existing markets
suggest that market processes work relatively well in allocating water between agricultural, municipal and industrial uses. Impacts on third-party water right holders
generally are incorporated into market decisions, though
procedures to protect water right holders vary considerably among the southwestern states. Instream flow and
water quality considerations not closely tied to vested
water rights are represented poorly in market processes,
as are environmental values in general. State laws that
allow private parties to purchase water rights for
instream flow or water quality maintenance give
recreational and environmental interests access to markets
but cannot resolve public good problems that can prevent
environmental values from being reflected fully in market
negotiations with agricultural, municipal, and industrial
water users.

Pervasive trade-offs were encountered in this evaluation of market processes. Water markets increase returns
to water use and facilitate economic development by
providing water to new users while fully compensating
sellers. On the other hand, markets are not without
costs. Aside from the costs of implementing any policies
which govern transfers, markets require enforceable
property rights in water. Enforceable rights in turn
require public agencies, courts and sometimes lengthy and
expensive adjudication proceedings.

The opportunity cost criterion for efficiency
requires that third-party and public interests be recognized in market processes. Implementation of this
criterion requires policies that impose transaction costs
on buyers and sellers as well as administrative costs.
Recognizing that policy is not costless, it is necessary
to weigh policy costs against the value of what policy
seeks to accomplish in order to avoid either of two

pitfalls--expensive policy solutions to small problems or inadequate policy solutions to significant third-party impacts of water transfers.

Do markets "work"? This evaluation of the efficiency and equity of southwestern water markets perhaps has raised more questions than it has answered. However, a few recommendations for further research and for policy development can be made. Additional research is needed on existing markets and actual transactions to identify private and social costs and benefits associated with transfers. Studies on potential gains from market transfers need to be balanced with studies on transaction costs and administrative costs associated with current and proposed policies to govern market activities.

Policy makers should focus on the third-party effects of market transfers rather than the private costs and benefits accruing to buyers and sellers, since buyers and sellers are already strongly motivated to weigh the private impacts of a transfer proposal but have little incentive to weigh third-party impacts. Public policy must seek a balance between unrestricted markets which can impose high external costs, and market restrictions which reduce external costs, but make transfers more expensive, both to market participants and to agencies which evaluate transfer proposals. Achieving such a balance will require much better information than currently is available on the nature and value of transfer impacts, returns to water in alternative uses, and costs of implementing transfer policies. Water markets will continue to be an important policy issue in the Southwest for many years to come. This research indicates that we are a long way from being able to identify and quantify the benefits and costs associated with market transfers in order to determine how and to what extent market outcomes should be governed by public policy.

NOTES

1. Examples may be found in T.L. Anderson, O.R. Burt and D.T. Fractor, "Privatizing Groundwater Basins," in Water Rights, ed. T.L. Anderson, Pacific Institute for Public Policy Research, San Francisco, 1983; J.W. Eheart and R.M. Lyon, "Alternative Structures for Water Rights Markets," Water Resources Research 19, 887-894, 1983; B.D. Gardner, "Institutional Impediments to Efficient Water

Allocation," Policy Studies Review 5, 353-363, 1985; H.J. Vaux and R.E.Howitt, "Managing Water Scarcity: An Evaluation of Interregional Transfers," Water Resources Research 20; 785-792, 1984; and B.C. Wong and J.W. Eheart, "Market Simulations for Irrigation Water Rights: A Hypothetical Case Study," Water Resources Research 19, 1127-1138, 1983.

2. Readers may wish to refer to Chapter 4 for a review of policies in the Southwestern states regarding beneficial use.

3. C.W. Howe, D.R. Schurmeier and W.D. Shaw, "Innovative Approaches to Water Allocation: The Potential for Water Markets." Water Resources Research 22: 431-445, 1986.

4. For instance, H.J. Vaux, "Water Scarcity and Gains From Trade in Kern Co., California," in Scarce Water and Institutional Change, ed. K.D. Frederick, Resources for the Future, Washington D.C., 1986; R.W. Wahl and R.K. Davis. "Satisfying Southern California's Thirst for Water: Efficient Alternatives," Scarce Water and Institutional Change, ed. K.D.Frederick, Resources for the Future, Washington DC, 1986; and N.K. Whittlesey and J.E. Houston, "Water Markets for Stream Flow Augmentation," Water Resources Bulletin, 11 139-146, 1984.

5. S.V. Ciriacy-Wantrup, "Concepts Used as Economic Criteria for a System of Water Rights," Land Economics 32:295-312, 1956; M. Hartman and D. Seastone, Water Transfers: Economic Efficiency and Alternative Institutions. Baltimore: John Hopkins Press, 1970; F.J. Trelease, "Developments in Groundwater Law," ed. Z.A. Saleem, in Advances in Groundwater Hydrology, American Water Resources Association, Minneapolis, 1976; L. Brown, B. McDonald, J. Tyseling and C. DuMars, "Water Reallocation Market Proficiency and Conflicting Social Values," in Water and Agriculture in the Western U.S., ed. Gary Weatherford, Westview Press, Boulder, Colorado, 1982; R.A. Young. "Direct and Regional Impacts of Competition for Irrigation Water in the West." Paper read at Conference on Impacts of Limited Water for Irrigated Agriculture in the Arid West, Pacific Grove, California 1982. Howe, Schurmeier and Shaw, op. cit.

6. These attributes of a property rights system were discussed in Chapter 2 where their importance for efficient market performance was noted. A. Randall, Resource Economics: An Economic Approach to Natural Resource and Environmental Policy. New York: John Wiley

258

and Sons, 1987. See Chapter 8, "Property Rights, Efficiency and the Distribution of Income," p.153-163.

7. The marginal value of water is the net benefit gained or lost by adding or deleting a unit of water to or from an existing use. M.M. Kelso, W.E. Martin and L.E. Mack, Water Supplies and Economic Growth in an Arid Environment. Tucson: University of Arizona Press, 1973.

8. Chapter 2 provides a hypothetical example of a transfer from agricultural use to municipal use which illustrates how an efficient market equates the marginal value of water in alternative uses.

9. J.P. Crouter, "Hedonic Estimation Applied to a Water Rights Market," forthcoming article in Land Economics, 1987; and R.A. Young, "Why Are There So Few Transactions Among Water Users?" American Journal of Agricultural Economics, 67, 1986.

10. D.B. Bush and B.C. Saliba, in "Commodity Identification and Price Behavior in Western Water Markets." Paper presented at American Agricultural Association Annual meetings, Reno, Nevada, August, 1986.

11. Opportunity costs are all of the net benefits sacrificed when one alternative, such as a water transfer, is chosen over other alternatives, including the alternative of continuing with the same water use patterns.

12. Arizona Agricultural Statistics, Arizona Agricultural Statistics Service, Phoenix, published annually.

13. M. Perez, Intermountain Power Project Management Engineer, personal communication, 1985.

14. D.B. Bush and W. E. Martin, "Potential Costs and Benefits to Arizona Agriculture of the Central Arizona Project," University of Arizona, College of Agriculture, Technical Bulletin No. 254, 1986; and W.E. Martin and J. Thomas, "Policy Relevance in Studies of Urban Residential Water Demand." Water Resources Research 22(13), 1735-1741, 1986.

15. Linda Micale, "The Total Direct Costs of Importing Avra Valley Water." Working Paper, Department of Agricultural Economics, University of Arizona, 1984.

16. Tucson currently is pumping and transporting less than 20 percent of its Avra Valley water rights each year for use in the city and will adjust its use of Avra Valley water in response to CAP delivery fluctuations and changing peak-load demands resulting from weather patterns and population growth. B.C. Saliba, D.B. Bush, W.E. Martin and T. Brown, "Do Water Market Prices Appropriately

Measure Water Values?" <u>Natural Resources Journal</u> 27, forthcoming, 1987.

17. Ariz. Rev. Stat., Vol.15, title 45 (1980) Ground-water Management Act.

18. Howe, Schurmeier and Shaw, op. cit.

19. Ariz. Rev. Stat., Vol.15, Title 45 (1980) Ground-water Management Act.

20. Chris Nunn, University of Arizona, Dept. of Hydrology and Water Resources, personal communication with author, 1987.

21. B.C. Saliba, "Market Transfers: Resolving the Tradeoffs--A Challenge for Public Policy," in proceedings of <u>Water Transfers: Arizona Issues and Challenges</u>, American Water Resources Association--Arizona Section, 1986.

22. R.L. Gardner and T.A. Miller, "Price Behavior In the Water Market of Northeastern Colorado." <u>Water Resources Bulletin</u> Vol. 19, No. 4:557-562, 1983.

23. Perez, M. See Note 12.

24. D. Hansen, Policy Statement on Underground Water Appropriation in Delta Area, Millard County, Utah Dept. of Natural Resources and Energy, 1982.

25. Price information is based upon interviews with buyers, sellers, public officials and water brokers in the basin.

26. Brown et al.,op. cit., See Note 5.

27. Howe, Schurmeier and Shaw, op. cit.

28. R. Young, J.T. Daubert and H.J. Morel-Seytoux, "Evaluating Institutional Alternatives for Managing an Interrelated Stream - Aquifer System." <u>American Journal of Agricultural Economics</u> 67:787-796, 1986.

29. Staff attorneys in the Legal Division, personal communications with author, 1986 and 1987.

30. B.C. Driver, "The Effect of Western Water Law on Water Transfers," in <u>Water Marketing</u>, ed. S. Shupe, University of Denver College of Law, 1986.

31. <u>Ibid</u>.

32. Arizona statutes contain provisions concerning third-party impacts resulting from inter-basin transfers of groundwater. An exporter of groundwater potentially is liable to pay damages to affected individuals in the basin of origin but the burden of initiating litigation and demonstrating injury falls on the protesting party. Ariz. Rev. Stat. Vol. 15, Title 45. (1980) Groundwater Management Act.

33. Bush and Saliba, op.cit.

260

34. The State of Arizona's rights to the flow of the Gila and San Francisco Rivers were clarified in State of Arizona v. State of California U.S. Supreme Court, March 9, 1964. Also see Grant County District Court Case Nos. 16290 and 16610, August 1967 for proceedings in New Mexico courts regarding water rights in the Gila-San Francisco Basin.

35. Howe, Schurmeier and Shaw, op. cit.

36. Readers may refer to Chapter 4 for a review of instream flow policies in the six southwestern states.

37. B.C. Driver, "Western Water: Tuning the System," report to the Western Governor's Association, Denver, 1986.

38. Public goods characteristics and their implications from instream flow protection are discussed in Chapter 6.

39. J.T. Daubert and R.A. Young, "Recreational Demands for Maintaining Instream Flows: A Contingent Valuation Approach." American Journal of Agricultural Economics 63:666-676, 1981.

40. C. Wilkinson, "Public Interest Constraints on Water Transfers," in Water Marketing, ed. S.J. Shupe, University of Denver College of Law, 1986.

41. Readers may refer to Chapter 4 for a review of public interest provisions in the water policies of the southwestern states and for a discussion of the Public Trust Doctrine and its potential implications for water transfers.

42. Ariz. Rev. Stat. Title 45, Chapter 289 (1986), Groundwater Recharge and Underground Storage Law.

43. Ariz. Rev. Stat. Title 49, Chapter 368 (1986) Environmental Quality Act.

44. Howe, Schurmeier and Shaw, op. cit.

45. "Colorado's Front Range Cities and the Arkansas Valley: What Happens When The Water Is Gone?" Water Market Update, S.J. Shupe and J.A. Folk-Williams (eds), Vol. No. 2, February, 1987.

46. House Bill 2257, codified in Ariz. Rev. Stat. Ann. Title 9 Chapter 4, Article 1 Section 404C, enacted in 1987.

47. Negotiations over Colorado's Windy Gap Project resulted in an agreement by project proponents to pay $550,000 to the U.S. Fish and Wildlife Service for work to protect endangered fish species in the affected watershed and an agreement to provide minimum streamflows in order to mitigate adverse impacts on fish species. L.J. MacDonnell, C.W. Howe, J.N. Corbridge and W.A. Ahrens,

"Guidelines for Developing Area of Origin Compensation." University of Colorado, Natural Resources Law Center Research Report 22-36, December, 1985.

48. The Hawaiian legislature enacted a state water code in May 1987. The code allows the transfer of permitted rights but only if the conditions of use of the permit remain the same. Transferors desiring a change in the conditions of use must seek a modification in permit terms. Further judicial and administrative interpretation of the new code will undoubtedly be necessary to clarify the conditions for water transfers. Market Update Vol.1 No.6, June, 1987.

49. T.L. Anderson, "The Market Alternative for Hawaiian Water." Natural Resources Journal 25:893-910, 1985.

50. Amendment to California constitution Article 13, Section 11. Added November, 1974.

51. Ariz. Rev. Stat. Ann. Sec. 45-472 and Sec. 45-473.

52. MacDonnell et al., op. cit., See Note 47.

53. Ibid.

54. R. Clark, "An Energy Industry View in Groundwater and Energy." Proceedings of the U.S. Dept. of Energy's National Workshop, Albuquerque, New Mexico, 1980.

55. T.L. Anderson. op. cit. See Note 48, B.C. Saliba, op. cit. See Note 21.

Index

Colorado: Aetna Group, 134;
Animas-La Plata Pro-
ject, 38, 197;
appurtenancy of water
rights to land in, 63;
area-of-origin issues
in, 69-70; Azure
Reservoir and Power
Project, 70;
beneficial uses of
water in, 62; Bessemer
Ditch Company, 138,
139; Black Squirrel
Basin, 136; Booth-
Orchard Canal Company,
137; Boulder (city),
117, 127; Broomfield
(city), 128, 132;
Busk-Ivanhoe Ditch
Company, 138; Catlin
Canal Company, 139;
Central Weld County
Water district, 128,
132; Colorado Canal
Company, 134, 135,
138; Colorado Foundry
and Iron Steel Corpo-
ration, 135, 137;
Colorado River, 115,
120-121; Colorado
Water Conservation
Board, 72, 76; compen-
satory storage in, 70;
Crowley Land and De-
velopment Company,
134; Denver (city),
176; Estes Park, 127,
128, 132; Fort Collins
(city), 117, 127, 128;
Foxley and Company,
136; Fountain (city),
117, 136-137; Fountain
Valley Mutual Irriga-
tion Company, 136-137;
Fountain Valley Pipe-
line, 136-137; Frying
Pan-Arkansas Project,
120, 126, 127, 137;
Game and Fish Commis-
sion, 139; Greeley
(city), 117, 127;
Henry Reservoir com-
pany, 134, 135-136;
Huerfano-Cuchares
Ditch Company, 138;
instream flow protec-
tion in, 76; legal
restrictions on water
transfers in, 62, 63,
65, 66, 69-70, 72,
121, 246, 247;
Longmont (city), 117,
127; Loveland (city),
117, 127; Meredith
Reservoir Company,
134, 135-136; mutual
water companies in,
59-60; North Poudre
Irrigation Company,
129-131; Northern
Colorado Water Conser-
vancy District, 116-
117, 127, 128, 129,
244; Otero Canal Com-
pany, 137; Platte
River Power Authority,
128; protection of
third parties in, 67;
Proxy Group, 134;
public interest and
public trust consider-
ations in, 72; Pueblo
(city), 117, 120, 134,
135, 137; Pueblo
Reservoir, 122, 136,
137, 138; Pueblo West
(city), 120, 134, 135,
137-138; Rocky Ford
Ditch Company, 138;
Rocky Ford Highline
Canal Company 137;
South Platte River
Basin, 116; South-
eastern Colorado Water

266

(Chino) mine, 158;
legal restrictions in,
62, 63-64, 65, 66, 70,
72-73, 76, 246; Middle
Rio Grande Conservancy
District, 70; Middle
Rio Grande Conservancy
District v. Cox, 70-
71; Mimbres Basin,
153, 155, 158, 160-61,
195; Phelps Dodge Cor-
poration, 155, 158-59,
161; protection of
third parties in, 67-
68; public interest
and public trust con-
siderations in, 72-73;
Redrock (town), 153,
156; Reserve (town),
153; San Francisco
River, 153; San
Francisco Subbasin,
156, 159; State Engi-
neer, 155-56, 157;
Silver city, 153, 155,
158, 159, 245; Silver
City wellfields
(Anderson, Franks,
Woodward), 160-61; use
and transfer of con-
served water in, 65.
See also Gila-San
Francisco Basin
Northern Colorado Water
Conservancy District.
See under Colorado

Opportunity cost, 12, 236,
239, 240, 255

Papago Indian tribe. See
Native Americans:
Tohono O'odham tribe
Pareto Efficiency, 13-14
Phoenix. See under Arizona

Prior appropriations doc-
trine. See Appropria-
tions doctrine
Price. See Water prices
Public goods, 192-95
Public interest, 71-74, 100
Public Trust Doctrine, 2,
73-74, 249; origin of,
74
Pyramid Lake Indian tribe.
See under Native
Americans

Reallocative processes, 2-4
Reclamation Act of 1902, 80
Recreational uses of water,
209,223-25
Reno (city), 139, 140, 142,
147, 151, 196, 245.
See also Nevada
Rental, of water. See
under Water rights,
leasing of
Reserved rights, federal.
See under U.S. govern-
ment
Resource allocation pro-
cess. See Markets:
allocation
Retirement of irrigated
lands. See under
Water uses: agricul-
tural
Riparian doctrine: in
California, 109, 110;
definition and
history, 36, 57; de-
velopment of, 37

Salt River Users
Association v.
Kavocich, 64
Sierra Pacific Power Com-
pany, 142, 143, 144,
145-48, 151-52, 196,
198, 245. See also
Nevada